Roosevelt's Revolt

ALSO BY JOHN C. SKIPPER
AND FROM MCFARLAND

*The 1964 Republican Convention: Barry Goldwater
and the Beginning of the Conservative Movement* (2016)

Frank Robinson: A Baseball Biography (2015)

*Billy Southworth: A Biography of the Hall
of Fame Manager and Ballplayer* (2013)

*Showdown at the 1964 Democratic Convention:
Lyndon Johnson, Mississippi and Civil Rights* (2012)

*The Iowa Caucuses: First Tests
of Presidential Aspiration, 1972–2008* (2010)

*Charlie Gehringer: A Biography of the Hall
of Fame Tigers Second Baseman* (2008)

*A Biographical Dictionary of the Baseball Hall
of Fame,* 2d ed. (2008; softcover 2015)

*Dazzy Vance: A Biography
of the Brooklyn Dodger Hall of Famer* (2007)

*Wicked Curve: The Life and Troubled Times
of Grover Cleveland Alexander* (2006)

*The Cubs Win the Pennant!: Charlie Grimm,
the Billy Goat Curse, and the 1945 World Series Run* (2004)

*A Biographical Dictionary of Major League
Baseball Managers* (2003; softcover 2011)

*Take Me Out to the Cubs Game: 35 Former Ballplayers
Speak of Losing at Wrigley* (2000)

*Umpires: Classic Baseball Stories
from the Men Who Made the Calls* (1997)

Roosevelt's Revolt

*The 1912 Republican Convention
and the Launch
of the Bull Moose Party*

JOHN C. SKIPPER

McFarland & Company, Inc., Publishers
Jefferson, North Carolina

All photographs are from the Library of Congress.

ISBN (print) 978-1-4766-6701-0 ∞
ISBN (ebook) 978-1-4766-3219-3

LIBRARY OF CONGRESS CATALOGUING DATA ARE AVAILABLE

BRITISH LIBRARY CATALOGUING DATA ARE AVAILABLE

© 2018 John C. Skipper. All rights reserved

No part of this book may be reproduced or transmitted in any form or by any means, electronic or mechanical, including photocopying or recording, or by any information storage and retrieval system, without permission in writing from the publisher.

Front cover: Theodore Roosevelt, head-and-shoulders portrait, facing front, speaking, 1912 (Library of Congress)

Printed in the United States of America

McFarland & Company, Inc., Publishers
Box 611, Jefferson, North Carolina 28640
www.mcfarlandpub.com

For John Lee,
who enjoys history as much as I do

Table of Contents

Preface — 1
Introduction — 7

1. Politics and Temperament — 15
2. The World in 1912 — 21
3. The Republican Evolution — 29
4. Teedie and Will — 36
5. The Roosevelt Presidency — 46
6. The Tragedy of Archie Butt — 52
7. The Great Divide — 58
8. LaFollette — 69
9. The Scheme and the Implosion — 74
10. Primary Considerations — 81
11. The Roosevelt Express — 87
12. The Republican National Committee — 99
13. An Unconventional Convention — 109
14. The Democrats — 123
15. The Progressives — 132
16. The Resolve of Taft — 140
17. Milwaukee — 146
18. Vast Differences in Approach — 154

19. Election Day	158
20. Retrospect	164
21. Reconciliation	171
Epilogue	177
Appendix A. 1912 Republican Primary Results	189
Appendix B. 1912 Democratic Party Platform (Summary)	190
Appendix C. 1912 Republican Party Platform (Summary)	196
Appendix D. 1912 Progressive Party Platform (Summary)	201
Appendix E. 1912 Socialist Party Platform (Summary)	208
Appendix F. Presidential Assassinations and Assassination Attempts	211
Chapter Notes	213
Bibliography	221
Index	225

Preface

The 1912 presidential election is the only one in American history that featured a president, a former president and a future president—William Howard Taft, the roly-poly, jovial Republican former jurist who would have much rather been on the Supreme Court than in the White House; Theodore Roosevelt, the former president who hand-picked Taft to be his successor and then tried to oust him four years later; and Woodrow Wilson, the Democrat and former president of Princeton University who looked and talked like a college professor.

Taft and Wilson emerged as their parties' candidates after raucous political conventions in which, for the Democrats, Wilson received the nomination on the 46th ballot and, for the Republicans, Taft was the victor in a process in which Roosevelt claimed the nomination was stolen from him, causing him to walk out and start a third-party candidacy.

Today's conventions are like elaborate stage productions—the political equivalent of a Broadway show with everything carefully staged and choreographed and a storyline in which there are few surprises and no surprise endings. They have become so predictable that the major television networks no longer broadcast them gavel-to-gavel, instead focusing on the major speeches every night.

It never used to be that way. Longtime political junkies remember times like the 1964 Republican convention when New York's liberal governor, Nelson Rockefeller, was booed so loudly by conservative Goldwater delegates, that his speech could not be heard, or when NBC commentator John Chancellor was carried out of the hall by security guards at the same convention because he apparently had not moved quickly enough when he was told to move out of an aisle.

In 1972, the Democrats ran so far behind schedule on the last night of their convention that George McGovern, whom they had chosen as their nominee for president, did not give his acceptance speech until about 2 a.m., Eastern time, when most of the nation had turned off their televisions and had gone to bed. At the 1980 Republican convention, there was a rumor that Ronald Reagan, the party's nominee, was going to select former president Gerald Ford as his running mate. There was so much anticipation about it that Reagan took the unprecedented step of coming to the convention on the night he was nominated to announce that George Bush was his choice to be on the ticket with him.

Nominations are taken care of on the first ballot these days. Not since 1956 has there been a need to go to a second ballot because no one got a majority on the first. In 1956, Democrats nominated Illinois governor Adlai Stevenson to be their presidential candidate, as they had in 1952, to run once again against Dwight D. Eisenhower. They deadlocked on their choice for vice president before nominating Senator Estes Kefauver of Tennessee on the second ballot. Perhaps the most significant factor in the vice presidential sweepstakes that year was that the man Kefauver defeated for the nomination was a young senator from Massachusetts, John F. Kennedy, who drew national attention, setting the stage for his run for the presidency four years later.

In this day and age, it is hard to imagine a political convention in which delegates brought their guns to the convention hall, planned fist fights to disrupt the proceedings, spoke from a podium with barbed wire strung around it to protect the speakers and ended with hundreds of delegates storming out in protest over the incumbent president receiving the nomination. But that's exactly what happened at the 1912 Republican convention in Chicago with the re-nomination of Taft, infuriating the backers of Roosevelt who, a month later, formed the new political party, the Progressives, and nominated Roosevelt as a third-party candidate.

All of this history was ample fuel for me, a political writer with almost a lifelong interest in presidential politics, to dig into it. The 1912 Republican convention, with all that led up to it, and all that followed, set the Republican Party on its ear and, in some ways, it has still not fully recovered from the bedlam that occurred a century ago. It is a story worth revisiting in today's political climate that rivals the venom of 1912.

It's hard to pinpoint when my interest in presidential politics began but I trace it back to a couple of things that occurred in my childhood more than 50 years ago. Not many people my age can claim this legacy: When I was a child in the 1950s, when kids my age had photos and bubblegum cards of Mickey Mantle, Willie Mays, Fess Parker (Davy Crockett) and George Reeves (Superman), I had a color photo on my bedroom wall of Dwight D. Eisenhower.

At my young age, I probably had trouble spelling "Eisenhower" but that didn't matter. He was president of the United States and therefore worthy of a place of distinction in my bedroom.

I don't know how my interest in presidents began. It might have been because of a ploy by my brother Jim, who was 11 years older than me. I liked hanging around with him whenever I could. But, not surprisingly, as I look back on it, there were times when he wanted to be with his friends without having to entertain his little brother. So he would try to find things for me to do to distract me from him.

On one of those occasions, instead of telling me to "scram," he said, "Why don't you go somewhere and memorize the presidents of the United States—in order."

And I did. I was proud to approach him a day or two later and recite for him, "Washington, Adams, Jefferson, Madison, Monroe…" all the way through to Eisenhower. Today, a half-century later, I can still do it, but it's a little more difficult because I'm a little older, my memory isn't as good as it used to be and there are 11 more presidents to recite.

Another childhood memory that is relevant is an auction I wandered into at the home of a woman who lived across the street and who had recently died. It was a typical auction in which furniture, appliances and other big-ticket items were being auctioned off. But there was some little stuff too, pots and pans and odd and ends that didn't fit any particular category.

One of the smaller items was a bowl the size of a cereal bowl. About the only thing you could see in it were spools of thread. Whatever else was in there was hidden by the spools on top. I had a couple of dollars in my pocket so, just for the heck of it, I bid on it—and I won. Apparently no one else wanted a bowl full of junk. I took it home and sorted through the stuff it contained—buttons and paper clips and colored toothpicks, as I recall. There was also a treasure for a kid like me. There, at the bottom of the bowl, was a William McKinley campaign button from 1896.

I was thrilled. With the encouragement of my parents, I began collecting presidential campaign buttons, finding many of them in second-hand shops and souvenir stores. I asked all of my parents' friends if they had any, to save them for me. I placed an ad in *Oak Leaves*, the weekly paper in my hometown of Oak Park, Illinois, asking townspeople to help me with my collection.

Every four years from the time I got the button in the auction, I made my way to local Republican and Democratic campaign headquarters and steadily added to my collection. Today, I have at least one button or pin from every presidential winner and loser since 1896. The old stickpins are out of fashion now, giving way to Velcro but that's about the only difference in them in the past 50 years.

As an adult, I began a newspaper career that has taken my family and me to several states but eventually led me to Iowa in 1984 where I have been ever since. Iowa's distinction in politics is that its caucuses every four years are the first-in-the-nation tests for would-be presidential candidates from both parties and have been the launching pad for many candidacies over the years. In 1976, a little-known peanut farmer from Georgia, Jimmy Carter, surprised the world by winning the Iowa caucuses on his way to winning the presidency.

My job as a political reporter in Iowa has afforded me the opportunity to interview or cover several past, present or future presidents—Gerald Ford, George H.W. Bush, George Bush, Bill Clinton, Barack Obama and Donald Trump among them—and dozens of presidential candidates including Al Gore, Bob Dole, John McCain, Steve Forbes, Pat Buchanan, Hillary Clinton, Joe Biden and nearly 50 others.

Having seen all of these candidates on the campaign trail has heightened my interest in the national political conventions of both parties because I have seen firsthand how it began for all of them. I have seen the candidates when they spoke before an audience of eight (Indiana senator Richard Lugar in 1995) and 1,800 (Senator Barack Obama in 2007).

These experiences have led to the publication of three of my books by McFarland: *The Iowa Caucuses: First Tests of Presidential Aspiration, 1972–2008*; *Showdown at the 1964 Democratic Convention: Lyndon Johnson, Mississippi and Civil Rights*; and *The 1964 Republican Convention: Barry Goldwater and the Beginning of the Conservative Movement*.

In doing the research for the convention books, two things were clear.—the conventions were contentious for a variety of reasons but were also emblematic of tensions in the country at those times, and, historians have agreed, all were tame compared to the Republican convention of 1912.

My own research confirms the historians are correct. In an atmosphere of fist fights, drawn guns, bribery and racism, Roosevelt, a former president, challenged Taft, the incumbent president, for the nomination. When it was apparent that Taft would win the nomination, Roosevelt claimed it had been stolen from him by party bosses. He and his followers stormed out of the convention and launched a third-party movement with Roosevelt at the top of the Progressive ticket (also called the Bull Moose ticket).

The split in the Republican Party between the conservatives of Taft and the progressives of Roosevelt handed the presidency to Democrat Woodrow Wilson. One hundred years later, scars from that election still haunt the Republican Party.

All of this background was ample fodder for the author, who so many years before had treasured his finding of a campaign button for William McKinley, the man who preceded Roosevelt in the presidency. Anyone involved in an extensive research project is indebted to the historians who preceded him, and this author is no exception. The bibliography at the end of this work is testament to that. In addition to books, magazines, radio and television transcripts and internet resources, several research institutions have been indispensable in putting the pieces of this book together.

The Library of Congress is an outstanding venue, filled with accurate, pertinent documents and photographs that are easily accessible. The same can be said for the Miller Center at the University of Virginia, a storehouse of history. The Theodore Roosevelt Center at Dickinson State University, Dickinson, South Dakota, was a third source of valuable information.

Also significant in this author's research are the letters that have been preserved for posterity. Long before emails and texting and Instagram and the like were even conceived, people sat down and wrote letters to one another, including influential individuals in the political wars of 1912. With these letters, the researcher gets an informed, insightful look at what people were thinking when they were either making history or observing it.

Examples are Roosevelt with his words embossed on paper with the use of a manual typewriter—one can almost hear his fingers pounding the keys; or TR's handwritten notes in swirling cursive; or Taft's more stately and straightforward prose, often lengthy and descriptive as he wrote to his beloved wife, Nellie; or the words of Archie Butt, the military aide to both presidents Roosevelt and Taft who was torn by the rift between the two men he served, admired and loved. He wrote scores of letters to his sister-in-law with the hope they would be preserved so that future generations would get a glimpse inside the White House and into the personalities of people whose words and actions shaped the world situations. His letters were preserved, providing fascinating and illuminating insights into the presidencies and personalities of two vastly different men who each became the leader of the nation.

The author also wishes to thank Bennett Smith, history instructor at North Iowa Area Community College, for his insights, editing, and perhaps most important, his encouragement, and to friends and colleagues, too numerous to mention, who all share the experience of having "heard" the book long before they will have had the chance to read it. My thanks to all for their perseverance.

Introduction

No guns.

That was the message from law enforcement to those attending the Republican National Convention in Cleveland in July of 2016, much to the chagrin of Second Amendment zealots who wanted to exercise their right to bear arms. Most of them came to the convention to enthusiastically support the nomination of Donald Trump who, four months later, was elected 45th president of the United States.

The notion of guns at a national political convention turned out to be just that—a notion. More than a century earlier, it was a reality at the raucous convention of 1912 when former president Theodore Roosevelt tried to wrest the nomination from President William Howard Taft, at one time his good friend and the man he ordained to succeed him in the White House.

At that convention in Chicago, to many of the delegates, some of them former Rough Riders with Roosevelt in the Spanish American War, carrying a gun was as common as wearing a wrist watch. Instead of police banning the weapons, the cops showed up in force at the Chicago Coliseum to do what they could to quell disturbances that were certain to break out. "Not since the Haymarket Riot have so many members of this fine body of constabulary been gathered in one place. They were in the galleries, they patrolled the aisles and mingled with the delegates, scrutinizing them with the familiar expression they wear when elbowing through a crowd of hoodlums."[1]

There are many relevant comparisons between the campaigns of 1912 and 2016. Each featured a New York man born into wealth, extraordinarily egotistical, obsessed with gaining power and influence, and who craved the limelight. Alice Roosevelt Longworth once said, "My father always wanted to be the corpse at every funeral, the bride at every wedding and the baby at every christening." Friends and foes alike would agree the same characteristics applied to Donald Trump.

One big difference between these two men who lived a century apart is that Roosevelt was a product of politics. In his time, he was both the message

Chicago police look as if they are posing for a class picture as they prepare to try to keep order at the Republican convention.

and the messenger, having been elected to the New York General Assembly, to the governorship of New York, to the vice presidency of the United States and finally to the presidency. Trump, who inherited a business empire and expanded it worldwide, had never before held public office.

In a television interview during the 2016 campaign, Trump was asked what he thought would happen if mainstream Republicans denied him the nomination. "I think you'd have riots," he said. And then he repeated it to emphasize his point. "I think you'd have riots."[2]

On another occasion, boasting about his popularity, he said he could shoot somebody in the middle of Fifth Avenue in New York and people would still vote for him. Some Republicans embraced and admired his bombastic nature. But many thought remarks like that were reckless and could plant the seed for violence.

In 1912, the Roosevelt forces actually planned a riot on the convention floor if Roosevelt was not nominated. The only reason it didn't happen was Roosevelt's floor manager, Missouri governor Herbert Hadley, who was designated to set off the disturbance while speaking from the floor, got cold feet and decided not to do it.

In his acceptance speech at the Cleveland convention, Trump outlined what he considered some of the nation's problems and declared, "I'm the only one who can fix it." In 1912, President Taft worried about Roosevelt's ego and what he thought was TR's belief that he was the only one that could do the job. In fact, Taft feared Roosevelt would seek to be re-elected every four years for the rest of his life.[3]

Trump gained fame through hosting a television program called *The Apprentice*, in which contestants sought his approval as if applying for a job. A catch-phrase from that show came from when Trump summarily ousted them by saying, "You're fired!"

In politics, he discovered early on how difficult it can be to "fix it" when dealing in a democracy rather than a board room. He couldn't "fire" Congress. Within the first 60 days of his administration, his bill proposing a major overhaul of the nation's health care system was pulled from consideration in the House because he did not have enough votes to pass it. When the House finally passed a health-care bill, it was considered "dead on arrival" in the Senate—and the stalemate continued.

Comparing Trump to Roosevelt, author Tim Bryan found some common ground. Both were "conceited to the point of bursting and opinionated beyond the resources of descriptive writing."[4] Former Speaker of the House John Boehner, a fellow Republican, said, "I think Donald Trump sees himself larger than life. He kind of reminds me of Teddy Roosevelt."[5]

The comparisons between the campaigns of 1912 and 2016 go far beyond the personalities of the candidates. "The party is riven between establishment and insurgents. The people's choice is prone to intemperate remarks and hot-headed declarations—to the delight of followers and the frustration of party leaders."[6]

Colorful American presidential campaigns are part of the fabric of democracy, ranging from the drab to the dramatic and even melodramatic. But the Republican campaign of 1912 and Roosevelt's obsession of winning back the White House, after stepping aside for four years, created a division within the Republican Party that remains more than 100 years later.

Historian Robert Novak, writing about Roosevelt's third-party run after being denied the nomination, said, "After this debacle, it would seem sensible for the Republican Party to forego ideological hairsplitting and instead effect a grand reunion of the party. But here is where the Republican Party begins to show a taint, an aberration, a sort of political masochism that plagues it to this day."[7]

Instead of uniting, Novak argues, the conservative wing of the party, despite losing the presidential election to Democrat Woodrow Wilson, rejoiced in casting aside the liberal faction of the party led by Roosevelt. "All of this, predictably enough, led to the permanent loss of the party's left wing with a cry of 'good riddance' from the conservatives. What the Old Guard didn't realize was that the Republican Party was descending into minority status, a party that could go to its right but not to its left."[8]

Another historian, Thomas Patterson, was blunt. He wrote, "A century ago, the Republican Party chose to become a permanent minority, not wittingly or directly but inevitably. It spent most of the succeeding decades trying without great success to overcome its mistake. Today's GOP is at a similar crossroads that could take it into the political wilderness for years to come."[9]

One big difference between Roosevelt in 1912 and Trump in 2016 is that Roosevelt lost and Trump won. Regardless, the split between the conservative and the moderate or liberal wings of the party still exists, and its roots can be traced to the Roosevelt-Taft showdown at the Chicago Coliseum in the summer of 1912.

While 1912 is remembered as the year Roosevelt led the Progressive movement in Republican politics, its aftermath was the Republican Party digging in its heels, shifting to the right and never looking back. In the aftermath of World War I, Republican candidates won elections in 1920, 1924 and 1928 but that is deceiving. Warren Harding won in 1920 at least in part by the voters distancing themselves from the eight years of Woodrow Wilson that included participation in a world war and consternation over his efforts to create the League of Nations. Harding was succeeded by Calvin Coolidge not because of popularity but because Harding died in office. Coolidge served out Harding's term and then was elected to a full term.

He chose not to run again in 1928. Herbert Hoover, popular because of relief efforts he led overseas during World War I and afterwards, was elected to succeed Coolidge. It was during his administration that the stock market crashed and America fell into what has come to be known as the Great Depression.

Democrats took over the White House in 1932 and held it for the next 20 years as the Republican Party flailed away, trying to find unity within the conservative and liberal wings of the party. They regained the White House with Dwight D. Eisenhower in 1952 but it was neither a conservative or liberal victory.

Eisenhower was a war hero from World War II whose politics were so middle-of-the-road that each party wooed him to be their candidate.

Along the way, there were periodic third-party and even fourth-party candidacies that made headlines—South Carolina governor Strom Thurmond and the Dixiecrats as well as former FDR cabinet member and vice president Henry Wallace of Iowa leading the Progressives, breaking away from Democrats in 1948; segregationist Alabama governor George Wallace in 1968; Illinois congressman John Andersen leaving the Republicans and running as an independent in 1980; Texas billionaire Ross Perot in 1992; and Ralph Nader taking crucial votes away from Democrat Albert Gore in the presidential race of 2000.

But all of them lost badly. Roosevelt remains the most successful third-party candidate ever. Conservative Republicans chose to let the Roosevelt supporters stew in their own juice and made no effort at unity. "The GOP had picked the wrong side of history and had misjudged the dynamics of a two-party system."[10]

The result was the Democratic Party, intact throughout the years, became the majority party in the country for generations to come with its liberal base while Republicans battled splits within the party that began with the Roosevelt defection in 1912.

That split was on public display in 1964 when the conservative wing of the party was strong enough to elevate its chief spokesman, the insurgent Senator Barry Goldwater of Arizona, as the Republican candidate, casting aside more liberal and mainstream candidates such as New York governor Nelson Rockefeller, Pennsylvania governor William Scranton and Michigan governor George Romney.

In 1976, Ronald Reagan, California's conservative governor, challenged President Gerald Ford, a moderate, for the Republican nomination, and fell short. But his campaign laid the groundwork for his successful run for the presidency in 1980.

The spotlight on the division within the party was once again evident in 2016 when Trump, the political newcomer, defeated Hillary Clinton, a former first lady, senator and secretary of state. The campaigns of both had been bitter, filled with name-calling, exaggerations, allegations of lies and with each candidate questioning the other's mental fitness for office—not unlike the Roosevelt-Taft tussle of 1912.

Trump, the multi-millionaire businessman with the ego and swagger of Roosevelt, championed himself as the agent for change, the man who would "make America great again" by "draining the swamp" in Washington. In his style of ignoring what he called "political correctness," he often said things on the campaign trail that offended many segments of the population but resonated with enough of the middle class to carry him to victory.

His speeches were laced with language not often heard in polite company. But Trump, who once authored a book called *The Art of the Deal*, like Roosevelt, knew the importance of branding and, in an age in which Americans were anxious for change, he branded himself as the change agent, much as Roosevelt had done. His campaign slogan was known in most households, Republican, Democrat or Independent: "Make America Great Again."

Clinton, who had run for the Democratic nomination in 2008, losing to Barack Obama, was once again attempting to be the first woman to be elected president—to "break the glass ceiling" as she often said. She was the embodiment of Washington establishment, just as President Taft was in 1912.

On November 8, 2016, she received three million more votes than

Trump, but Trump secured enough electoral votes to win the election. In 1912, Roosevelt was the winner in nine of 13 primary elections and got more than one million more votes than Taft in those primaries. But Taft had secured enough delegates in the other states—by hook and crook, according to the Roosevelt forces, to win the election.

Roosevelt was furious and abandoned the Republican Party even as its convention was still going on. He ran as a third party candidate on the Progressive ticket, often called the Bull Moose, that insured victory for Democrat Woodrow Wilson and drove the wedge through the middle of the Republican Party.

More than 100 years later, Trump amassed more primary votes than any Republican in history. But along the way, he alienated mainstream Republicans who tried to wrestle the nomination away from him. Longtime traditional Republicans feared a Trump candidacy would result in what happened in 1912—the end of the Republican Party as they had known it.

Seventeen candidates entered the Republican primary field and Trump disposed of all of his foes, often with nasty name-calling and labeling during a series of debates.

When the GOP faithful met for their convention in Cleveland, many Republican heroes were conspicuous by their absence. Former presidents George H.W. Bush and George W. Bush stayed home. So did the two most recent Republican presidential candidates, Senator John McCain of Arizona and former Massachusetts governor Mitt Romney. Other no-shows included Senator Lindsey Graham of South Carolina, Ohio governor John Kasich, whose state was hosting the convention and former Florida governor Jeb Bush, all of whom were defeated by Trump in the primaries and were subjects of his ridicule. Senator Ted Cruz of Texas, another of Trump's primary opponents, did speak at the convention, but when it became obvious he was not going to endorse Trump, the audience booed. The division within the party was on full display, just as it had been in 1912.

The campaign of 1912 has another distinction that seems routine in today's political spectrum but was unique in its day. For the first time in American history, presidential preference primaries were held with the goal of letting the people decide who the candidate should be rather than having him picked by party bosses.

Roosevelt, who was president from 1901 to 1908, used his enormous popularity to help propel his old friend and secretary of war in his cabinet, William Howard Taft, to succeed him. Taft defeated the Democrat, William Jennings Bryan, to win the presidency and presumably to inherit the legacy of Roosevelt and to expand on it. But Roosevelt became increasingly disenchanted with how Taft was handling that legacy.

After several months of stewing, he decided to challenge Taft for the

Introduction

Republican nomination in 1912. Roosevelt was politically savvy enough to know he had to do something to overcome Taft's influence on party bosses throughout the country. So he became an advocate of presidential preference primaries because he believed he would easily win the popular vote. And he was right. There were 13 primaries and Roosevelt won nine of them. Wisconsin senator Robert LaFollette won two as did Taft—a miserable showing for an incumbent president.

The focus of this book is on the Republican National Convention of 1912 in which Roosevelt accused Taft of "stealing" the nomination from him, causing him to defiantly run as a third-party candidate—the Progressive or "Bull Moose" party. The result was a divided Republican vote, gifting the presidency to Democrat Woodrow Wilson. The many events leading up to the convention, including the primary elections, help give context to what happened at the convention and after it.

The 1912 convention changed the equilibrium of a major political party for generations to come, creating the schism that has affected the GOP from TR to Trump. To fully understand how that occurred, it is necessary to examine the events leading up to it as well as the events that occurred afterward, including the Roosevelt and Taft presidencies, the fractured relationship between the two men, the advent of presidential primaries, the controversial decisions of the Republican National Committee, the bitter convention and the formation of a third political party. "Destiny is the one artifice that can use all tools and that finds a shortcut to its goal through ways mysterious and most devious."[11]

The following pages provide a play-by-play of this fascinating, mysterious and most devious political game.

1

POLITICS AND TEMPERAMENT

"We hold these truths to be self-evident; that all men are created equal, that they are endowed by their creator with certain unalienable rights; that among these are life, liberty and the pursuit of happiness." Jefferson and the framers of the Declaration of Independence set out not only the principles of a new nation but the tone of how they would be carried out—firm, forthright and passionate.

Self-evident truths. Unalienable rights. Equality. The forefathers of the nation expressed through their words a philosophy for governing a new nation and a certain temperament for the country and for those who would lead it. It is something that has been part of the American political being from the beginning. In presidential campaigns, it is personal and it is telling.

In 1860, Abraham Lincoln was seen by voters to have the temperament to guide a divided lnation. More than 150 years later, in 2016, Democrats and even some Republicans questioned whether Donald Trump, the GOP candidate, who was impulsive, insulting and often profane on the campaign trail, had what it took to be president. Was a man whose words offended women, Latinos, Muslims, Democrats and even moderate Republicans suited to be the person who one day might be entertaining foreign dignitaries and delivering State of the Union addresses? The voters said yes.

Many Americans had the same skepticism about the Democratic candidate, Hillary Clinton, a former first lady, former U.S. senator and former secretary of state. She was linked in one way or another to many scandals and was the subject of an FBI investigation for her questionable use of a private server in her home to deal with sensitive and perhaps classified State Department emails.

Going into the election of November 8, 2016, each candidate questioned whether the other had the temperament to be president.

In 1964, when President Lyndon Johnson was opposed by Republican Barry Goldwater, the Johnson campaign ran a television ad showing a little girl in the foreground, innocently picking petals off of daisies while, in the background, a fiery huge mushroom cloud, representing a nuclear bomb, filled the sky behind her. The image clearly portrayed Goldwater as a dangerous war monger and an extremist who did not have what it took to be president.[1]

In 1960, during the first televised presidential debate, Vice President Richard Nixon, the Republican candidate, who had recently been ill and was still feverish, looked gaunt and uncomfortable and sweated profusely. Senator John Kennedy, his Democratic opponent, had a becoming tan, a broad, infectious smile and seemed totally in control of the moment.

In each of these campaigns, the nation was asked to judge the candidates on an important variable, a quality that is hard to define but easy to recognize—temperament.

Regardless of background, experience, past controversies and positions on important issues of the times, candidates are often judged on whether they have the right combination of personality and grit to be leaders of the free world.

Researchers David Keirsey and Ray Choiniere formulated various categories of human temperaments and then evaluated American presidents based on their findings. They said, "Temperament is a lifelong predisposition toward certain identifiable patterns of behavior." They also said, "Character arises from the interplay of our environment and our temperament."[2]

Often, Americans identify temperament through the writings and speeches of candidates and presidents. President Franklin D. Roosevelt exuded confidence, when, in the midst of the Great Depression, he reassured a troubled nation, saying, "The only thing we have to fear is fear itself."

His successor, Harry S Truman, was a plain-spoken, no-nonsense politician, not given to fancy oratory with his nasal-sounding voice. But he is well remembered for a sign he had on his desk in the oval office which read, "the buck stops here."

On January 20, 1961, President John F. Kennedy, in his inaugural address, struck optimistic themes for the future and asked Americans to do their part, saying, "Ask not what your country can do for you; ask what you can do for your country."

Exactly 20 years later, newly-sworn in President Ronald Reagan proclaimed the greatness of America, comparing it to "a shining city on a hill."

On an entirely different level, on November 17, 1973, in the midst of the Watergate scandal that would eventually lead to his resignation, a defiant President Richard Nixon told Associated Press managing editors at their annual meeting, "I'm not a crook."

Reagan often showed a sunny disposition but also showed stern leadership as when he gave a speech in West Berlin, Germany, on June 12, 1987. Referencing the Berlin Wall which separated communist East Berlin from

1. Politics and Temperament

Theodore Roosevelt and William Howard Taft, once the best of friends, became bitter rivals for the Republican presidential nomination in 1912.

West Berlin, Reagan gave a directive to the Soviet leader, saying, "Mr. Gorbachev, tear down this wall."

At the start of the 20th century, Theodore Roosevelt, a brash, egotistical, boisterous former cowboy, police commissioner and governor of New York, was elected vice president of the United States and was thrust into the presidency upon the assassination of President William McKinley in September of 1901. Roosevelt is often remembered for his one-sentence philosophy of governing: "Speak softly but carry a big stick."

When Roosevelt won election in his own right in 1904, he said he would not seek another term. He reasoned that serving seven years was tantamount to serving two terms and, following the precedent set by George Washington, believed two terms were enough. It was a statement he would come to regret.

In 1908, Roosevelt threw his support to his longtime friend, William Howard Taft, who had been his secretary of war and his confidante, to succeed him. Taft was a lawyer and judge who had served effectively as governor of the Philippines, a U.S. territory, doing all of this before becoming part of Roosevelt's cabinet. More than any other government official, Taft was a Roosevelt loyalist who often became the president's spokesman, traveling around the country as the chief advocate of administration policies.

Roosevelt was extremely popular and whoever he might choose to be his successor had a distinct advantage over any opponent. Taft won easily in the election of November 1908. But it wasn't long before Taft started to drift from Roosevelt's agenda, preferring to compromise with Congress rather than fighting it tooth-and-nail.

When he left office, Roosevelt purposely tried to detach himself from American politics by going on an African safari. But word of some of his successor's actions reached him overseas and Roosevelt became more and more discontent with Taft. He came to believe he had made two great mistakes as president—pledging not to run for another term and choosing Taft to succeed him.

The division between these two men became so great that Roosevelt decided to, in his words, "throw his hat in the ring"—a western rodeo term—and try to wrest the nomination away from the incumbent president in 1912.

Roosevelt offered a strange rationalization for his decision to run again, in effect retracting his pledge not to seek a third term. "Frequently, when asked to take another cup of coffee at breakfast, I say 'No thank you. I won't take another cup.' This does not mean that I never intend to take another cup of coffee during my life; it means I am not accepting the offer as applying to that breakfast and that my remark is limited to that breakfast."[3]

The struggle between the two men was epic. Historians say it changed the dynamics of the Republican party for generations. They also point out that, at the heart of their differences, at the very core of how they approached the problems of the country and, for that matter, their reaction to each other, came down to a matter of temperament. "Roosevelt and Taft's temperaments could not have been more different. Where Roosevelt was a politician, activist and warrior, Taft was an executive, mediator and judge. Taft had been a talented and loyal lieutenant serving brilliantly as governor of the Philippines before joining TR's cabinet as secretary of war. But he had never run for a major elective office."[4]

Roosevelt's good friend, New York Senator Elihu Root, who had served in TR's cabinet, told him he wouldn't be able to keep his pledge to not run for president again "because of your temperament; because of the urgent need of your nature for prompt decision and action which must make an attitude like this for you a condition of unstable equilibrium.... No thirsty sinner ever took a pledge harder to keep than it will be for you to maintain this position."[5]

Root proved to be correct and, ironically, presided over the convention in which Roosevelt sought unsuccessfully to get the nomination. "Taft was not a pugnacious fighter. He hated combat.... Colonel Roosevelt was rather careless of his innuendo. He said things that were hard for Taft to forget. And Taft kept making unconscionable blunders that were elephantine insults to all that Roosevelt believed. Temperamentally, the two men could not be reconciled once a quarrel had started."[6]

When he left office, Roosevelt preferred to be called "colonel," a reference to his military days in the Spanish-American War, rather than "president," because he believed the country only had one president at a time. So he was called "colonel" often by those who knew him, out of respect for him and at his request.

Roosevelt had perhaps the best rapport with members of the press than any other president. He considered many of them confidantes whose advice he sought, part of his inner circle who helped write and edit his speeches and spread his message all over the country. His coziness with the media was unique and yet an asset to both. Roosevelt used the press for his advantage and the press used the president for their advantage—and they both knew they were using one another. It was an improbable, incredible relationship that required, on the part of Roosevelt, a unique personality in order to pull it off. "No president ever lived on better terms with the newspapermen than Roosevelt did. He treated them all with perfect fairness, according no special favors, no 'beats' or 'scoops' to anyone, so they regarded him as 'square,' a man of his word."[7]

Perhaps because of his background as a jurist, Taft preferred to keep the press at a comfortable distance from him. "He was simply 'not constituted' as Roosevelt was to expound upon his thoughts and vent his feelings with members of the press. It was, as Taft came to realize, a matter of temperament."[8]

In their research Kiersey and Choiniere identified four specific temperaments in human beings: (1) Artisan—generally colorful, adventuresome, brave; (2) Guardian—generally careful, unexciting and exercising great self-control; (3) Rational—generally intelligent, ethical, philosophical, given to careful, thoughtful consideration; and (4) Idealist—generally optimists who are given to be big dreamers as a direct result of their optimistic natures. Interestingly, the researchers could find no idealists among the 45 presidents.

They conclude that Roosevelt was the adventuresome Artisan, Taft the laid-back Guardian, temperaments that created a balance in their early personal friendship but ultimately crushed the friendship when push came to shove on the political stage. Oil and water.

Perhaps the differences in their approach to government is best expressed through their own words. Taft, the former jurist who did not like confrontation and sought to be loved and respected, was chagrined when he went out on the campaign trail. He once said he might as well give up being a candidate because so many people in the country didn't like him. As a candidate for re-election, Taft rarely went on the campaign trail, believing it was unbecoming for a president to do so. But it also gave him a convenient excuse to avoid the discomfort he felt in engaging in verbal combat.

By contrast, Roosevelt loved a good fight. His view on political wars was included in a speech he gave at the Sorbonne in Paris in 1910, a passage that many politicians in future generations have adopted as their mantra: "It is not the critic who counts, not the man who points out how the strong man stumbles or where the doer of deeds could have done them better. The credit belongs to the man who is actually in the arena, whose face is marred by dust and sweat and blood, who strives valiantly, who errs, who comes short again and again—because there is no effort without error and shortcoming, but who does actually strive to do the deeds, who knows great enthusiasm, the great devotions, who spends himself in a worthy cause, who at best, knows in the end the triumph of high achievement and who, at the worst, if he fails, at least fails while daring greatly so that his place shall never be with those cold and timid souls who know neither victory or defeat."[9]

2

THE WORLD IN 1912

It was big, haughty and seemingly unsinkable.

In many ways, the *Titanic*, the first-of-its-kind massive luxury ocean liner, represented the transformation taking place in the United States and other parts of the world in 1912—a flamboyant advance in technology, science, nautical acumen, expectations and in power and influence. It spewed success.

The *Titanic* set off on its much-heralded maiden voyage from Southampton, England, on April 10, with 2,224 passengers, the highest of high society and richest of the rich aboard. There were also newsmen among the throngs, ready to report the details of the journey to the rest of the world as the ship headed for New York.

The *Titanic* was emblematic of the times. America had experienced a whirlwind of changes since the end of the Civil War. In the next four decades, Thomas Edison introduced his countrymen to the marvels of electricity; Alexander Graham Bell developed a new way of communicating with a device he called the telephone; forms of travel were advancing from horse and buggy to railroads to Henry Ford's automobiles to Orville and Wilbur Wright's flying machine they called an airplane—and to luxury ocean liners such as Thomas Andrews' *Titanic*. America and the world were on the move.

The inventive spirit was infectious and produced both survivors and victims in its wake. As the industrial revolution swept across the nation, entrepreneurs had a passion to build something better and cheaper. They built factories to manufacture new and better products for their willing consumers and hired as many workers as they could to meet the demands for their goods. One of the results was a work atmosphere in which men and women took low-paying jobs in unsafe and unhealthy working conditions while their bosses became wealthy and influential. An affluent America had become a nation where the rich got richer and the poor got poorer. As successful as these business tycoons were, many of them became known as "robber barons" because of their greed and how they treated their employees.

"Capitalism had generated a wave of miraculous changes in everyday life—railroads, electric lights, telephones, automobiles—and raised the overall standard of living, but it also opened up a large gap between rich and poor and caused a great deal of suffering, social unrest, corruption and dislocation."[1] "From the ashes of the American Civil War sprung an economic powerhouse.... After the war, beginning with the railroads, small businesses grew larger and larger. By century's end, the nation's economy was dominated by a few, very powerful individuals. In 1850, most Americans worked for themselves. By 1900, most Americans worked for an employer."[2]

Among the tycoons who emerged and held immense power because of the industries they built, the products they produced and the jobs they provided were John D. Rockefeller, founder of the Standard Oil Company; Andrew Carnegie, whose steel company provided the raw materials for much of what made the American economy operate; and Cornelius Vanderbilt, who provided the means to transport those raw materials as well as finished products throughout much of the country first through his steamboat company and later through his railroad empire.

The era between the end of the Civil War and the start of the 20th century, roughly about 35 years, came to be known as the Gilded Age as all the new technology fueled the American economy. Railroads were at the heart of the surge because they literally provided the movement of goods and services. It was railroads that provided the means to transport all manner of manufactured products as well as their individual parts; food and dairy products; and merchandise for store shelves all over the country.

Equally important, people were able to travel hundreds of miles quickly compared to the time it took to get from one place to another by horseback, horse and buggy and stagecoach. It is estimated that at the end of the Civil War, the U.S. had 35,000 miles of railroad track. By 1900, that number had jumped to 200,000. With the rise of importance of railroads came the rise of the barons who ran the railroads and, in time, that became a political problem that helped spawn the Progressive movement toward more government regulation of big business and more championing of the rights of the consumer.

Rockefeller used his wealth to purchase other oil companies and thereby eliminate competition, a process known as horizontal integration. Carnegie used his fortune to buy companies that were suppliers of products he needed for his steel operation—vertical integration. Whereas Rockefeller was known for his stinginess and poor treatment of his workers, Carnegie created profit-sharing plans for his employees.

In 1901, Carnegie sold his interests to J.P. Morgan for $500 million. Morgan created U.S. Steel Corporation. In retirement, Carnegie donated more than $350 million to public foundations. He built Carnegie-Mellon University in Pittsburgh and donated to the construction of 3,000 libraries throughout the country. He also funded the construction of Carnegie Hall in New York.

Vanderbilt started building his fortune in the steamboat industry and later became a hugely successful railroad magnate, creating the New York Central Railroad and having interests in many other rail companies. Like Carnegie, he donated millions to worthy causes including the university that bears his name.

Historian H. Roger Grant described Vanderbilt in a way that could also be applied to many industrialists of his time: "Contemporaries hated or feared Vanderbilt or at least considered him an unmannered brute. While Vanderbilt could be a rascal, combative and cunning, he was much more a builder than a wrecker."[3]

In the second half of the 19th century, the growth of the American economy was astounding. Competition was fierce. The industrialists who couldn't keep up were bought out by their bigger, richer competitors or were forced into bankruptcy.

By 1912, some dramatic changes had taken place. Theodore Roosevelt, president of the United States from 1901 to 1908, was a crusader intent on using the powers of his office to give the nation a "square deal" in their workplaces and in their quality of life outside of work. His energy was boundless and his enthusiasm contagious.

He had first used the term "square deal" in an Independence Day speech he made in Springfield, Illinois, in 1903. He proclaimed, "A man who is good enough to shed his blood for his country is good enough to be given a square deal afterward. More than that no man is entitled to, and less than that no man shall have."[4]

Roosevelt understood the importance of big business in stimulating the American economy but also did not hesitate to try to stop it from strangling the average citizen with its power. That was the essence of not only the "Square Deal" but the birth of the Progressive political movement in America.

William Allen White, editor of the Emporia, Kansas, Gazette, wrote, "[It] was a time of tremendous change in our national life, particularly as it affected our national attitudes. The American people were melting down old heroes and recasting the mold in which heroes were made."[5]

White said newspapers, magazines and books closely monitored the changes taking place. He wrote, "The people were questioning the way every rich man got his money. They were ready to believe he was a scamp who pinched pennies out of the teacups of the poor by various shenanigans, who was distributing his largess to divert attention from his rascality."[6]

Magazine and newspaper writers exposed the horrid conditions in many of the nation's workplaces as well as corrupt businessmen and government officials, setting the stage for a social crusade.

S.S. McClure, a magazine publisher, hired a stable of writers who had a single mission—to tell the truth about what White referred to as "shenanigans" in business and government. These were the writers, White among them, who Roosevelt called "muckrakers," which was at first a derogatory term but one that McClure and the writers took pride in. In time, Roosevelt came to respect their work and developed a close relationship with some of them who actually helped shape some of the president's policies.

Among them was Lincoln Steffens, who wrote extensively about corruption in government and wrote a masterful piece for McClure's in 1902 titled "Tweed Days in St. Louis." It was later published in a book that included many of his writings.

Not mincing any words, Steffens wrote, "The riffraff, catching the smell of corruption, rushed into the municipal assembly, drove out the remaining respectable men and sold the city—its streets, its wharfs, its markets ... to the now greedy businessmen and bribers.... When the leading men began to devour their own city, the herd rushed into the trough and fed also."[7]

S.S. McClure published a magazine that exposed dangers and health hazards in businesses run by America's most powerful industrialists.

Ida Tarbell exposed Rockefeller as a money-grabbing, miserly dictator in her "History of Standard Oil" in 1908. Quoting congressional testimony on a price-fixing scheme, she wrote, "The railroad companies have combined with an organization of individuals known as the Standard Ring; they give to that party the sole and entire control of all the petroleum refining interest and petroleum shipping interest in the United States and consequently place the whole producing interest entirely at their mercy."[8]

Similarly Ray Stannard Baker's "The Right to Work" in McClure's in 1903 informed the nation about dangerous conditions existing in coal mines and the power of unions. In his work, Baker often used the words of the workers themselves such as in the plight of a non-striking miner who was shot at while he stood in his front yard late at night. "I claim my right as a free man to do what my conscience approves ... to work for my home and loved ones. If I am murdered for this, I ask my enemies to face me in daylight ... and not in the dead of night."[9]

Upton Sinclair's 1906 book, *The Jungle*, exposed dangerous and unhealthy conditions in the meat-packing industry that led Congress to pass the Pure Food and Drug Act and the Meat Inspection Act.

Sinclair also focused on how workers were treated. "The man who told tales and spied upon his fellow workers would rise, but the man who minded his own business and did his work, why they would speed him up till they had worn him out, and then they would throw him into the gutter."[10]

The result of these types of conditions on the worker was heart-wrenching, according to Sinclair. "So he went on, tearing up all the flowers from his soul, and setting his heel upon them."[11]

McClure was a man with "restless enthusiasm and "manic energy." He wanted his writers to "begin their research without preconceived notions, to carry their readers through their own process of discovery. As they educated themselves about social and economic inequities, rampant in the wake of teeming industrialization, so they educated the entire country."[12]

Their work brought on an era of reform that the informed public welcomed. "A sudden new interest in the underdog was manifest in the land. He was not exalted but universally the people began to understand what slums were, what sweatshops were, what exploited labor was, what absentee landlordism had become in our urban life, what railroad rates were doing to the farmer and to the consumer."[13]

In 1912, Americans went about their business, having no idea the country would be swept into a world war in five years that would dramatically change many of their lives in ways muckrakers could do nothing to expose or prevent.

It was the year in which New Mexico and Arizona became the 47th and 48th states, the year Fenway Park opened in Boston and the year the Red Sox celebrated their new ballpark by winning the American League championship and the World Series.

The average citizen made ends meet on an income of $1,200 a year, up from $500 a year 25 years ago. They could mail a letter with a two-cent stamp, get a tooth filling for 50 cents and keep themselves healthy by going to places like Dr. Johnson's Institute in Denver where, for $5 to $10, they could be treated "for all acute and chronic diseases under written guarantee."[14]

In Baltimore, a chubby, uncouth 17-year-old boy was arousing a lot of local interest by how hard he could hit and throw a baseball. Two years later, George Herman "Babe" Ruth would be pitching for the Boston Red Sox and still later would be known as the "Sultan of Swat" with the New York Yankees.

It was a year in which people sang and danced to many new songs including "When Irish Eyes Are Smiling" and "Be My Little Baby Bumblebee." William Frawley, a vaudeville singer who later gained fame for his portrayal of Fred Mertz on the *I Love Lucy* television program, introduced a song by George Norton and Ernie Burnett called "Melancholy Baby." Another catchy tune published that year was called "It's a Long Way to Tipperary."

Also of note—a 24-year-old songwriter named Irving Berlin, who was born in Russia, wrote "Alexander's Ragtime Band," one of 21 songs he published that year. He would go on to have a 60-year career as one of America's most prolific and popular song writers.

Americans were also entertained by Harry Houdini, a daredevil magician and escape artist who was born in Budapest, Hungary and who in 1912 allowed himself to be handcuffed, put in leg shackles, stuffed into a crate that was nailed shut and lowered into the East River in New York. It took him 57 seconds to free himself and emerge from the river.

When the *Titanic* left Southampton on April 10, many wealthy, influential Americans were its guests in first class. Among them were John Jacob Astor IV, a real estate developer, inventor and financier whose buildings included what came to be known as New York's Waldorf-Astoria Hotel. Also aboard was Isador Strauss, owner of Macy's Department Store in New York City and his wife, Ida; industrialist Benjamin Guggenheim as well as his mistress, valet and chauffeur; Archie Butt, military aide to President William Howard Taft; Henry B. Harris, theatrical manager and producer; James Clinch Smith, well-known New York sportsman; William T. Stead, a British editor; Margaret "Molly" Brown, a millionairess from Denver; J. Bruce Ismay, president of the White Star Line company that owned the *Titanic*; and Thomas Andrews of Harland and Wolff Corporation, the ship's builder.

The largest passenger steamship ever built—883 feet in length with weight measured in hundreds of tons—was deemed "unsinkable" by *Shipbuilder* magazine. It had made stops in Cherbourg, France, and Queenstown, Ireland, and was headed for New York on the night of April 14, four days into its spectacular journey when suddenly, a ferocious jolt knocked passengers to the ground, tossed dishes and furniture as if they were dollhouse trinkets and, more significantly, brought in an unending tide of seawater that spelled certain death if it was not stopped. And it was not stopped. The ship had hit an iceberg and, within a very few moments, a glorious adventure turned into unspeakable tragedy. By 2:20 a.m. on the morning of April 15, after an insufficient number of lifeboats were afloat with as many passengers as possible, the *Titanic* plunged two miles to the ocean floor. More than 1,500 passengers perished. Legend has it that as the ship was going down, the band, still performing, played "Nearer My God to Thee." In the end, the unthinkable happened. The unsinkable had sunk.

2. The World in 1912

Wealth, influence and ego could do nothing to stop the force of the sea. "The technological aspects of the tragedy aside, *Titanic*'s demise has taken on a deeper, almost mythic meaning in popular culture. Many view the tragedy as a morality play about the dangers of human hubris."[15]

Eleven years earlier, Roosevelt had risen to the presidency because of a tragedy at home. President William McKinley, the Ohio Republican, was shot and killed in September 1901, becoming the third president to be assassinated in 36 years and the second in the past 20 years. Vice President Roosevelt, the brash former "Rough Rider" of Spanish American War fame who could cajole political opponents and unify supporters with his electrifying speeches, was sworn in as McKinley's successor. At age 42, he became the youngest president in American history.[16]

He served the remaining three years of McKinley's term and then won election in his own right in 1904. Upon his election in 1904, he announced he would not seek another term in 1908. It was his view that no president should serve more than two terms, a tradition that began with George Washington. Roosevelt felt that since he had served three years of McKinley's term—in effect, nearly a full term—that he should serve no longer than 1908. It was a decision he would come to regret.

President William McKinley was assassinated in September 1901, elevating Vice President Theodore Roosevelt to the presidency.

Roosevelt selected his longtime close friend, William Howard Taft to succeed him, and the voters went along with his wishes. Taft, a former judge who had been Roosevelt's secretary of war, won election easily. But he did not have the Roosevelt personality or grit and was comfortable trying to reach agreement with congressmen rather than taking them on as Roosevelt loved to do. Whereas Roosevelt embraced the press and used them for his purposes, Taft was uncomfortable around them.

When Roosevelt left office, he went on an African safari to take him far away from politics where he would not be second-guessing his successor or competing with him for headlines. But some of his political insiders in Washington found ways of keeping him informed of political trouble at home. When he returned to America, he was shocked by how his old friend Taft had drifted away from the policies that he had fought for and how Taft had dumped some government officials who had been part of his predecessor's inner circle.

At the core of the problems between Roosevelt and Taft was a basic difference in philosophy. Roosevelt never backed away from a good fight. He used the power of the presidency to try to ramrod his programs through Congress by either flattering or intimidating those who stood in his way or using what he called "the bully pulpit"—his ability to use his flamboyant personality and oratory to win over the press and the public.

Taft was a jurist, a conciliatory person, who respected the three branches of government, and was willing to compromise with Congress in the belief that half a loaf was better than no loaf at all. Whereas Roosevelt was a galloping Progressive, Taft was a slow-moving and methodical moderate and, in Roosevelt's view, a willing tool of the conservatives.

So Roosevelt, who had pledged not to seek another term in office and who had practically ordained his close friend to take the reins of the presidency, decided he had no choice but to "throw his hat in the ring," as he called it, and challenge Taft for the Republican presidential nomination in 1912.

In effect, he set out to reverse two serious mistakes in judgment he believed he had made as president—the decision not to run again and the selection of Taft as his successor.

Hence, Roosevelt re-entered political life and with that, the Republican Party was about to experience a political *Titanic* that would affect its fortunes for several generations.

"The one great error Roosevelt committed during his presidency was the designation of William Howard Taft as his successor," wrote historian Robert Novak. "But it was a fatal error. Roosevelt was so much more clearly popular than President Taft within the party that the Progressive wing was probably stronger under Roosevelt's leadership than the conservative wing under Taft's."[17]

More than 50 years later, Novak concluded that the debacle of the 1912 Republican convention "provoked the schism from which the Republican party never has recovered."[18]

3

THE REPUBLICAN EVOLUTION

Most every presidential election brings with it allegations of fraud, lies and deception by supporters of all candidates and, in some cases, by the candidates themselves. Each election carries its own brand of unsavory dialogue that may seem new but, in truth, is as old as the first time two political candidates challenged one another. Sometimes the political sparring is between candidates of the same party as was the case in 2016 when Donald Trump bested 16 other candidates for the Republican nomination in a campaign of dueling tongues.

Chicanery is nothing new to the Republican Party. President Abraham Lincoln is regarded by historians as one of the nation's greatest presidents. But in his time, Lincoln was hardly the darling of the Republican Party.

He was the newly-formed party's first president, a fact well-noted in American history. A side note often forgotten in political discourse is that it took three ballots to nominate Lincoln in 1860. Senator William Seward of New York, a former two-term governor, was the favorite as Republicans gathered for their convention in Chicago. It took 233 votes to win the nomination and Seward and his people felt confident they had two-thirds of what they needed locked in before they arrived in the Windy City.

Seward had a distinguished political career and was noted for being an outspoken opponent of slavery. Carl Shurz, a well-known and respected journalist, described Seward as "one of those spirits who sometimes will go ahead of public opinion instead of tamely following its footprints."[1]

But winning the nomination on the first ballot would be tricky because of the number of other candidates. They included Simon Cameron of Pennsylvania, Salmon P. Chase of Ohio, Edwin Bates of Missouri and Lincoln, a favorite-son candidate from Illinois.

Cameron was a senator from Pennsylvania who was not held in as high regard as Seward. In fact, Thaddeus Stevens, a colorful congressman from Vermont, considered him a thief. Asked about Cameron's honesty, Stevens said with sarcasm, "Well, I don't think he would steal a red-hot stove." When

Cameron demanded an apology, Stevens said, "I believe I said he would not steal a red-hot stove. I will now take that back."[2]

Next to Seward, Chase was the candidate with the best credentials to be president. He was a senator and former governor of Ohio and was instrumental in the formation of the Republican Party. He is credited with helping write a document that best explained Republican principles.

Bates was an anti-slavery lawyer and politician from Missouri who gained fame in the estimation of some, notoriety in the opinion of others, for his legal efforts on behalf of slaves in several celebrated cases.

The candidates stayed away from the convention but their operatives were there, cajoling and conniving. The Lincoln people influenced party officials in charge of seating arrangements for the convention and had Seward's New York delegation seated at the back of the hall, making it more difficult for them to converse with—and convert—delegates for other candidates.

On the third day of the convention—nomination day—Seward supporters marched triumphantly to the convention hall behind a brass band they had hired which played "Oh, Isn't He a Darling." When the enthusiastic bunch arrived at the hall, ready to rally for Seward, they were turned away. Lincoln's people had distributed counterfeit tickets to their people who filled all the empty seats.[3]

On the first ballot, Seward prevailed with 173 votes, 60 short of the required number. Lincoln was second with 102. Cameron had 50, Chase 49 and Bates 48. On the second ballot, Seward picked up 11 votes but Lincoln surged, adding 79. Seward still led with 184 to Lincoln's 181. The wheeling and dealing continued and on the third ballot, Lincoln tallied 231½, coming just shy of the 233 he needed for the nomination. Then, at the last moment, Ohio changed four of its votes to Lincoln, giving him the nomination. In November, he was elected 16th president of the United States.[4]

So the Republican Party was off and running in presidential politics but it wasn't easy and it was just a harbinger of what was to come. The journey of the GOP in presidential politics has been a hectic one from the days of Lincoln to the rocky 2016 nominating process. One issue, more than any other, led to the formation of the party.

By the middle of the 19th century, slavery was the core issue that divided the nation geographically and politically. Government made well-meaning but feeble attempts to legislate a solution.

The Missouri Compromise of 1820 divided the country at the 36/30 parallel between the pro-slavery, plantation-filled south and the more industrial-centered, anti-slavery north. There was sound political reasoning for dividing the nation by such an unusual method on the map. It was a way of admitting Missouri to the union as a slave state while admitting Maine as a free state. That was the essence of the compromise. Missouri was actually north of the

3. The Republican Evolution

36/30 line but was still added as a slave state to balance out the addition of Maine. The compromise was limited to territory included in the Louisiana Purchase.

In 1854, the Missouri Compromise was repealed by the Kansas-Nebraska Act which created the territories of Kansas and Nebraska. The policy of "popular sovereignty" was included in the Act, allowing settlers in each territory to determine whether to permit slavery. It was considered a sovereign way of doing things since a public vote decided it in each territory. (Kansas became a state in 1861 and Nebraska in 1867.)

Three years later, the Dred Scott decision changed everything again—dramatically. Scott was the slave of an Army doctor and had lived in Missouri, a slave state and had also lived for a time in Illinois and the Northwest Territory, both slave free, before returning to Missouri and being considered a slave. Scott sued in 1846, claiming his years in free territory allowed him to be a free man. Through delays and appeals to higher courts, the case came before the United States Supreme Court in 1857.

Slavery had been the subject of legislative review for nearly 40 years. Now, the highest court in the land was to decide whether it was constitutional for the federal government to exclude it from the territories, as the Missouri Compromise had done.

The court ruled that Scott's "sojourn," as it called it, into free territory and the free state of Illinois did not make him free upon his return to Missouri. Further, it ruled black people were excluded from U.S. citizenship and therefore could not sue. Finally, and emphatically, the court ruled Congress had no right to bar slavery in the territories because it denied people's property rights in violation of the Fifth Amendment. In other words, the court ruled slaves were property, not people. And slave owners could take their "property" into free states without being at risk.

It was against this backdrop that a growing group of anti-slavery northerners decided they needed to unite and try to right the wrongs that slavery represented. The result was the forming of a new political party that started with a meeting in Ripon, Wisconsin, on March 20, 1854. It is generally regarded as the date of the founding of the Republican Party. The first organizing convention took place in February of 1856 with the first nominating convention in Philadelphia in June of 1856. John Fremont secured a place in political history by becoming the first Republican candidate for president. He lost to James Buchanan. Lincoln became the first Republican president with his election in 1860.

The party actually got its name through an editorial written by Horace Greeley, editor of the *New York Tribune* on June, 24, 1854, about three months after the meeting in Ripon: Greeley wrote, "We should not care much whether those thus united (against slavery) were designated Whig, Free Democrat or something else, though we think some simple name like Republican would more fitly designate those who had united to restore the Union to its true mission of champion and promulgator of Liberty rather than propagandist of Slavery."[5]

Republicans won the White House in all but eight years of the first 52 years of their existence, and in that time, only one Democrat beat them—Grover Cleveland in 1885 and 1893. But the dominance came with some pain and anguish.

Lincoln was shot and killed by John Wilkes Booth while attending a play at Ford's Theater on April 14, 1865. His assassination was part of a plot by southern sympathizers to kill Lincoln, Vice President Andrew Johnson, Secretary of State William Seward and Union Army Gen. Ulysses S. Grant. While Booth snuck into the theater and shot Lincoln, co-conspirator Lewis Paine went to Seward's home and viciously stabbed Seward, his two sons and an Army nurse, all of whom survived. Another conspirator, George Atzerodt, was assigned to kill Johnson but lost his nerve and got drunk in the same hotel in which Johnson was staying. The plan to kill Grant was thwarted when the general left town unexpectedly earlier in the

Journalist Horace Greeley is credited with coming up with the term "Republican" for the new political party.

Abraham Lincoln, nominated on the third ballot, became the first Republican president.

3. The Republican Evolution

day. Mary and John Surratt, mother and son, were masterminds of the planned mass murders. For her part, Mary Surratt became the first woman to be executed in the United States.

Johnson, the Democrat-turned-Republican who ascended to the presidency upon the assassination of Lincoln, was hounded by members of his own party as he dealt with Reconstruction issues and state's rights. Congress put new restrictions on the presidency and when Johnson was accused of overstepping his authority, the House of Representatives voted 11 articles of impeachment against him. He was tried in the Senate and was acquitted by one vote.

Chase, the Ohio politician who lost the presidential nomination to Lincoln in 1860, served as Lincoln's secretary of the treasury and was later appointed chief justice of the United States by Lincoln. He presided over Johnson's impeachment trial.

Grant, the general who led Union forces to victory in the Civil War, was a hero to President Lincoln but he sided with radical Republicans who opposed Johnson. He was elected president in 1869 and served two terms but was often criticized for being easily led and not exercising the leadership qualities that made him a successful general.

Another Republican, Rutherford B. Hayes followed Grant into the White House but his election did not lack drama or controversy. Democrat Samuel Tilden won the popular vote by nearly 300,000 votes but the electoral votes in Louisiana, South Carolina and Florida were challenged. Hayes needed to win all three states to be elected. The dispute went on for weeks.

In January of 1877, Congress established a special 15-member commission to weigh all considerations and determine a winner. In an effort to make it a bi-partisan group, it was made up of seven Republicans, seven Democrats and a member of the Supreme Court. "It was understood that the crucially important swing

Rutherford B. Hayes won the presidency as a result of a one-vote margin of a special commission formed to decide the outcome of the election.

member would be Justice David Davis, an appointee of Lincoln, who was widely respected for both his fairness and his nonpartisanship. With him on the commission, it appeared likely that at least one of the disputed electoral votes would be awarded to Tilden, thus making the Democrat president."[6]

Not long after the commission was formed, the Illinois Legislature, under Democratic control, had to fill a vacancy in the U.S. Senate—and it chose Davis, making him ineligible to serve on the commission. Justice Joseph P. Bradley, described as "an independent-leaning Republican," was named to replace Davis on the commission. "Bradley did not exhibit any such independent traits. He joined with the seven other Republicans to constitute an eight-vote majority, awarding the disputed electoral votes in every state to Hayes, the Republican."[7]

With the 8–7 vote, Hayes was declared to be the 19th president of the United States in what remains the closest electoral victory in U.S. history. His wins in Louisiana, South Carolina and Florida gave him 185 electoral votes to Tilden's 184.

Hayes had pledged to serve only one term and he kept his word. Nominating his successor proved to be no easy task. At the convention, James A. Garfield of Ohio, a longtime congressman who had recently been elected to the Senate, was the campaign manager for Secretary of the Treasury John Sherman and gave the nominating speech for him. Other candidates nominated were Grant and James G. Blaine. None of the candidates could secure a majority of the delegates' votes.

The nominating process went on for days. Finally, on the 36th ballot, Garfield was nominated as a compromise candidate. He won election in November, took the oath of office in March. He was assassinated six months later.

Vice President Chester Arthur served out the remainder of his term. It was during this time that a division occurred within the GOP regarding patronage—the age-old practice of office holders giving out jobs to friends and supporters, regardless of their qualifications. Some reformers within the party wanted the merit system to determine who got the jobs. In the parlance of the time, those seeking reform were denigrated as "Half-Breeds" while those supporting the cronyism were called "Stalwarts." In the convention of 1880, the deadlock was between Stalwart candidate Grant, trying for a political comeback and James G. Blaine, the reform-minded Half-Breed. In the end, after 36 ballots, Garfield, a Half-Breed, prevailed as the compromise candidate. With Garfield's death, Arthur, who had been a Stalwart, took office and surprised his supporters by initiating civil service reform.

Cleveland, the Democrat, broke the Republican string by winning in 1884 but Republicans retook the White House with Benjamin Harrison four years later. Cleveland ran again and won again in 1892. One of the reasons

3. The Republican Evolution

for Cleveland's election in 1884 was the defection of some Republicans who did not support Blaine, the GOP candidate. They came to be known as "Mugwumps" which, to traditional Republicans, meant "turncoats."

Republican William McKinley won in 1896, was re-elected in 1900 but became the third victim of assassination in 36 years a year later. His vice president, Theodore Roosevelt took over and was elected in his own right in 2004. Roosevelt had vowed early on not to seek another term, a promise he was to regret. His friend and successor, William Howard Taft won easily in 1908.

So politically, Republicans dominated for a half-century, a turbulent time of great social, industrial and economic change in America. But another movement was emerging within the party—an effort to put constraints on the entrepreneurs who were inventing great things and heaping big profits at the expense of the common man who was in the factory making these products at low wages and long hours as well as the consumer who had to pay for them on their meager wages. "At the start of Roosevelt's presidency in 1901, big business had been in the driver's seat. While the country prospered as never before, squalid conditions were rampant in immigrant slums, workers in factories and mines labored without safety regulations and farmers fought with railroads over freight rates."[8]

Roosevelt, whose appetite for reform dated back to his days as New York police commissioner and whose yearning for a good fight served him well as a "rough rider" in the Spanish American War, was ripe for the challenge of changing the American way of life. His brashness and his passion for leadership made him a curious choice for vice president except to his detractors, who believed the vice presidency would make him a political eunuch. But with McKinley's assassination, fate had put him in the position for which his supporters felt he had been divinely ordained. "By the end of Roosevelt's tenure, much had been accomplished. The Sherman Anti-Trust Act had been revived, vast acres of land had been protected from exploitation, and railroads had been prevented from continuing long-standing abuses. Congress passed workmen's compensation, a pure food and drug law and a meat inspection act."[9]

It would be up to Taft, Roosevelt's great friend, to carry on the Roosevelt legacy.

4

TEEDIE AND WILL

Theodore Roosevelt was a sickly child, beset with illnesses that made him weak and often struggling for breath, who became a bookworm and naturalist because of his health limitations. He grew up to be a cowboy, New York police commissioner, governor, vice president, president, and, in the minds of many, national statesman, to others, national bully. He was nominated to be vice president because even his most ardent supporters believed it was a "safe" position where he could do little harm. Roosevelt ascended to the presidency as a result of the assassination of President William McKinley and was the victim of an assassination attempt himself after he left office and became a candidate again on the third party Progressive ticket.

William Howard Taft, like Roosevelt, achieved a lot in a relatively short period of time. Growing up in Cincinnati, he was assistant prosecutor for Hamilton County, Ohio, at age 23, collector of internal revenue in Cincinnati at age 25, judge of the state superior court at 29, solicitor general of the United States at age 32, federal circuit court judge at 34, first U.S. civil governor of the Philippines at 42, secretary of war for President Roosevelt at 46, president of the United States at 51 and chief justice of the United States at 64.

Comparing the distinguished careers of these two men, one fundamental difference stands out. Roosevelt rose to political fame through elective office; Taft rose through the ranks through appointments to important positions. Indeed, the only elective office Taft ever held was the presidency, and it resulted in the most unhappy four years of his life.

By contrast, Roosevelt reveled in his presidency but had decided he should not seek re-election after serving nearly two full terms. He all but bequeathed the office to his good friend Taft but was itching to get back into the political fray four years later when he challenged President Taft for the nomination.

Both Roosevelt and Taft were born into families of privilege and benefited throughout their lives by strong family ties from parents, siblings, spouses and children.

4. Teedie and Will

Roosevelt was born October 27, 1858, the second child of Theodore and Martha Roosevelt. He had an older sister, Anna, a younger brother, Elliott, and a younger sister, Corinne. His father, whom he idolized, was a wealthy glass importer and philanthropist who was highly regarded in New York society. Young "Teedie" suffered from severe asthma as a youth that prevented him from any strenuous activities such as sports. Often, his father would take the youngster out on long carriage rides at night in an effort to get fresh air into his lungs. It was perhaps because of one-on-one outings such as these, father and son, that young Roosevelt developed such devotion to his papa.

Theodore Roosevelt was a veteran campaigner who was said to have made two mistakes: deciding not to seek re-election in 1908 and picking Taft to succeed him.

"My father, Theodore Roosevelt, was the best man I ever knew," Roosevelt wrote in his autobiography. "He combined strength and courage with gentleness, tenderness and great unselfishness. He would not tolerate in us children selfishness or cruelty, idleness, cowardice or untruthfulness."[1]

It is clear Roosevelt grew to take on many of the traits of his father, significantly his disdain for cowardice. As an adult, Roosevelt often described how busy he was by describing the "crowded hours" in his day. It is a trait he recognized in his father: "My father always excelled in improving every spare half-hour or three-quarters of an hour, whether for work or enjoyment," he wrote. "I never knew anyone who got more joy out of living ... or who more whole-heartedly performed every duty; and who approached his combination of enjoyment of life and performance of duty."[2]

Because he was homebound for much of his youth, Roosevelt developed what became a lifelong interest in natural history, even writing books about it. He never attended public schools, instead being taught at home by his mother and his aunt, Anna Bulloch. A private tutor was hired to prepare him for college and he enrolled at Harvard in the fall of 1876.

Aside from his health problems, young Roosevelt led a privileged life—a loving, caring family, well traveled, most every need easily fulfilled. That world crumbled around him in 1878, when he was a natural history major at Harvard. His father died of stomach cancer. Young Theodore said at the time he had lost the greatest man he had ever known.

When he returned to Harvard, he changed his major from natural history to history and government. Roosevelt decided to pursue a career in public service because he had developed a keen interest in politics. Also, he thought a career in public service would be a fitting tribute to his late father.

In 1879, Roosevelt met Alice Hathaway Lee and fell madly in love with her. It was an unusual pairing—he a rumpled, bespectacled, opinionated, self-possessed extrovert, she a lovely, beautiful, proper young lady who seemingly could have her pick of all the young men who wooed her. But she chose Theodore, who long ago had shed the "Teedie" nickname. They were married on October 27, 1880, Roosevelt's 22nd birthday.

After graduating from Harvard, he enrolled in law school at Columbia University but found it did not suit him so he dropped out after just one semester. Roosevelt decided to pursue his career in public service and was elected to the New York Assembly in 1881. Though he was often scoffed at, laughed at or scorned because of his boisterous nature on the floor of the Legislature, he was re-elected in 1882 and 1883. He was elected minority leader in 1882 but his colleagues chose not to give him that responsibility the following year.

Young Roosevelt was riding high. He had established himself in New York politics and was even being observed in Washington, D.C., as someone with great potential. At home, he was excited by the news that he and Alice were expecting their first child.

On February 12, 1884, Roosevelt was having a typical day, engaging in a spirited discussion in the Assembly in Albany when he received a telegram from his sister informing him he had become a father. He and Alice had a little girl who would also be named Alice. Roosevelt was elated. He would return home as soon as he could. A short time later, a second telegram arrived, telling him to come home immediately. His wife was seriously ill.

Roosevelt boarded a train and returned home where he learned the situation was worse than he could have ever imagined. Not only was Alice deathly ill from kidney disease, but his mother, in another part of the house, was dying from typhoid fever. She died in the middle of the night. Twelve hours later, Alice passed away. He had not only lost his wife and his mother, he had lost them on the same day in the same house.

On the death of his beloved Alice, Roosevelt said, "The light has gone out of my life." He is said to have never mentioned her by name again and there is no mention of her in his 600-page autobiography.

Roosevelt chose not to run again for the Assembly in 1884 and instead headed for the Dakota territories, where he had been once before and enjoyed it immensely. He loved the adventure of surviving in the wilderness and it seemed to revitalize him. His infant daughter was back home in New York, staying with his sister. "It was a land of vast, silent spaces, of lonely rivers and of plains where the wild game stared at the passing horsemen," Roosevelt wrote. "It was a land of scattered ranches, of herds of long-horned cattle and of reckless riders who, unmoved, looked into the eyes of life or of death."[3]

The combination of being away from family, away from the tragic homefront, and being in a place of adventure, a place where staying focused was essential, seemed to provide him with the break he needed, the space he needed to occupy and navigate at a critical time in his life. He no longer had his father to give him strength and guidance and now he had lost his wife and mother suddenly. He desperately needed to find himself, and he did, in the land of rugged terrain and cattle ranchers. "We knew toil and hardship and hunger and thirst; and we saw men die violent deaths as they worked among the horses and cattle or fought in evil feuds among one another. But we felt the beat of hardy life in our veins and ours was the glory of work and the joy of living."[4]

In 1886, he decided to head back home and before long, he was immersed once again in New York politics. He ran unsuccessfully for mayor of New York City—but he always considered the loss a win because he was back in the limelight, a force to be reckoned with. During this time he became reacquainted with a childhood friend, Edith Carow. Their friendship blossomed into romance and they were married not long after the mayoral defeat. In the next ten years, they had five children.

In 1889, President Benjamin Harrison appointed Roosevelt to the U.S. Civil Service Commission where he worked diligently to reform the system to institute a merit system for job promotions rather than political patronage and favoritism. He moved his family to Washington and served on the commission for six years. It was during this time that he met William Howard Taft, a burly mustachioed judge from Cincinnati, who had been appointed solicitor general of the United States. They were neighbors, both new to Washington, about the same age—Taft was a year older—and both had young families. They enjoyed each other's company and became fast friends.

The two men, so different in physical appearance and temperament, shared a respect for public service and in reward for a man's abilities instead of for his knowing the right people. While Roosevelt's forthrightness was based on principle as he reformed the Civil Service and later the New York Police Department, Taft had a more personal experience. In Cincinnati, he had resigned his position as revenue collector rather than bow to demands to fire devoted, hard-working underlings because of their political affiliations. Taft described the essence of his friendship with Roosevelt, saying simply, "Common views and sympathies."[5]

Roosevelt and Taft began walking to work together, creating a fascinating study for those who might see them on their morning jaunt—Roosevelt, about six inches shorter and very animated, waving his arms as he talked, often flashing a smile that revealed a set of upper teeth that were so straight, they looked like perfectly lined-up tiles; and Taft, looking ever judicial as he always did, walking slower than his companion for he was carrying much more weight, but with a certain dignity similar to the posture of a military officer except for the excessive paunch.

Often, they would meet for lunch and once again their differences in style were on public display. "Roosevelt did most of the talking, finding scant pleasure in his food. 'Whether absorbed in work or play,' one reporter observed, 'Roosevelt would eat hay and not know it whereas Taft savored his meals.' Profound differences in manner and metabolism never diminished the delight they found in each other's company."[6]

Roosevelt resigned from the Civil Service Commission in 1895 to become police commissioner of New York City. There he instituted the same kinds of reforms he had with the Civil Service Commission, putting ability and merit over patronage in awarding promotions.

McKinley appointed him assistant secretary of the Navy which gave him the opportunity to maneuver himself into a situation where he could take part in the Spanish American War. It was then that he led a band of renegade volunteers up San Juan Hill, giving him a place in military history of the era.

The thrill and challenge of politics was a constant motivating factor for him and he ran and was elected governor of New York in 1897. Three years later, he agreed to be President William McKinley's running mate, prompting Ohio Senator, Mark Hanna, a Republican but a Roosevelt critic, to say, "Don't you realize that there's only one life between this madman and the White House?"[7]

In September of 1901, President McKinley was assassinated—the third assassination in 36 years—and that "madman' was suddenly President of the United States.

Like Roosevelt, Taft was born into a family of wealth and respect and in which discipline and adherence to strong family values was expected. Unlike Roosevelt, Taft rose in prominence through being appointed to high-level positions whereas Roosevelt's rise was primarily through being elected. It was said that Roosevelt found government service while government service found Taft.

Taft was born September 15, 1857, in Cincinnati, Ohio, the son of Alphonso and Louisa Taft. His father was a distinguished lawyer who was one of the founders of the Republican Party in Cincinnati at about the time Will was born. Alphonso served as both attorney general and secretary of war in President Ulysses Grant's cabinet and as an ambassador to Austria-Hungary and to Russia in the administration of President Chester A. Arthur. He also served on the Cincinnati City Council and sought the Republican nomination for governor in 1875. Alphonso was "sensible, kind, gentle and highly Victorian a man who kept his emotions under rigid control."⁸

Taft had five siblings—two half-brothers from his father's first marriage, and two brothers and a sister born to his mother. Alphonso expected big things from all of them. He chided his children when he thought they should be doing better in school and once wrote a note to Will, telling him "the anxiety for your success is very great and I know there is but one way to attain it and that is by self-denial and enthusiastic hard work."⁹

For Will and the other children, a motivating factor in their lives was the fear of disappointing their father. Taft understood and appreciated his father's influence on his life. "I got my political pull, first, through my father's prominence," he said.¹⁰

The family achieved amazing success. Taft's brother Henry became a senior partner in a prestigious law firm. Another brother, Horace, went into education and founded a school in Con-

William Howard Taft, who had never run for public office until he sought the presidency, would rather have been on the Supreme Court.

necticut. A third brother, Charles, became publisher of the *Cincinnati Times-Star* newspaper and was one of the investors in the Chicago Cubs baseball team. A fourth brother, Peter, was valedictorian of his class at Yale University but struggled with depression and died at a young age in a sanitarium.

Taft remained close to his brothers all of his life and once put off accepting a government appointment until he could discuss it with them. Horace in particular was a confidante and Charles backed him financially in some of his endeavors, including contributing nearly $1 million to his 1908 presidential run.

Louisa Taft subscribed to the same values as her husband and had the same expectations for her children. But she was more adventuresome than her husband, willing to take on challenging projects and displaying an attitude and temperament geared toward achievement.

She was a well-organized woman who had noticeable leadership and managerial abilities in an era where those qualities held little importance because she was a woman. She organized a movement that led to the formation of kindergartens in Cincinnati and later statewide. When her son was president of the United States, he told her admiringly, "When woman's field widens, mother, you must become president of a railway company."[11]

Will finished second in his graduating class at Woodward High School in Cincinnati and then went on to Yale where once again he finished second in his graduating class. He could have been part of the influential east coast establishment or ventured to Washington where his father had made a name for himself. Instead, Taft chose to return to the family roots in Cincinnati where he received his law degree from the Cincinnati Law School which one day would become part of the University of Cincinnati.

His first public office came in 1881, when, at the age of 24, he became assistant prosecutor for Hamilton County, Ohio. Six years later, he became a superior court judge in Cincinnati, his first step in what he hoped would be a lifelong journey in the judiciary in which, eventually, he aspired to be appointed to the United States Supreme Court.

In 1890, he was appointed solicitor general of the United States in which he argued cases before the Supreme Court. He held that position for about two years but it was a pivotal time in his life because it was during this time that he became a friend and neighbor of the young Civil Service commissioner Theodore Roosevelt.

In 1892, a federal appeals court was established in Cincinnati and President Benjamin Harrison appointed Taft to be the judge. He held that position for eight years and developed traits and skills that became part of his DNA on the bench. "In his judicial career, he was known for the quality of his opinions and for his diligence. He found great satisfaction in the 'writing up' of appellate decisions. His ability to marshal detail into a coherent whole served him well in appellate work."[12]

While back in Cincinnati with the appeals court, Taft also served as the first dean of the newly-formed University of Cincinnati Law School which gave him a special satisfaction since the new school was formed from a merger with the Cincinnati Law School, his alma mater.

Without doubt, one of the first things people noticed about Taft when meeting him for the first time was his size. He was about six feet tall but weighed 300 pounds or more most of his adult life. He dieted from time to time but his love for food constantly won the battle over self-discipline.

One story about him when he was president concerns a train trip he took from Washington to Ohio where he was to give a speech. He was accompanied by many of his aides but not by his wife Nellie or his physician—the two people who kept watch over his diet and cajoled him into eating properly.

It wasn't long before Taft motioned to the conductor and asked him about the food in the dining car. The conductor apologized but said there was no dining car on this particular train. Taft was livid. He is said to have told the conductor and C.D. Norton, his traveling secretary, "I am president

4. Teedie and Will

of the United States and I want a dining car attached to this train at the next stop. I want it stocked with food. You will see that we get a diner. What's the use of being president if you can't have a train with a diner on it?" He got his diner at the next stop.[13]

In 1905, when Taft was Roosevelt's secretary of war, he wrote to Dr. Nathaniel E. Yorke-Davies of London, England, reportedly an expert in diet and health care. Taft told the doctor he thought his excessive weight was causing him heartburn, indigestion and sleepiness. He sought suggestions on how to lose weight.

Davies sent him a list of foods he should eat, foods he shouldn't eat and told him to weigh himself every day. He was to write to the doctor every week with a progress report.

Dr. Yorke-Davies put Taft on a diet with a specific schedule. He was to sip a cup of hot water with lemon at 8 o'clock each morning, about an hour later, have a breakfast of biscuits and lean meat. His diet also included stewed fruit, cooked vegetables and clear soup every day. Within a year, Taft's weight dropped from 314 pounds to 255 pounds and he reported to the doctor that he was feeling much better.

Taft's only complaint was that he was constantly hungry. As time went by, he reverted back to his old ways and in 1909, when he took the oath of office as president, he reportedly weighed 354 pounds.[14]

Despite his gerth, he enjoyed dancing and playing golf and did both reasonably well. He also engaged in academic activities such as book clubs which he enjoyed immensely. Another trait: He also possessed what one biographer called "the most infectious chuckle in the history of politics" and often laughed at himself. "The popular image of the jolly fat man fooled many into believing that Taft's core was of petroleum jelly rather than tempered steel. And TR, while they were still friends, said Taft was 'one of the best haters' he had ever known."[15]

He met Helen "Nellie" Herron at a sledding party. The two were a good match, both smart and ambitious and coming from influential families. Nellie's father had been a college classmate of President Benjamin Harrison and a law partner of President Rutherford B. Hayes. Her mother's father had been a member of Congress and so had an uncle, her mother's sister.

A well-known story about Nellie Herron is that when she was 17 and a guest with her parents of President and Mrs. Hayes at the White House, she determined she would live there someday because she would marry someone who would be elected president. When she married Will Taft, an up-and-coming lawyer and judge, she was confident her childhood dream would become a reality. It was a unique circumstance in that Will's ambition was to someday be chief justice of the Supreme Court while his wife had her sights on him becoming president.

Taft was solicitor general for about two years but could not resist accepting appointment as a federal judge back in Cincinnati. He was immersed back in his successful judicial career when President McKinley asked him to be the governor of the Philippine Islands, an American territory. It would take some persuasion to take a man who was comfortable and successful in his chosen profession and convince him to move him and his family thousands of miles away to try to create a civil government out of potential chaos. "He finally succumbed to duty and the president's assurance that 'if you give up this judicial office at my request, you shall not suffer.' To Taft, this sounded very much like a promissory note for the next Supreme Court vacancy."[16]

The lives of Taft and Roosevelt were once again interwoven, as they were when they were young men, as Taft accepted the position of civil governor of the Philippines. Tension on the islands was high because one of the results of the Spanish American War, in which Roosevelt fought, is that the Philippines had become a U.S. territory. Thousands of U.S. soldiers were fighting to put down a rebellion by Filipino nationalists. This was the environment that Taft inherited when he and his family moved there.

Taft immediately determined that the American military involvement was too brutal and ordered changes, including a change in command. He removed Gen. Arthur MacArthur, father of future Gen. Douglas MacArthur (who President Truman removed from Korea a generation later).

In his three years in the Philippines, Taft instituted many reforms, much to the chagrin of many military officials there who preferred their own rule to that of a politician. The reforms included drafting of a Constitution that included a Bill of Rights very similar to the first ten amendments of the U.S. Constitution; a civil service system; a judicial system; public schools in which English was taught; and a health care system. Taft became immensely popular with most of the natives who were leading better lives because of their portly governor.

The challenges facing Taft played to his strengths—finding solutions through a strong organizational structure and a results-oriented system. The arbiter was in his element.

The Philippine situation existed at least in part due to the Spanish American War in which Col. Roosevelt, assistant secretary of the Navy, pushed all the right buttons to get himself into it—in which he was in his element. The war only lasted three months, from May to July 1898, but Roosevelt made the most of it. He received government permission to form a volunteer regiment that would fight under the direction of Roosevelt's friend, General Leonard Wood. Roosevelt recruited what has been described as a rag-tag group of hunters, cowboys, athletes and native Americans. Together, they formed the "Rough Riders" and earned fame by winning a battle on San Juan Hill.

McKinley was assassinated in September 1901 and Roosevelt, the vice

4. Teedie and Will

president whom Senator Mark Hanna had described as a "madman," was now the most powerful man in America. He offered his old friend, Taft, the job he had sought all his life, a seat on the Supreme Court. But Taft felt so loyal to the people of the Philippines, and was dedicated to seeing his programs to fruition, that he turned down the new president. It was a decision that must have gnawed at his inner being because he might have passed up his only chance to be on the Supreme Court.

Later, Roosevelt offered his old friend a cabinet position, secretary of war, and Taft accepted it because the war department had jurisdiction over the Philippines. He became Roosevelt's trusted advisor and advocate in the cabinet and when Roosevelt decided that he would not seek re-election in 1908, he enthusiastically endorsed Taft to succeed him. And that was good enough for the American public. Taft was easily elected—the first time in his life in which he had been a candidate for elective office.

Nobody could have foreseen the problems that would develop and that a hearty friendship would be crushed. Roosevelt believed it was the duty of the executive branch to exercise whatever power necessary to accomplish its goals. Taft, the jurist, believed in the sanctity of the three branches of government and that the president had no power that wasn't specifically assigned in the Constitution.

When Taft took office, Roosevelt went on a year-long safari to Africa, partly to give his successor a free hand without the colonel looking over his shoulder and partly because it was a new sense of adventure for someone who craved adventure. Although the circumstances were completely different, Roosevelt's decision to get away and focus on vast, potentially dangerous lands he had never experienced was not unlike his decision to head to the Dakotas 22 years earlier when he needed to clear his head.

His admirers missed his infectious zeal. His detractors welcomed his departure. Said one in toasting Roosevelt's newest adventure, "To the lions!"

5

THE ROOSEVELT PRESIDENCY

American history is replete with examples in which fate has intervened and bulldozed diplomacy, statesmanship and logic. There are no greater examples than how the course of history was changed three times in 36 years by a bullet. On the night of April 14, 1865, President Abraham Lincoln was shot in a conspiracy that involved the attempted murders of other government officials as well. When Lincoln died the next morning, Vice President Andrew Johnson, a southerner, a tailor who was functionally illiterate was thrust into power, succeeding the man who freed the slaves and guided the country through a civil war. In 1881, when President James Garfield was gunned down after just a few months in office, his successor was Vice President Chester A. Arthur, a nondescript individual who is remembered in history chiefly as the man who succeeded Garfield. And then in 1901, President McKinley was slain, elevating Theodore Roosevelt, a man once described by Senator Mark Hanna as a "madman" into the highest office in the land.

Roosevelt pledged to continue the policies of the slain president but it was not in his nature to be a caretaker. Action was his oxygen. It had been from his early days in the New York Assembly and in the western wilderness where he learned how to be a rancher and a cowboy; to the days when he was New York police commissioner when he initiated reforms after personally witnessing misconduct; and when he led a band of "rough riders" up San Juan hill during the Spanish-American War.

Soon after taking the oath of office, Roosevelt promised the country, "I shall continue absolutely unbroken the policy of President McKinley for the peace, prosperity and the honor of the country." A few days later, in an off-the-record meeting with reporters, the new president said, "I am president and shall act in every word and deed precisely as if I and not McKinley had been the candidate for whom the electors cast the vote for president."[1]

And so it was that as president, it wasn't long before the new president shed the cloak of being McKinley's successor and returned to the persona he loved the most—allowing Roosevelt to be Roosevelt.

5. The Roosevelt Presidency

Within months after taking office, Roosevelt began establishing his reputation as a "trust buster" when he instructed the Justice Department to break up Northern Securities, a massive holding company that controlled the nation's railroads.

In 1901, railroad tycoons James J. Hill and Edward Harriman both sought to gain control of the Chicago, Burlington & Quincy Railroad, each having the motive of solidifying their railroad interests in the Midwest. Hill owned the Great Northern and Northern Pacific railroads. Harriman was itching to expand his business ventures into the railroad industry. At the height of their bidding war, Hill and Harriman came in contact with banker J.P. Morgan and millionaire John D. Rockefeller. Together, the four created Northern Securities, a holding company with controlling stock in the Chicago, Burlington & Quincy, the Northern Pacific, the Great Northern and several smaller railroads affiliated with the big ones.

At age 42, Theodore Roosevelt was the youngest man to become president.

Roosevelt believed Northern Securities was a monopoly that could cause restraint of trade and asked the Justice Department, using the Sherman Anti-Trust Act, to dismantle it. Northern Securities sued. In a long battle in the courts that eventually went to the Supreme Court, the government prevailed in a 5–4 decision that was issued in 1904.

The president took on the railroads once again in 1903 with passage of the Elkins Act which ended the activities of railroads granting shipping rebates to certain companies of their choosing. The rebates gave the railroad tycoons the right to ship their products for much lower rates than their smaller competitors could do. Later in his administration, he was able to spearhead the effort that led to passage of the Hepburn Act which gave the Interstate Commerce Commission control over railroads to further prevent the owners from padding their own pockets at the expense of taxpayers.

Roosevelt also found himself in the unusual role of being a mediator in 1902 when workers in the anthracite coalfields of Pennsylvania went on strike. Roosevelt realized that, among other things, the strike could prevent millions of Americans from getting the source of heat they would need during the winter months. He recognized also the potential for civil unrest and violence. So he asked parties on both sides of the dispute to meet with him in Washington. He urged them to reach a settlement, to avoid "untold misery with the certainty of riots which might develop into social war."[2]

It was a difficult situation but in the end, the workers went back on the job and Roosevelt, the cowboy, the rough rider, the warrior, had been the peace maker. It was not only a unique position for him, it was unusual in American history for a president to break up a strike without sending in federal troops.

A priority early on of the Roosevelt administration that lasted for his entire tenure was conservation of the nation's lands. He said, "When I had lived in the west, I had come to realize the vital need of irrigation for the country and I had been both amused and irritated by the attitude of eastern men who obtained from Congress grants of national money to build harbors and yet fought the use of the nation's power to develop the irrigation work of the west."[3]

He found similar concerns from Congressman Francis Newlands of Nevada and Gifford Pinchot, a forester who would one day head the U.S. Department of Forestry. The Newlands Reclamation Act of 1902 set aside the proceeds of the sales of public lands to be used for reclaiming waste areas of the arid, useless lands by irrigating them and making them suitable sites for building homes. "Roosevelt identified the American character with the nation's wilderness regions, believing that our western and frontier heritage had shaped American values, behavior and culture. The president wanted the United States to change from exploiting natural resources to carefully managing them."[4]

To this end, he worked with Pinchot to stop big industries from buying up empty western lands and commercializing them to the detriment of conservation. Through executive orders, the federal government took over management of 172 million acres of land in the western United States. Roosevelt created national parks, national monuments, wildlife refuges and national forests. He established the cabinet position of Commerce and Labor, which was later separated into two entities He also created the National Forestry Service within the Department of Agriculture.

In looking out for the consumer, Roosevelt considered one of the greatest achievements of his administration passage of the Meat Inspection Act and Pure Food and Drug Act of 1906. These bills were in response to revelations by muckraking journalists of substandard health and safety issues in factories and meat-processing plants.

Roosevelt had developed a good working relationship with many of the muckrakers—so labeled because of their ability to recognize "muck" in

5. The Roosevelt Presidency

American business practices and write about it. One of the most important works in this era was Upton Sinclair's *The Jungle* which vividly described the practice of filthy materials being ground into meat and sausages that Americans were eating every day. The legislation established national standards in food production through government regulations.

It was not without its opponents, however. In the Senate, Senator Nelson Aldrich of Rhode Island asked if the government was now going to tell the American people what they could eat or drink—and penalize the producers if their goods did not meet the standards of chemists in the Agriculture Department. The pressure of the president and the groundswell of support from the public answered that question. The landmark bill became law.

Aldrich, who served in the Senate for 30 years, was one of its most influential members at the peak of his career. As chairman of the Senate Finance Committee, he controlled what spending bills made their way to the floor of the Senate. He was involved in major legislation involving U.S tariff policies.

In foreign affairs, Roosevelt wanted to make the United States a world power and it was in this context that he developed the philosophy to "speak softly but carry a big stick." Part of the control he wanted had already been achieved after the Spanish-American War when Spain turned over Puerto Rico, Guam and the Philippines to U.S. jurisdiction. McKinley appointed Taft to become the first civilian governor of the Philippines. Taft characteristically was gracious but methodic in establishing a democratic government with an elected legislature. Taft became so dedicated to his job and to the people of the Philippines that he turned down a possible appointment to the Supreme Court—his dream job—so he could complete the work he had started in the Philippines.

During the Spanish-American War, American ships in the Pacific Ocean had to go all the way around the tip of South America to meet up with U.S. vessels in the Atlantic near Cuba. It was a venture that took two months. What was needed was a pathway between the Atlantic and Pacific oceans through Central America. Roosevelt believed the solution was to build a canal through Panama, which was controlled by Columbia. The Columbia government resisted at first but after many developments, including a revolt by Panamanians against Columbia, supported by the U.S., a treaty was signed which allowed for the canal to be built, for the U.S. to have perpetual control for a $10 million payment and annual payments of $250,000.

It was a steep price and it took eight years to build but when it was completed, "it shortened the voyage from San Francisco to New York by more than 8,000 miles. The process of building the canal generated advances in U.S. technology and engineering. The project also projected the Panama

Canal Zone into a major staging area for American military forces, making the United States the dominant military power in Central America."[5]

In 1902, a Latin American hotspot developed in a dispute between Venezuela and two adversaries, Germany and Britain. The European countries had loaned money to Venezuela, and when it became apparent that the Venezuelan dictatorship had no intention of paying back, Germany and Britain sent ships to blockade the coastline of Venezuela. Roosevelt was concerned about possible military action and stepped into the fray, demanding that the disputing countries agree to arbitration. Santo Domingo (which is now the Dominican Republic) appealed to the United States to help. Roosevelt arranged for the U.S. to take control of customs houses and collect duties to help pay off the debts.

His actions resulted in what came to be known as the Roosevelt Corollary to the Monroe Doctrine. The Monroe Doctrine, crafted in 1823 in the administration of President James Monroe, had as its guiding principle that the United States would not tolerate European intervention into Latin or Central America. Roosevelt realized that failure to repay debts could easily lead to military intervention so, as a corollary to the Monroe Doctrine, declared the U.S. would intervene in serious economic problems in Latin America.

The corollary meant "the United States would serve as the 'policeman' of the Western Hemisphere, a policy which eventually created much resentment in Latin America."[6]

Roosevelt's reputation as a fighter, someone who thrived on aggression, was well earned from his days on the western frontier, to leading his band of renegades up San Juan Hill in the Spanish-American War to his trust-busting in the White House. But he was also a skilled negotiator, someone who was willing to move in and be a mediator, as he had been in the Venezualan dispute, when he thought American interests were at risk.

In 1904, war broke out between Russia and Japan and as casualties mounted on both sides, Roosevelt offered to intervene and act as a peacemaker if he could. After initial resistance from both sides, they eventually agreed to meet with the president in 1905 at Portsmouth, New Hampshire. He was able to convince both sides to reach agreement and end the war. For his efforts, Roosevelt was later awarded the Nobel Peace Prize.

The nearly eight years of the Roosevelt administration were filled with "crowded hours," an expression the president was fond of using, and when his time was up, when he fulfilled his pledge not to seek another term, he left a hefty legacy for the man he had chosen to succeed him, his good friend and Secretary of War, Taft. "It was on election night, Nov. 8, 1904, that Roosevelt, excited about winning the presidency that he had inherited nearly four years earlier, looked ahead for years as he said, "the wise custom that limits the president to two terms, regards the substance and not the form, and under no circumstances will I be a candidate for and accept the nomination for another."[7]

In the years to come, Roosevelt supporters would say the colonel made two big mistakes in his presidency. One was his decision not to run and the other was his selection of Taft to succeed him.

6

THE TRAGEDY OF ARCHIE BUTT

The election of 1912 made the Roosevelt-Taft feud a public spectacle with both men having ardent supporters within the same political party. But one man, perhaps more than any other, was torn by the dispute. Archibald Butt was Roosevelt's military aide in the White House, taking care of numerous details and frequently being at the president's side, much like a modern day chief of staff. When Roosevelt left office, President Taft asked Butt to stay on and serve the new president as he had for his predecessor.

Butt was a magnificent public servant whose military background helped hone two characteristics that were engrained in his being—duty and loyalty. He not only served both presidents with distinction but he loved working with them and for them. As the rift between the two men escalated, Butt became distraught to the point of being grief stricken, and he eventually fell into a depression that he could not shake.

The breach between Roosevelt and Taft was perhaps inevitable, given the personalities of the two men and the politics of the times. Nobody saw the animosity develop sooner than Butt and no one was more heartbroken because of the love, devotion and loyalty he had for both men.

As a military aide to both presidents, he was with each of them more than any other individual with the exception of their spouses. They both confided in him and often sought his counsel. He was at their sides when they entertained dignitaries or met with senators and congressmen on important legislative issues. He knew who they liked and disliked and how they handled themselves in joyous situations and in despair.

Butt enjoyed watching Roosevelt captivate friends, colleagues and people he was trying to win over with his gift for story-telling, how they would seemingly hang on his every word as he told how he took on both outlaws and critters in the wild west or how he led his men up San Juan Hill in the Spanish-American War or how he finessed a congressman to help get one of his bills through.

6. The Tragedy of Archie Butt

But he also saw the belligerent Roosevelt who minced no words in attacking his political enemies and how he would show his contempt for someone as they talked by cutting them off in mid-sentence and begin a conversation with someone else. To Roosevelt, the ends always justified the means.

Butt knew Taft and his habits and tendencies, just as well. He saw firsthand how Taft preferred compromise to conflict, how he often let his underlings do his political bidding for him, so as to honor the office of the presidency by staying above the fray. Butt understood the differences in personality between Roosevelt, his old boss, and Taft, his new one, and could see trouble brewing between the two men but felt helpless to do anything about it.

Presidents Roosevelt and Taft are shown in happier days shortly after Taft was elected president in 1908.

Butt enjoyed it when Taft confided in him as the two were on the golf course, which was often, or when they motored around Washington to give the president a time to relax and reflect. He was concerned and yet sometimes amused by Taft's half-hearted attempts at dieting to see if he could shed some weight off of his 300-pound body and his penchant for dozing off, a signal to guests that their meeting with him was over. And Butt, like most everyone else in the company of the president, loved Taft's infectious chuckle that frequently took the tension out of a room.

During his tenure with both presidents, Butt corresponded almost daily with Clara Butt, wife of his brother, Louis. His letters to her, kept for posterity and later published, are like a diary of life in the White House, depicting the hardball politics of the time and Butt's angst as he witnessed the bitter demise of the friendship between two men whom he had served and adored.

"It is all a game of politics and there is nothing lower in the universe," he wrote in August 1910. "I ought to be above them and calmly look on and say to myself, let the biggest rascal win."[1]

As he witnessed the deterioration of the long friendship between the two men, Butt's reactions, which he kept to himself except in his letters to Clara, ranged from disappointment to anger to despair. He was a military man who understood the importance of duty and loyalty to both a president and an ex-president, a situation that eventually took a toll on his own health.

Butt was born in Augusta, Georgia in 1865 into a family with a rich military tradition. His grandfather served in the Revolutionary War and his great-grandfather served in the Continental Army. His uncle was a general in the Confederate Army during the Civil War.

After graduating from the University of the South in Tennessee, Butt pursued a journalism career and covered national news for several newspapers in the south. Butt was outgoing and ambitious and made some important connections through his work. When one of his Washington acquaintances, former Senator Matt Ransom, became U.S. ambassador to Mexico in 1895, he hired Butt to be the embassy's secretary, a position he held for two years.

In 1898, with the onset of the Spanish-American War, Butt was commissioned as a lieutenant in a volunteer group overseen by the U.S. Army, carrying on the family military heritage into yet another war. Eventually he enlisted in the Army and his military service took him to the Philippines where his personality and his literary talents won the praise of many people, including Taft who was governor of the islands at the time.

In 1904, he was ordered back to Washington where he was depot quartermaster and two years later was asked to be quartermaster in Cuba and to organize logistics there. President Roosevelt was impressed with Butt for several reasons. He knew of his service in the Spanish-American War and of his reputation for being well organized and efficient in most everything he did. Plus, Taft, who was secretary of war in Roosevelt's cabinet, was familiar with Butt from the time they both were in the Philippines and thought he was a fine man. Based on all of this, Roosevelt chose him to be his military aide. A year later, when Taft became president, he asked Butt to stay on.

In his letters to his sister-in-law, he often gave revealing insights into the two men. He told her the Roosevelt haters had never been in "the charmed circle of Mr. Roosevelt" or "felt his hypnotic influence" or saw his "personal purity."[2]

Of Taft, he said, "In many ways, he is the best man I have ever known, too honest for the presidency, possibly too good-natured or too trusting or too something on which it is hard just now for a contemporary to put his finger on, but on which the finger of the historian of our politics will be placed."[3]

Butt was present during many political discussions between Taft and his advisers and it troubled him to hear Taft's personal secretary, C.D. Norton, and others making disparaging remarks about Roosevelt and try to set traps

6. The Tragedy of Archie Butt

to make him look foolish. And while he understood Taft's reluctance to personally get involved in what Butt called "the whirlpool of petty schemes," he was dismayed at how often Taft allowed himself to be dragged into the fray.

Taft appreciated the position Butt found himself in, torn between loyalties to two men he considered great public servants. After one particularly bitter conversation in which Roosevelt was assailed, Taft took Butt aside and told him how troubling it must have been to listen to all of that. The president told him he appreciated Butt's "dignified silence."

There were good times, too, such as the opportunities to be a part of living history—watching how two presidents, using their respective skills, helped shape the destinies of millions of Americans; and the funny incidents such as when Taft threw his golf club after making a bad shot or when he would go off his diet and sneak a treat when he was not within the eyesight of Nellie.

Butt was a great story teller and he had a lot of them. Among his favorites: George Gould, president of the Missouri Pacific Railroad, came across one of his trains and decided to personally inspect it. An old railroad fireman was nearby and Gould asked him about the condition of the wheels.

"As poor as they can possibly be," said the fireman.

"And what about the rails," Gould asked.

"They will do for the wheels," the fireman said.

Gould continued: "What about the cars?"

"They are no better than the wheels or the rails," the fireman said.

"You can't know who I am," said Gould.

"Yes I do," said the fireman. "You are George Gould, president of the railroad. Your father was Jay Gould, president before you and he will be president again some day."

Gould said, "My father will never be president again because my father is dead.

"Oh yes, said the fireman. "He will be president again someday because this railroad is going to hell."[4]

Taft was at his presidential retreat in Beverly, Maryland on July 5, 1910, when he was informed of the death of Chief Justice Melville Fuller. He told Butt, "If the judges would only retire when they recognize themselves that their faculties have become impaired, one could grieve sincerely when they pass away and you would not feel like such a hypocrite as you do when going through the formality of sending telegrams of condolence and giving out interviews for propriety's sake."[5]

Taft had many conversations with Butt about his relationship with Roosevelt, expressing distress and feeling "deeply wounded" and how the prophet of the square deal was not playing squarely with him.

On Aug. 20, 1910, he confided to his sister-in-law: "I throw up my hands, dear girl. I had hoped things might be otherwise. But they are now apart and how they will keep from wrecking the country between them, I scarcely see. Possibly, it may land a good Democrat in the White House which may bring back sanity to the people.... Damn politics anyhow."[6]

In November, Roosevelt was in Washington and it was anticipated that he might attend the annual Gridiron Dinner at which Taft was also attending. Butt suggested to Taft that he invite the colonel to stay at the White House as an overnight guest as a way of reconciling their relationship. The reunion did not occur. In a letter to his sister-in-law, Butt once again related how his loyalty to both men was ever present and the dissention between the two was devastating to him.

"If I can only help to bring about peace between these two men, I will be willing to retire with only the blessing which is promised to the peacemakers," he wrote. "Nothing shakes my belief in the other man ... and I feel certain that in his heart, the president has an affection for his predecessor."[7]

In February of 1912, Roosevelt made it official, unveiling what had become the worst kept secret in politics—he was throwing "his hat in the ring" and would challenge his old friend for the Republican nomination for president.

For Butt, the turmoil was so great and his personal feelings so raw that he began having serious health problems. He lost weight, he became withdrawn and appeared to be on the verge of a breakdown. A White House doctor noticed Butt's declining health and told him, "I don't see how you stand the strain you are constantly under. I have been expecting to hear of your breaking down, and since I have been in attendance on the president, and seen what you have to do, I marvel more and more how you keep up."[8]

Taft also became concerned about Butt's well-being. When it was suggested he take a leave of absence to get some rest and relaxation, Butt decided to do it.

He arranged to go abroad with his friend and housemate, Francis David Millet, to get away from politics and have some fun before the presidential primaries began. On March 1, they left on a six-week vacation to Europe to experience the cultures of different lands, dine in fine restaurants, see architectural marvels of the different countries and, perhaps most important, have some fun.

On February 27, Butt wrote a letter to his Aunt Kitty, Mrs. John D. Butt, in response to a letter she had sent him. In it, he kidded her about some insecurities she had about driving and then told her of his upcoming plans.

"I am very tired and really need a rest," he wrote. He said he was reluctant to go and at one point decided to cancel his plans but Taft talked him out of it. "He does not want to see me go but I think he feels I will break down just when he needs me the most if I don't go now."[9]

6. The Tragedy of Archie Butt

In March, he boarded the S.S. *Berlin* in Hoboken, New Jersey, sailed directly to Naples and spent some time with friends in Rome. On April 10, refreshed after a long-overdue vacation, it was time to return home. The last vacation treat he would enjoy was coming home on a ship making its maiden voyage—the R.M.S. *Titanic*.

He was reportedly playing cards in the first-class smoking room when the ship hit an iceberg on April 14 and sank. Nearly 2,000 passengers died. Butt reportedly helped women and children into lifeboats, unconcerned about his own safety. But being a military man to the end, Butt went down with the ship.

7

THE GREAT DIVIDE

One of the big differences between President Roosevelt and President Taft was in their approach to governing. Roosevelt was an aggressor, a rough rider who imposed his will on Congress as if it was a fundamental right of the executive branch. Taft was a former judge and a lifelong disciple of the judicial branch of government and a respecter of the legislative branch. He preferred compromise to confrontation, a total opposite temperament to the man he succeeded.

His critics joked that if Taft was the pope, he would appoint some Protestants to the College of Cardinals. One of their areas of disagreement was Taft's role in the passage and implementation of the Payne-Aldrich Tariff Act of 1909—the first tariff reform since 1897. "In all tariff legislation, the true principle of protection is best maintained by the imposition of such duties as will equal the difference between the cost of production at home and abroad together with a reasonable profit to American industries."[1]

Like many Progressives, Roosevelt believed that high tariffs were hurting the American economy from many different directions—protecting big business and special interests, cutting competition and, the end result, hurting the pocketbooks of consumers.

Though it was a divisive issue between the conservative and Progressive wings of his own party, the Republican platform called for tariff reform and Taft called Congress into special session not long after his inauguration in 1909. But he knew he had a mountain to climb in the House, where the bill would originate and where House Speaker Joseph G. Cannon ruled with an iron fist.

Cannon served in the House for 46 years, a record at the time of his retirement, and was Speaker of the House from 1903 to 1911, also a record tenure for a Republican speaker at the time. Cannon, a conservative, was an abrasive, dominant leader who was also chairman of the House Rules Committee. With his dual roles, Cannon appointed chairmen of all House committees and determined who would serve on those committees. He could therefore control which bills made it out of committee and on to the House floor and then control the amount of debate each bill would receive.

Cannon did not mince words in evaluating politicians he did not like. He did not like Roosevelt's use of executive power, saying, "he has no more use for the Constitution than a tomcat has for a marriage license."[2]

Cannon did not favor tariff reform but was facing a political problem that threatened his power. Progressives in the House were mounting a campaign to oust him as speaker. President Taft had to decide whether to get into the fray. He considered Cannon an arrogant, vulgar man whom he did not like. But he had to determine which was the worst option politically—to get involved and lose or to not get involved and lose. Rather than doing either, he decided to meet with Cannon and get his approval on a moderate tariff reform bill. His hope was

Joseph "Uncle Joe" Cannon was an iron-fisted speaker of the House who controlled committee assignments and chairmanships so that he could control the fate of legislation.

that in exchange for Cannon giving tacit approval to a new tariff bill, Progressive Republicans would drop their attempts to oust the speaker. "Perhaps it was inevitable that Taft's temperament—his aversion to dissention and preference for personal persuasion—would ultimately lead him to work within the system rather than mobilize external pressure from his bully pulpit."[3]

When the special session called by Taft opened, members of the House and Senate and the press were eager to hear the president's clarion call for reduced tariffs with all the reasons he believed it would be good for the American people. Instead, they got a 340-word message—it took about two minutes to deliver—urging Congress to give immediate consideration to the tariff bill.

Hoping to avoid starting his administration with a fight with Congress—something Roosevelt would have relished, Taft chose to start his relationship with "no loud noises, no explosions, no disturbances of the atmosphere."[4]

The bill was introduced in the House by Congressman Sereno Payne, a New York Republican, a conservative and chairman of the House Ways and Means Committee. The Senate sponsor was Nelson Aldrich, a Republican from Rhode Island, chairman of the Finance Committee who had a reputation of being the Senate's guardian angel over big business.

Payne and Aldrich worked for months to craft a bill, meeting in committee rooms often filled with supporters of special interests who had something to gain from the legislation. "Neither Payne nor Aldrich had the slightest idea that to fix tariff rates to enrich special interests and firms was a most corrupt practice. When a Republican senator, who honestly supposed that the revision would be downward, privately remonstrated, the reply he heard was 'Where shall we get our campaign funds?'"[5]

The bill sailed through the House and Senate. Taft was not totally satisfied with it but considered it a step in the right direction. It put some items on the "free list," reduced the tariff on other items, kept some tariffs as they had been and raised the tariff on a few items. The *New York Evening Post* called it "a more enlightened and promising measure than any tariff measure ever fathered by the Republican Party," and said it was enacted with the consumer in mind.[6]

The Senate bill had added dozens of amendments to the House bill that in effect negated much of the reforms passed by the House. In order to placate Aldrich and other conservatives, Taft sent two other pieces of legislation to the Congress—one creating a tax on corporations, the other a federal income tax. Both were revenue producers that Taft hoped would sooth the nerves of conservatives concerned about lost revenue in the tariff bill.

In the end, the watered-down Senate bill passed by nine votes and went to a conference committee to work out differences and send the bill to the president. One provision of the final bill created a tariff board that was to study future proposals and make recommendations to Congress and the president. Taft signed the bill, realizing it was better than nothing, but lauded it publicly as a great tariff reform bill, as promised before he was elected.

Progressives felt betrayed. While Roosevelt was on safari in Africa, his successor had let them down in his first test as president, they felt. Progressives thought Taft should have imposed his will, in Roosevelt style, on Congress. True to form, Taft believed the legislative branch should be left to act on its own.

"I knew the fire had gone out [of the Progressive movement]," said Gifford Pinchot, a Roosevelt ally. "Washington was a dead town. Its leader was gone and in his place was a man whose fundamental desire was to keep out of trouble."[7]

The Payne-Aldrich Tariff Bill not only displayed the differences between the two wings of the Republican Party but also the difference in style between

7. The Great Divide　　　　　　　　　　　　　　　61

Roosevelt and Taft. "Mr. Roosevelt believes that the President ... went in with the Reactionary leaders to secure a tariff board of such limited powers as to cause the people to regard it with suspicion; that the president has consulted the tariff board when he wished to find excuse for executive disapproval of the tariff legislation."[8]

In his campaign of 1912, Roosevelt claimed Taft used the tariff board to stifle changes rather than to promote them and had therefore not kept his campaign promises or stayed with the platform pledges of the Republican Party.

Roosevelt said his position on the tariffs hadn't changed—that he supported tariff reform in accordance with the Republican platform of 1908. "I believe tariff benefits should not stop at the front office but those benefits should go on through the entire establishment of the profit of every wage worker. It is high time the consumer, as well as the special interests, was considered in the making of a tariff law."[9]

After the bill was signed into law, Taft went on a two-month, cross-country speaking tour, traveling by train from one city to another, explaining the new tariff law, in some cases extolling its virtues, in other cases doing his best to defend it. Because it raised tariffs on some goods, Progressives felt that Taft had gone against the party platform. Because it lowered tariffs on other products, conservatives considered it a bad bill. Taft, who was not as adept at public speaking and winning over crowds as his predecessor was, did the best he could at laying out the facts.

But the trip was grueling and sometimes the president let down his guard. At a speech in Winona, Minnesota, a tired Taft told the crowd, "On the whole, I am bound to say that I think the Payne tariff bill is the best bill that the Republican Party ever passed."[10]

It was a statement that no one on either side of the issue or either side of the aisle in Congress believed, and it made headlines throughout the country, hurting the new president's trustworthiness. "His critics and his friends alike had thrust upon them this dilemma: Either he knew the Payne-Aldrich Tariff had been arrived at by corrupt ways and was not a revision downward, in spite of which he pronounced it the best ever; or he did not know its nature and the means used in framing it."[11]

In other words, he was either insincere and dishonest or ill-informed and not competent. Either way the credibility of his presidency was damaged early on in his administration. "The shock caused by the Winona speech vibrated through the country; never after that did the public fully trust Mr. Taft. It knew that the Interests had crawled back and dictated the Payne-Aldrich Tariff and it surmised that, although he prosecuted the Trusts diligently, they did not feel greatly terrified."[12]

Taft's personal life had been dealt a heavy blow during the tariff debate when his beloved Nellie suffered a stroke that paralyzed part of her body and made her unable to speak. The president had to balance his professional duties with his concern for his stricken wife, and his time away from her was devastating to him.

More trouble was brewing on the political front when he returned home after 57 days on the road. As most new presidents do, Taft replaced many of Roosevelt's cabinet members with people of his own choosing. One of them was the appointment of Richard Ballinger, a former mayor of Seattle and commissioner of the General Land Office, as secretary of interior, replacing James R. Garfield, the Roosevelt appointee.

One of the hallmarks of the Roosevelt administration, heralded even 100 years after he left office, was his devotion to conservation—the preservation of land for its aesthetic value for the people. He was also perhaps a century ahead of his time in his recognition of the value and the eventual need of renewable energy.

He was also a "trust buster," eager for the federal government to break up monopolies that stifled competition and made rich corporate giants even richer.

To that end, in the waning days of his administration, Roosevelt delivered a message to Congress promoting hydroelectric power—the electrical transmission of water over large distances. While supplies of materials such as oil, gas and coal could eventually reach their saturation point, hydroelectric power was infinite.

But Roosevelt feared that large corporations such as Westinghouse and General Electric could dominate the industry, controlling prices and accessibility—in effect becoming the kind of monopoly that he had fought against for much of his administration.

Working with Garfield and Gifford Pinchot, head of the Forestry Department, Roosevelt issued a series of executive orders that prohibited private development of 1.5 million acres of land along 16 rivers in six western states. The result was government control over lease agreements on the land—the heartland of potential hydroelectric development.[13]

When Ballinger took over as interior secretary early in 1909, he took action to negate Roosevelt's executive orders, thereby freeing millions of acres for private development. His reasoning, obviously with Taft's approval, was that Roosevelt had overstepped his bounds by putting the land under federal control without the consent of Congress.

What came to be known as the Ballinger Affair set off a political firestorm. While Roosevelt's critics had accused him of taking socialist actions in grabbing the land, Progressives feared that Ballinger's actions played into the hands of greedy, corporate America. Either way, the American consumer could be caught in the squeeze.

Taft, the lifelong jurist, believed there was nothing in the Constitution that justified the executive branch exercising control over the lands—and if the Constitution didn't specifically grant a right to the federal government, that right automatically went to the states. Taft considered himself to be a champion of conservation, just as Roosevelt was, but, unlike Roosevelt, Taft did not believe the ends justified the means.

Pinchot had been on a speaking tour when he received word of Ballinger's actions. When he returned to Washington, he immediately conferred with Taft to express his concerns over what Ballinger had done. Taft respected Pinchot but believed him to be someone who had a huge ego and had been part of Roosevelt's inner circle. But he acquiesced to the point of telling Ballinger to hold off on any further withdrawals of the Roosevelt executive orders.

But the battle lines had been drawn and were clearly visible when both Pinchot and Ballinger were among the speakers at the National Irrigation Conference in Spokane in August. On August 9, the day before Pinchot was to speak, United Press came out with a story accusing Ballinger of dragging his feet in curtailing his actions on the conservation issue, allowing big companies to make huge land grabs in Montana.

The next day, when Pinchot spoke, he seized upon the opportunity presented to him by the United Press story. He assailed Ballinger and warned his audience that waterpower monopolies were almost certain to become a reality.

Then he invoked the name of the man who Progressives worshiped on the altar of conservation. "I stand for the Roosevelt policies," Pinchot told the crowd, "because

Gifford Pinchot was an expert forester and ally of President Roosevelt whose ouster by President Taft furthered the animosity between the two presidents.

they set the common good in all of us above the private gain of some of us."¹⁴

The next day, it was Ballinger's turn at the podium. His audience as well as the press anticipated a fiery response to the United Press story and to Pinchot's remarks. But instead, Ballinger gave a rather drab report without mentioning any of the accusations about him that had become so public.

Later, it was determined the United Press story was in error, that the writer had misplaced a decimal point in reporting the land acquisitions which were actually minuscule in comparison to what had been reported.

But the damage was done. The wounds were open and they were to get worse as the Pinchot-Ballinger feud escalated and was, in effect, becoming a Roosevelt-versus-Taft policy war even though Roosevelt was thousands of miles away on safari and Taft tried in vain to be a mediator.

Another scandal erupted when Louis R. Glavis, who worked for Pinchot in the Department of Interior, told Pinchot he had been doing some research which showed that Ballinger was about to allow 5,000 acres of coal land in Alaska to be purchased by a syndicate headed by Clarence Cunningham, a developer from Seattle, Ballinger's home town. Further, Glavis said Ballinger had been working with Cunningham's people to put the deal together.

Pinchot went to Taft with the Glavis information but word had already leaked out to the press, presumably from Pinchot's Forestry Department, that Ballinger had accepted fees from Cunningham who expected favorable treatment in return.

Taft arranged to meet with Glavis to hear the accusations firsthand and then met with Attorney General George Wickersham. The attorney general advised the president to forward Glavis's report to Ballinger and require a response from him.

Ballinger responded with a 10,000-word defense of what he had done—and hadn't done. Taft read the Ballinger account and determined Glavis had no worthwhile evidence to substantiate his accusations against Ballinger. As such, he gave Ballinger permission to discharge Glavis for disloyalty and insubordination, and Ballinger complied.

But Taft had another tiger he had to tame. He sent a letter to Pinchot, Roosevelt's good friend, assuring him he remained in good stead and that the Glavis situation did not reflect badly on him. The president did not want to fire Pinchot or have him resign because he did not want to incur the wrath of Roosevelt and other Progressives.

Unfortunately for the president, neither Pinchot nor Ballinger were willing to give up the fight. Pinchot, working with others in the Interior Department, arranged to have Glavis's side of the story published in the November issue of *Collier's* magazine. *Collier's* ran the story, including the firing of Glavis and exoneration of Ballinger, under the headline "The Whitewashing of Ballinger," and did not contact Ballinger for a response.[15]

Taft, who hated confrontation, wanted the ordeal to end so that everyone involved could move on. But an irate Ballinger wanted his reputation back. He contacted some friends in the Washington congressional delegation and asked for an investigation into his actions—and he got his wish.

Unsolicited, Pinchot sent a letter to congressional investigators expressing his views. Taft believed Pinchot had overstepped his bounds by acting on his own without the approval of his boss, Agriculture Secretary James Wilson. Taft directed Wilson to fire Pinchot. Two underlings in the Interior Department who had helped supply information for the *Collier's* article were also fired.

Taft, who never trusted Pinchot, suspected the old Roosevelt ally tried to set up a circumstance in which Taft would be forced to fire him. Writing to Nellie on October 3, 1909, Taft said, "I am convinced that Pinchot with his fanaticism and his disappointment at my decision in the Ballinger case plans a coup by which I will be compelled to dismiss him. And he will be able to mark out martyrdom and try to raise opposition to me on Ballinger's account."[16]

The congressional hearings ended in May 1910 with the conclusion that Ballinger had done nothing illegal. Still, there was pressure on Taft to ease Ballinger out of the cabinet because he had become a political liability. The challenge was to do it in a way that would appease both Progressives and conservatives, the kind of dilemma Taft abhorred.

Archie Butt wrote to his sister-in-law, "To sacrifice Ballinger without due cause would, I am sure, lessen the president in the respect of very many people."

Butt wished Taft's mother was still alive because he believed "she was a stern counselor and offered her son good advice. His brother Horace told me that their mother often said that love of approval was Will's besetting fault and she always strove to correct it in him when they were children," Butt wrote. Taft had told Butt that when he went to the Philippines, his mother advised him to go ahead and do what he thought was right and let approval or disapproval follow as it might.[17]

The situation resolved itself when nine months later, Ballinger resigned and returned to private life.[18] Meanwhile, Theodore Roosevelt, who would be returning home soon, had been fully advised of the situation by his friend, Pinchot. The former president did not mince words. He said, "Mr. Ballinger, as secretary of the interior in this administration, did all he could to destroy a great public policy. Yet he was vindicated by Mr. Taft.... Gifford Pinchot, a peculiarly fine public servant, who, more than any one man, initiated the conservation policy of the preceding administration, was dismissed from office."[19]

There were other issues that irritated Roosevelt. He considered passage of the Pure Food and Drug Act and legislation regulating meat inspections as great achievements of his administration. So when the National Wholesale Liquor Dealers Association, makers of imitation whiskey, lobbied to weaken the law, Taft, the old jurist, tried to mediate by inserting changes of his own.

Roosevelt was furious. "It gave the imitation whiskey interests all that they had ever demanded," he said. "Under this new and strained construction of a beneficent law, it would be possible to mix coffee and chicory and call it blended coffee or to mix tea and willow leaves and call it blended tea."[20]

He also took issue with Taft on changes made to a railroad rate bill that he claimed nullified verified findings of the Interstate Commerce Commission.

But clearly, the concessions included in the Payne-Aldrich tariff bill and the fight over land conservation were catalysts for the clash that was imminent.

Pinchot was a devoted Roosevelt disciple and each held each other in the highest respect. In his autobiography, Roosevelt wrote that he was "the foremost leader" and breaking new ground in the struggle to achieve a national conservation policy. "I believe it is but just to say that among the many, many public officials who under my administration rendered literally invaluable service to the people of the United States, he, on the whole, stood first."[21]

The tariff meltdown, the conservation fight and the firing of Pinchot were the biggest sparks in the political fire that brought Roosevelt, who had been on his African safari, back into the jungle of American politics.

He arrived back in the U.S. to a tumultuous welcome at New York harbor and intended to stay out of hardball politics, at least for a while. But it was not in his nature. Taft had appointed New York governor Charles Evans Hughes to the Supreme Court. Before he left office, Hughes wanted the state legislature to pass a bill calling for direct primary elections. Roosevelt agreed to help him.

After much wrangling in the state General Assembly, the bill was defeated. Hughes had lost his last hurrah as governor and Roosevelt had lost his first foray back into American politics. He was furious.

He decided to run for the temporary chairmanship of the New York State Republican Convention. The title was misleading because the job was one of prestige. The temporary chairman helped develop the platform, helped nominate the party's candidates and delivered the keynote speech. It was a tailor-made job for someone with the personality, the ego, the drive and the ambition of Roosevelt.

But the former president ran into obstacles he had not anticipated. He was a progressive traveling in territory that was still the stomping grounds of the conservative element of the party. The party bosses nominated James Sherman, a longtime Republican conservative to run against Roosevelt. Sherman also happened to be Taft's vice president. Roosevelt was certain Taft had encouraged the nomination of Sherman, and when Sherman won, Roosevelt blamed Taft though the president had stayed clear of the whole process.

While Roosevelt was apparently angry at what he thought was Taft's influence in his defeat, Taft was upset that Roosevelt assumed the worst without ever consulting or confronting his old friend about the circumstances. "I am deeply hurt," Taft told Archie Butt. "The proper thing for him was to give me the opportunity to explain my position and to thrash it out as we had done so many times in the past. It is inconceivable that I, the president of the United States should go to him on my knees, so to speak, and ask his approval."[22]

Now the political fires were ablaze inside Roosevelt. He went on an extensive speaking tour, traveling by train from one city to another, just like in the old days. At Osawatomie, Kansas, he gave what came to be known as his "New Nationalism" speech, espousing direct primary elections, a ban on corporations from funding political initiatives, advocating an income tax and inheritance tax on the rich and calling for child labor laws.

He was sounding more and more like a candidate. "Though every special interest is entitled to justice, not one is entitled to a vote in Congress, to a voice on the bench or to representation in any public office," he said.[23]

In the summer of 1911, Taft put together a coalition with France and England that, in essence, was an arbitration agreement that would go into effect any time a major problem existed between the three countries. Taft, whose inner fiber was that of jurist, a mediator, and arbiter considered the arbitration treaty as one of the hallmarks of his presidency.

Roosevelt rebuked him, saying national honor was never subject to arbitration. He said it would be like watching a man slap your wife and then asking an arbiter to settle the matter. Taft said the disagreement—the latest one between him and Roosevelt—was an example of the differences in their approach. He said Roosevelt was a fighter who didn't believe in peace.[24]

Still another dispute between the two men occurred when Taft's Justice Department filed suit against U.S. Steel Corporation, claiming it was a monopoly acting illegally in restraint of trade and stifling competition. It sought dissolution of nearly 40 companies and subsidiaries including its purchase of Tennessee Coal and Iron Company in 1907.

That deal had been approved by President Roosevelt because he believed it served the nation's best interests at the time. He said Taft supported the action when he was in Roosevelt's cabinet so he was being a hypocrite now.

When Roosevelt was president, he had a reputation of being a "trust buster," specifically breaking up Standard Oil. He believed his trust-busting was breaking up big corporations to show them they were not above the law. He believed Taft was breaking up big corporations just because they were big.

Taft was disappointed in Roosevelt's attacks on him and was disgusted with how his opponents used Roosevelt's image as a weapon against him. He wrote to his wife, "This disposition to use Roosevelt's reputation and popularity as a club to beat me is not, of course very agreeable. But it is something which I might have expected and did expect."[25]

He was aware that he was elected in the enormous shadow of the man who preceded him but hoped on the basis of his accomplishments that he would be judged on his own merits. Taft was enough of a realist to know his legacy would be a combination of the two. He wrote that he hoped to be able "to obtain from a reasonable number of my constituents support because of myself and not because I happened to have adopted anyone else's policies, though the latter of course is the source of my strength at present and I am quite willing to recognize it."[26]

The two old friends were constantly at odds now, with neither of them having a kind word for the other. Chauncey Depew, ex-senator from New York, businessman and heavyweight in Republican politics, saw the split in the Republican Party and between Roosevelt and Taft. He was soon to say prophetically, "the only question now is which corpse gets the most flowers."[27]

But while these two Republican giants bickered, another Republican was rising fast on the horizon.

8

LaFollette

While Roosevelt and Taft were born into well-to-do families with nurturing parents and cultures that provided opportunities for personal growth and development, Robert LaFollette was born in a log cabin in rural Primrose, Wisconsin. His father died when he was one. His mother remarried to a man who paid little attention to his stepson.

Upon the death of his stepfather, his mother sold the family farm and moved to Madison. It was there that young Robert began to blossom. He went to the University of Wisconsin where he was described as a "very mediocre student who enjoyed social activities."[1]

It was at the university that he met John Bascom, university president, who took a liking to LaFollette and became a trusted adviser and mentor, shaping his views on morality and social justice. It was as if Bascom had become a father figure to a young man who was searching for one.

LaFollette developed an interest in public speaking and became an excellent debater. In his senior year he won an oratorical contest, competing with other student orators from throughout the Midwest.

After graduation, he went to law school and soon opened a practice in 1880. His passion for issues he believed in and his gift of oratory led him into what would turn out to be a life in politics. In November of 1890, he was elected district attorney for Dane County, Wisconsin. He served two two-year terms and then decided to try to make the leap to bigger political challenges. He was elected to the U.S. House of Representatives in 1895 and served three terms in which he championed, among other things, the rights of minorities.

In 1891, his first year as district attorney, an incident occurred that impacted the rest of his career. LaFollette claimed Senator Philetus Sawyer of Wisconsin approached him, trying to get him to help exonerate some former state officials who were involved in a scandal. Whatever was said between the two men, LaFollette felt like he was being bribed and flatly rejected him. But being that close to corruption in government spurred him to be a watchdog over questionable government actions, even within his own party, for the rest of his life.

"Nothing else ever came into my life that exerted such a powerful influence on me than that affair," he said. "It was the turning point, in a way, of my career. Sooner or later I probably would have done what I did in Wisconsin. But it would have been later. It would have been a matter of much slower evolution. But it shocked me into a complete realization of the extremes to which this power that Sawyer represented would go to get the results it was after."[2]

LaFollette became convinced that government power had to be stripped from the special interests and into the hands of the people. In the House, he formed a group within his own party, who came to be known as "the Insurgents," who opposed the government-as-usual "Stalwarts" and instead pushed for reforms such as direct election of public officials rather than appointment by the powers-that-be as well as an array of policies aimed at consumer rights.

Wisconsin senator Robert LaFollette organized the Progressive movement in the living room of his home.

LaFollette ran for governor in 1896 and 1898, unsuccessfully both times, but became well known throughout the state for his fiery oratory, often delivered from the back of a backboard wagon. His speeches were sometimes two hours long and he gave hundreds of them.

In 1900, he ran again, this time with a more organized band of Insurgents backing him. He is said to have to traveled to 61 counties, delivering more than 200 speeches, reaching more than 200,000 in total crowd size. He was elected by a margin of 100,000 votes and was re-elected in 1904.

His administration became nationally known for its emphasis on reform and also for the flamboyancy of the man in the governor's office. Through his "Wisconsin Idea," LaFollette worked with the University of Wisconsin to put together a coalition of citizens who would identify problems, determine solutions and recommend legislation to combat them. Wisconsin became "a laboratory for democracy" and "the most important state for the development of progressive legislation."[3]

The Wisconsin Idea even drew praise from Theodore Roosevelt, who said, "Following LaFollette, a number of practical workers and thinkers in Wisconsin have turned that state into an experimental laboratory of wise governmental action. They have initiated the kind of progressive government which means not only the preservation of true democracy but the extension of the principle of true democracy into industrialism as well as into politics."[4]

Another feature of the LaFollette era was a campaign tactic in which he would travel from county to county and emphatically deliver a "roll call"—reading the names of legislators who opposed him on bills that advanced the Progressive movement—a national theme by 1912 but had been part of the Insurgent movement in Wisconsin for several years.

In 1905, there was an opening for a U.S. Senate seat. One of the perks of being governor was being able to nominate whoever he wanted to fill the position. LaFollette nominated himself and was easily confirmed by the state senate. The flashy orator from Primrose, full of ideas and gusto, now had a national stage on which to perform.

LaFollette did what he could to advance the Insurgents agenda for consumer rights and protections. He was hampered because Sen. Aldrich, the powerful leader of the conservative wing and a man of great influence, made sure the cocky young senator was assigned to committees that had little impact.

The Progressive movement was gaining steam in the Republican Party with President Theodore Roosevelt setting the tone with his trust-busting policies to keep large companies from overpowering competitors and controlling prices.

LaFollette, who, as a freshman senator, had trouble making the splash in Washington that he had envisioned for himself, resorted to some of the tactics that had worked well for him in Wisconsin. Because of his temperament, his colleagues began calling him "Fighting Bob." When Congress adjourned, he went on a nationwide speaking tour, utilizing his oratorical skills and his amazing stamina to spread the Progressive message throughout the land. He also "called the roll," announcing to his large crowds the names of the senators who had voted with the old guard and special interests.

When Roosevelt did not run for re-election in 1908 and Taft succeeded him in the White House, it represented two important shifts. With Roosevelt on safari in Africa, LaFollette became the leading Progressive voice in America. But instead of the zealous Roosevelt being the leader in the White House, the torch had been passed to Taft, the amiable former judge and Roosevelt loyalist who preferred compromise to confrontation.

With Roosevelt out of the picture—or at least out of the country—LaFollette became the leading spokesman for Progressive ideals and ideas—and it wasn't long before he started contemplating a run for the presidency. His ambition didn't change after Roosevelt returned and toyed with getting back into political life.

LaFollette and his backers, which now included former Roosevelt stalwarts such as the deposed Gifford Pinchot, believed LaFollette would wrest the nomination away from Taft in 1912 and put another Progressive in the White House. "Roosevelt and LaFollette wanted, on the whole, about the same things but they were poles apart in their methods. Roosevelt would make a noisy fight, and in the end would compromise when he had gone as far as he could. LaFollette never compromised."[5]

On January 21, 1911, LaFollette met with a group of his supporters at his home in Washington. The talk was mostly about Progressive ideas but also how those ideas could grow into a national movement. There was no formal announcement of a LaFollette candidacy but clearly a path had begun. It was the start of what would become the National Progressive League, supporting, among other things the direct election of senators and delegates to the national convention; direct primary elections instead of caucuses controlled by the special interests; and advocacy of the recall of public officials when necessary.

The charter members included James Garfield and Gifford Pinchot, both former Roosevelt cabinet members deposed by Taft; muckraking journalist Ray Stannard Baker; Kansas journalist William Allen White; nine U.S. senators and 13 congressmen.

Many in the press saw it as an anti–Taft movement. Some saw it as an anti–Roosevelt movement. But it wasn't. In fact, LaFollette tried to get Roosevelt to join the new organization. Roosevelt declined to join but he did endorse it in the *Outlook*, the magazine for which he was now a regular contributor.

The two men were playing political games with one another. They did not like each other personally and were suspicious of one another politically.

Roosevelt toured the country, energizing his political juices and giving the impression he did not want to rock the boat but would consider it his duty to run again if that's what the public demanded.

"Fighting Bob" was not ambiguous about his intentions. On June 17, 1911, he announced his candidacy for president. "A fire-breathing orator from the farms of Wisconsin ... his huge pompadour and sharp suits made him instantly recognizable as he fought to limit corporate power and concentration and for laws to protect consumers and workers. If anyone symbolized and stood for progressive reforms, it was Bob LaFollette."[6]

Taft was well aware of LaFollette's disdain for him. "His enmity towards me is becoming so intense that it is overshadowing every other motive or plan on his part. The public is coming to recognize this and his attacks are understood," the president wrote in a letter to his wife.[7]

Nine days later, LaFollette still occupied the president's thoughts. "The bitterness against me by LaFollette and his friends is ecstatic and there is nothing they will not stop at to besmirch me, but I shall have to stand it."[8]

8. LaFollette

LaFollette's bitterness toward Roosevelt was even greater because he believed the former president, just as energetic, flamboyant and tireless as LaFollette, was stealing his thunder as a Progressive trailblazer.

With all of these political and personality clashes in place, one thing was clear. As 1911 drew to a close, LaFollette's political stock was definitely rising.

9

The Scheme and the Implosion

While LaFollette made the rounds publicly, boasting he was the man with the plan, Roosevelt worked behind the scenes with a plan of his own. Not wanting to appear to selfishly inject himself on the American public after a four-year hiatus, the old rough rider devised a "movement" on his behalf that he would not be able, in good conscience, to refuse. "Continuing to insist that he would neither seek the nomination nor take a single step to secure it, Roosevelt softened his tone and told supporters that if a genuine popular demand for his nomination indicated conviction that he was the man to do the job, he would of course accept."[1]

Roosevelt contacted Governor Chase Osborn of Michigan, one of his loyal supporters and asked him to write a letter urging Roosevelt to get into the race and to get as many governors as he could to co-sign the letter. With that kind of support and call to duty, how could he refuse? Roosevelt even helped write the letter.

On January 22, LaFollette spoke to a packed house at Carnegie Hall in New York. Waving his arms and using the oratorical skills that his crowds came to expect and even anticipate, it was a good showing for the senator. "Got on good terms with the audience and never lost it," the *New York World* reported.[2]

Despite the warm reception that night at Carnegie Hall, when LaFollette supporters met with him afterward for dinner at the Plaza Hotel, they had some disturbing news for him. Roosevelt's momentum was building, they said, and if he got in the race, Roosevelt and LaFollette would split the Progressive vote and assure Taft of being re-nominated. They thought he should consider withdrawing his candidacy.

LaFollette, buoyed by the tremendous support he had received at Carnegie Hall, reacted with defiance. "The senator could no longer suppress his rage that Roosevelt had been using him as a 'stalking horse' all along, testing President Taft's political strength."[3]

9. The Scheme and the Implosion

He vowed to stay in the race to the end and carried on a strenuous schedule of speaking engagements that was beginning to take its toll.

On February 2, he was one of the speakers at a convention of the Periodical Publishers Association in Philadelphia. Physically exhausted and also worried about surgery his daughter was to undergo the next day, LaFollette dropped his guard and resorted to his worst instincts.

He was the fourth speaker of the evening, following New Jersey governor Woodrow Wilson, a leading contender for the Democratic nomination; California governor Hiram Johnson, a prominent west coast Progressive; and Philadelphia mayor Rudolph Blankenburg. Wilson, a former Princeton University president and professor, gave a relatively short talk spiced with humor that the audience enjoyed. Johnson, a Roosevelt stalwart, gave a more rousing, political speech. Blankenburg's remarks were those of gracious host to the convention.

By the time LaFollette stepped up to the podium, the hour was late and the audience was hopeful of being inspired by this great orator, whose reputation preceded him. He had prepared a typical LaFollette speech, forceful and flamboyant and with a clear message. He was to tell his audience that the great issue facing Americans was control over their own government because of the influence of special interests and big money.

"The Progressive movement reflects a conflict as old as the history of man," he was to tell them, "the fight to maintain human liberty, the right of all people." But inexplicably, this seasoned, brilliant speaker became an angry, almost incoherent man. LaFollette veered off script and began rambling, telling this audience of writers and editors that he would read his speech and distribute copies of it because he was tired of being misquoted in the press. As he read his speech, droning on and on, he frequently looked up from it and spewed out spontaneous remarks that were off-topic and insulting to those he was addressing. Many in the audience began to leave.

LaFollette's presidential hopes tumbled as a result of a rambling, insulting speech he made in Philadelphia.

When he returned to his text, several times he lost his place and repeated parts of it he had already read. One observer said he read the same section seven times. By the end of his talk, which lasted more than two hours, he was "denouncing the empty chairs" and "insulting the empty cups and cigar stubs" on the floor in front of him.[4]

Kansas editor and Progressive proponent William Allen White was there. He said there were times when LaFollette read for five minutes or more passages of his speech he had already read. "For nearly two hours, fumbling occasionally with his manuscript, he raged on and on, saying the same thing over and over at the top of his voice. It was a terrible spectacle. The progressive leadership of the United States that night received such a shock as it never had."[5]

When LaFollette was done, he sat down in a nearby chair, angry, perplexed and exhausted. Many believed his campaign was done as well. The next morning, he was back in Washington with his family for his daughter's surgery and, after a few days off for rest, he returned to the Senate.

But rumors spread about his "nervous breakdown" in Philadelphia and there were concerns about his overall health. Throngs of would-be supporters, who had been unsure as to whether to back LaFollette or Roosevelt, now had an excuse to jump ship and go with the colonel even though he had not yet announced his candidacy.

While LaFollette remained in the race—for he was anything but a quitter—his campaign never had the steam it needed after the Philadelphia experience. Many who had followed him and supported him were now a bit afraid of him. "He was a great leader, a brave, wise uncompromising leader.... No other left-wing leader ever impressed upon the laws and institutions of his country and upon the purposes and impulse of the American people in his time so strong, definite and considerable an achievement as Robert LaFollette Sr."[6]

La Follette believed that the original text of his Philadelphia speech, which didn't get much publicity because of his antics in delivering it, was so important in espousing his political beliefs, that he included it in its entirety in his autobiography.

While LaFollette's campaign was sputtering, the Roosevelt machine was chugging along. The colonel had not formally announced his candidacy but those who knew him knew the challenge would be irresistible. Roosevelt biographer William Roscoe Thayer wrote his denial was like "the consummate actor or the prima donna, whom the world applauds, sincere in bidding farewell to the stage forever. Nevertheless, which of them is conscious of the strength of the passion, which long habit and supremacy and the intoxication of success have evoked, dwells in them? Given the moment and the lure, they forget their promise of farewell."[7]

9. The Scheme and the Implosion

Roosevelt wanted to be asked to run, and with the help of Governor Osborn in Michigan, he was about to receive the outpouring of support he not only craved but had carefully orchestrated.

Seven governors—Osborn of Michigan, Robert P. Bass of New Hampshire, Herbert S. Hadley of Missouri, William Glasscock of West Virginia, Robert D. Carey of Wyoming, Chester Aldrich of Nebraska and Walter Stubbs of Kansas—had signed a letter of support, urging Roosevelt to run.

Historians differ as to how much direction the colonel gave in drafting this letter of support for him. Some say he wrote it and had Osborn distribute it. Others say he contributed ideas to it or that he edited it before it was distributed. But none deny that the former president concocted this "spontaneous" display of adoration for him. "Roosevelt's enemies insinuated that the seven governors had been moved to act at his own instigation. No doubt he was consulted; no doubt being a very alert student of political effects, he suggested many things. But the rush of enthusiasts to him was genuine and spontaneous."[8]

The former president's exuberance was legendary and could take many forms. "He could not describe even a butterfly without vividness which easily passed into vehemence but he was in no sense mentally overwrought. His humor flashed out but he had the underlying gravity of one who knows that he is about to make a very important decision."[9]

Roosevelt was invited to address the Ohio Constitutional Convention in Columbus on February 22. This body was about to discuss and debate changes in its state constitution—which made it a perfect setting for Roosevelt to inform them, and because of the press coverage, the rest of the nation, his progressive vision on the responsibilities of government. Though he had not made any formal announcement about his own political intentions—for he had not yet unleashed his "outpouring" of support for his candidacy, he offhandedly responded to a reporter's question by saying, "my hat is in the ring."

A big part of the Roosevelt philosophy, aside from his belief in a strong executive branch, was his belief in the power of the people to run their own lives, to get a "square deal" from government and for them to have means to have a greater role in making sure they got their square deal. This philosophy came to be known as "let the people rule." He had touched on it in his "New Nationalism" speech in Kansas but he laid it out in greater detail in Columbus.

Invoking the name of Abraham Lincoln 15 times in his speech, Roosevelt began by telling his audience, "We Progressives believe that the people have the right, the power and the duty to protect themselves and their own welfare; that human rights are supreme over all other rights; that wealth should be the servant, not the master of the people. We believe that if representative government does not absolutely represent the people, it is not representative government at all."[10]

Therefore, he admonished the legislators to provide a means in their constitution for the public to easily amend it if they discover injustice in it. He reiterated much of the Progressive platform: workmen's compensation for those who deserved it; reasonable working hours for women and children; and safe and healthy working conditions for one and all.

"The people have nothing whatever to fear from giving any public servant power so long as they retain their own power to hold him accountable for his use of this power they have delegated to him," said Roosevelt.[11]

He called for direct election of delegates to national nominating conventions; direct election of United States senators; and ballot initiatives and referendums to "correct" representative government, when necessary.

He had pretty well followed the party line of the Progressives with his characteristic gusto—voice rising, finger pointing, toothy grin displayed from time to time. But then he went a step further, and to many it was a step too far. The colonel advocated the recall of judges and of judicial decisions by popular vote.

"When a judge decides a constitutional question," he said, "when he decides what the people as a whole can and cannot do, the people should have the right to recall that decision if they think it is wrong. If there must be a decision by a close majority, then let the people step in and let it be their majority that decides."[12]

Some Progressives loved the speech, such as Governor Hiram Johnson of California, whose state had already initiated some forms of recall. But the speech drew much criticism from some of Roosevelt's longtime political allies such as Elihu Root, Henry Stimson and Senator Henry Cabot Lodge. Root, a well-respected senator from New York had served in two positions in Roosevelt's cabinet—secretary of war and secretary of state. Stimson, a distinguished lawyer and politician, had been appointed by Roosevelt as U.S. attorney for the southern district of New York and was currently Taft's secretary of war. Lodge, a senator from Massachusetts, had been a friend of Taft for most of their adult lives.

Roosevelt thought so highly of Root that he was his first choice to succeed him as president in 1908 but made Taft his final choice. While he thought Root would make a better president, he believed Taft had a better chance of being elected. "Given Root's belief that democracy needed constitutional restraint for survival, he was understandably appalled at Roosevelt's program of constitutional reform which would have struck directly at the heart of such restraints."[13] "Many [critics] were lawyers steeped in legal training and thinking and perhaps influenced by their association with corporate clients. They

9. The Scheme and the Implosion

believed deeply in the sanctity of the courts to protect the rights and processes guaranteed by the Constitution."[14]

One of the people who believed deeply in the sanctity of the courts was President Taft who had to be appalled at Roosevelt's notion. Senator Lodge said, "Roosevelt's Columbus speech has turned Taft from a man into a principle."[15]

Taft confided to Archie Butt that he was going to have to fight his old friend Roosevelt and that he would probably lose but "don't think me capable of quitting. I can fight just as well when losing as when certain of victory."[16]

He said he planned to answer Roosevelt in Ohio, the president's home state but, more to the point, the same state in which Roosevelt had laid down the gauntlet. Taft said he hoped the fight would not get personal but firmly believed Roosevelt had gone too far, especially with his proposal to recall judges if the public disagreed with their decisions. That concept hit close to home for the former judge. He told Butt, "he will either be a hopeless failure if elected or else destroy his own reputation by becoming a socialist, being swept there by force of circumstances just as the leaders of the French Revolution were swept on and on, all their individual efforts failing to stem the tide until it had run itself out."[17]

Roosevelt's Columbus speech also provided Taft with a certain sense of relief because he could now take on the former president on the issues rather than engaging in personal attacks—a campaign based on ideas and not personalities.

One of the colonel's most loyal supporters, newspaperman William Allen White, said the call to recall judicial decisions was "indefensible" and wondered who advised Roosevelt to say it. "It hurt him; probably it crippled him more than any other one thing that he did in his life," wrote White. "For the speech shocked millions of his countrymen whom he had gathered about him as followers, and it attracted only the radicals who are never dependable to follow any man's train nor to pursue any consistent course."[18]

Newspapers assailed him. The *New York Sun* accused him of wanting to turn the judiciary into "a court of the crowd."[19]

The *St. Louis Republic* said his comments demonstrated "Mr. Roosevelt's inability to grasp a legal proposition."[20]

The *New York World* said Roosevelt was trying to "out-demagogue all demogogues."[21]

Roosevelt was undaunted by the criticism he was receiving from the press and old-guard politicians because he was convinced the public was behind him and, in the end, he was confident to "let the people rule." This was not unlike the approach that Donald Trump took a century later in his march to the presidency,

On Sunday, February 25, Roosevelt had one of those "crowded hours" days in which he met with supporters to set in motion the campaign that he had not yet publicly announced; attended a dinner; went to a meeting of the Harvard Overseers; and then ended the evening at the home of an old friend from his college days, Judge Robert Grant.

During that day, the colonel had authorized an announcement be made public that he had received a letter signed by seven governors urging him to run for president once again for the good of the American people. Further, Roosevelt wanted it known that he was humbled by this surprise show of support (that he had carefully orchestrated) and felt duty-bound to accept the nomination if it was offered to him.

Meanwhile, the guests at Judge Grant's home that night, unaware of the candidacy announcement being distributed to the press, expressed their concerns about a possible Roosevelt run, especially in light of his controversial remarks in Columbus.

Roosevelt listened to his friends politely, sometimes flashing that toothy grin, but it was clear his mind was made up. Finally, he said, "What do I owe Taft? It was through me and my friends that he became president. I had him in the hollow of my hand and he would have dropped out." Then the colonel retired to the guest room and went to bed.[22]

10

Primary Considerations

Though Theodore Roosevelt espoused the philosophy of "let the people rule," he was not a proponent of primary elections until he realized the expediency of them for his own political gain. Indeed, his initial attitude toward them revealed a part of his character not widely known and not enhancing to his public image.

Roosevelt's political success was due in large part to his dominant personality and his ability to attract the attention and support of powerful influences within the Republican Party. By opening up the nominating process to the public as a whole, Roosevelt believed unqualified people could be elected by people unqualified to vote for the best candidates.

He expressed his thoughts in correspondence with Dwight Willard, a leading Progressive in California who was a strong advocate of primary elections because they represented a way to let the people rule. Roosevelt responded by giving one example after another of where the people were not intelligent enough to vote, such as Haiti; or where necessary reforms were voted down, such as in Switzerland; or where corrupt politicians were elected by a well-meaning but unsuspecting citizenry, such as in New York.

"If you literally applied this without reservation or qualification in California," he said, "it would of course mean that the Chinese and Japanese should come in in unlimited quantities and should rule you."[1]

He said the same thing was true in the south where primary elections would give undue strength to undeserving negroes. In other words, Roosevelt told Willard, "only certain people are fit for democracy."[2]

The framers of the U.S. Constitution did not envision the creation of political parties nor the need for nominating conventions or the means of electing delegates to those conventions. By practice and not by law, delegates to the national conventions were most often picked at state conventions whose delegates were selected at district conventions. It was a system from start to finish that allowed rich, influential political bosses to control the delegate selection.

Things started to change at the start of the 20th century. In 1901, Florida became the first state to have a presidential primary election. Four years later, under the leadership of Governor LaFollette, Wisconsin had a direct open primary and required direct election of national convention delegates. In 1910, Oregon passed a law creating a presidential preference primary and requiring delegates to the national convention to support the winner of the primary.

As the 1912 presidential campaign drew near, the biggest supporters of primaries were LaFollette, now a firebrand senator from Wisconsin who had announced his candidacy for president, and Jonathan Bourne, an eccentric, little-known senator from Oregon who, like LaFollette, had convinced lawmakers in his own state to hold primary elections and believed every state should hold them.

Bourne, a fast-talking, cigar-chomping Progressive, arrived in Washington in 1907 and became a devout admirer of President Roosevelt, trying to see him just about every day and writing to him frequently. When he tried to mount a movement to get Roosevelt re-nominated in 1908, even though Roosevelt had vowed he would not run, Roosevelt dismissed him as "a sincere fanatic."

Roosevelt became annoyed at Bourne's constant attempts at attention, saying he was "the worst kind of insurgent—good for nothing except to insurge."[3]

Bourne reacted like a spurned lover and grew to detest Roosevelt. He became a follower of LaFollette and was one of the original members of the National Progressive Republican League which Roosevelt had declined to join. Political battles were now boiling within the Republican Party that divided the opposition to Taft, which had the potential to help the incumbent president. Essentially, Roosevelt would be out to stop Taft while LaFollette, Bourne and others were out to stop Taft and Roosevelt.

Several factors were beginning to tilt in Roosevelt's direction. He had the adulation of much of the public, even more than the usual respect Americans show former presidents. He had the division within the party toward Taft. He was the beneficiary of LaFollette's meltdown during his speech in Philadelphia. He had the "endorsement" of seven governors—Osborn of Michigan, Bass of New Hampshire, Hadley of Missouri, Glasscock of West Virginia, Carey of Wyoming, Aldrich of Nebraska and Stubbs of Kansas—through the letter that was Roosevelt's idea, that they all signed, urging him to run. He had the support of many Progressive leaders such as Gov. Hiram Johnson in California and William Allen White, the influential newspaper editor from Emporia, Kansas, as well as old political friends such as Henry Cabot Lodge in Massachusetts. And he had the experience of having already run—and won—a presidential campaign.

Because of his political experience, he knew the built-in advantages Taft enjoyed. Incumbent presidents develop broad support through appointments they make to cushy government jobs; through the gratitude of state and local candidates they have helped get elected all over the country; and through legislation they have helped enact that has benefited particular areas in which voters will express their gratitude on election day. Presidents exert enormous power and influence by just saying "yes" or "no." And they have a captive audience in that when they speak, a whole nation and much of the world listens. It is the stuff of which political machinery is built and flourishes.

By 1912, more states were favoring primary elections as the process to nominate their delegates to state and national conventions. New York, North Dakota, Nebraska and New Jersey were now onboard to go along with Oregon and Wisconsin. And while Roosevelt recognized what he perceived to be weaknesses in primary elections, he also saw them as a way of showing the tremendous popular support he still enjoyed and therefore could be a springboard for him to overtake Taft in delegate strength at the national convention. Roosevelt was a man of principles—and one of his principles was that the ends justify the means when the national interest was at stake—as it certainly was, in his view, in the 1912 presidential race. So he became an advocate of primary elections.

Taft was thought of, by his detractors, as a jolly fat man who had been a good judge and cabinet member but was out of his element and overmatched by the rigors of the presidency. In truth, he had his faults but he was not dumb; he had political capital that he had saved up and he was proud enough to put up a good fight for his integrity and legacy. "By waiting until Feb. 25, 1912 to announce his candidacy, Roosevelt allowed Taft to have a significant head start. Taft had spent the last year building a huge lead in delegates from states where there were no presidential primaries, particularly in the south, where White House patronage, rather than cotton, was the political king."[4]

Roosevelt took advantage of having developed so many friendships over the years with members of the press and engaged them in his campaign. They might have been objective reporters during the day, or given that impression, but in their off-hours, they were busy churning out pro–Roosevelt press releases and stressing the importance of all states having presidential preference primaries, to "let the people rule."

The Republican Party was facing a potentially crippling split involving three different factions—the Taft regulars (conservatives); the LaFollette Progressives, who were down but not out; and the Roosevelt Progressives who were mounting a charge. The question that voters would ultimately decide is which faction would prevail or, put another way, which factions would not survive. "There comes a time in every sect, party or institution when it stops

President Taft engages in conversation with some of the Washington political elite at a gathering in 1912. House Speaker Joe Cannon is second from left.

growing, its arteries harden, its young men see no visions; its old men dream no dreams. Unable to adjust to change and new conditions, it falls back into the past, as an old man drops into his worn-out armchair."[5]

Republicans were about to find out how it would play out. North Dakota was to hold the first-ever presidential preference primary on March 19 followed by New York a week later and then 11 more in rapid succession, ending with South Dakota on June 4, just a few weeks before the Republican National Convention.

While many states were joining the primary parade, almost three times as many still picked their candidates through state conventions and caucuses—and those provided an advantage to Taft because of patronage, one of the oldest political perks. It was a common practice in America for presidents to appoint friends and allies to influential positions and for those appointees to staff their offices with grateful job seekers—all of whom owed their livelihoods to the man at the top. And that man would be rewarded on election day. Patronage was the engine for political machines.

At many state conventions, the politics was personal, passionate and sometimes violent. Hardball politics meant winning at any cost with the ends justifying the means without decorum or dignity. Though Taft prevailed at many of the conventions, his hope of a campaign based on ideas played little part in his victories. As for Roosevelt, he felt compelled to send a message to some of his surrogates that bribery was not an acceptable tactic.

In Michigan, nearly 2,000 men tried to cram into an arena that held less than 1,500, leading to fist fights and rioting. As men were literally being tossed around and beaten, the state police were called in to restore order. When the convention finally got under way, the Taft forces, who far outnumbered Roosevelt's, prevailed.

At a district convention in Missouri, there was only one entrance to the hall and Roosevelt supporters were prevented from entering by Taft men wielding baseball bats. In Oklahoma, a man nearly created a riot when, dressed as a Rough Rider, he came into the convention on a horse and rode down the center aisle all the way to the speakers platform. Later, that same meeting was interrupted when fireworks were set off.

In Guthrie, Oklahoma, there was violence. Frank Knox, a newspaper publisher who was one of Roosevelt's Rough Riders in the Spanish American War, described the tension-filled battle for delegates. "One man dropped dead and two or three were carried out unconscious. The state chairman, Harris, was told if he tried to put over any crooked deals ... he wouldn't get out of the hall alive.... Gun-play was expected."[6]

As primaries approached, Roosevelt felt confident. His publicity machine was feeding press releases every day to a waiting public that seemed always interested in what the colonel was up to from one day to the next. North Dakota was a good launching pad for him in the primaries. He had spent much time in the "badlands" as a young man and had written extensively and lovingly about his days there. He was confident the people would remember him and support him.

New York, holding the second primary, also seemed to bode well for Roosevelt. It was his home state, the place where he grew up, where he cut his political teeth in the state legislature, where he was a swash-buckling police commissioner and later governor.

The path seemed smooth for the former president who, just months earlier, had criticized the primary election process because it allowed ignorant people to help pick the nation's leaders. Now he had surrogates in key states touting his candidacy and lining up votes for him. In states that weren't looking so good, particularly in the south, the strategy was to challenge the legality of delegates pledged to Taft or at least to threaten to do so to slow down any express that might be mounting.

Roosevelt wanted to stay off the campaign trail as much as he could to keep up the appearance of being the somewhat reluctant candidate, someone who was in it to satisfy the public demand rather than to feed his own ego.

But if he had to fight for it, he would, because as one pundit put it, Roosevelt needed a battle like most men need oxygen.

One thing he hadn't counted on—most political observers hadn't—was the resurgence of Sen. LaFollette. Many presumed him politically dead after his disastrous Philadelphia speech but he paid little attention to those writing his political obituary.

LaFollette had grown to hate Roosevelt. He was angered that the colonel had refused to join the Progressive League that LaFollette had started and yet now was considered the darling of the Progressives, stealing the limelight from the Wisconsin senator. Further, Roosevelt had been an early opponent of primary elections, which LaFollette had long endorsed and of which Wisconsin was a pioneer in using. Yet now, when Roosevelt saw political gain for himself, he was in favor of primaries.

LaFollette had a plan to get even with Roosevelt, to set him back on his ears and at the same time give a spanking to President Taft. LaFollette was a Midwest boy through and through, raised in a small Wisconsin town, educated in Wisconsin schools, devoting much of his professional life to improving conditions in his home state.

Midwest values are hard to define but voters know them when they see them, LaFollette believed. And he was confident his lifetime of being immersed in those values would more than offset Roosevelt's legacy of life in the badlands. The stage was set for LaFollette to defeat Roosevelt, as well as Taft, on March 19 in the nation's first primary in North Dakota.

11

THE ROOSEVELT EXPRESS

LaFollette was smart enough and shrewd enough to know he had probably squandered his chance to win the Republican nomination with his sputtering utterances in Philadelphia. "But he was so angry at TR's tactics, so contemptuous of his opportunistic support of progressive principles, so convinced that he should have been the party's standard bearer—and perhaps so furious at those who had deserted his campaign—that he was determined to deny Roosevelt the nomination."[1]

And so it was that on March 19, 1912, a day in which it was raining in Fargo, Williston and Bismarck and most everywhere in North Dakota, LaFollette rose from the political dead and scored a decisive victory in the nation's first presidential primary.

The totals were stunning: LaFollette 57.2 percent, Roosevelt 39.7 percent, Taft 3.1 percent.

There were many significant elements to the historic vote. Not only had LaFollette rebounded from his freefall the previous month, but the incumbent president had been thrashed, with about 97 percent of the voters choosing someone else. While most political observers recognized Taft's popularity had waned and his chances for overall victory were slipping, the extent of his defeat in the first primary was overwhelming.

The *New York Times* focused on what it thought was the most important aspect—the LaFollette win over not Taft, but the colonel. Its headline was "Beat Roosevelt in North Dakota."[2]

The *Washington Post* put it in perspective. "The small vote count for President Taft means very little," it reported, "as he was not fighting for recognition in the primaries as were Roosevelt and LaFollette. In a nutshell, the outcome is decidedly embarrassing to Roosevelt, encouraging to LaFollette and the subject of mixed amusement and satisfaction to Taft."[3]

"Strange as it seemed, LaFollette was back in the campaign and in a position to attract some Progressive voters who would otherwise have supported Roosevelt by default. LaFollette is a wonder. What other man on earth could collapse as he did, not only physically but politically, and come back as he has done?"[4]

Roosevelt had no time to lick his wounds. The New York primary was a week away.

New York and North Dakota could not have been more culturally different. While North Dakota was a state with a city here and there and wide open spaces in between, New York, and particularly New York City, was big and bawdy, and what empty spaces existed were on someone's drawing board to fill up with tall buildings and other centers of commerce.

In fact, in early 1912, T. Kennard Thomson, an ambitious engineer, was promoting his idea to fill in the East River, add 1,400 acres of land to New York City and extend Manhattan by 10 blocks, creating what he believed would be a mecca for economic development. The plan was widely discussed but went nowhere. Nonetheless, Thomson was the personification of what New York was in the early 20th century, a place where ideas were born and nurtured.

North Dakota had just as proud a culture, but it didn't have the big city swagger. It had wide open spaces, a certain grit and a wholesomeness that was far from the fast-paced juggernaut of New York.

While North Dakota's main sports were rodeos, New York had two major league baseball teams. One was the Highlanders, a team stuck at the bottom of the standings in the American League, with players name Cozy (Doan), Stubby (Magner) and Hippo (Vaughn). The other was the Giants, perennial powerhouse of the National League, managed by John McGraw and led by two future Hall-of-Fame pitchers, Christy Mathewson and Rube Marquard.

New York also had something that North Dakota didn't have, nor did any other state in the country. It had Broadway, the most famous entertainment center in the east. In March of 1912, George M. Cohan was starring in his own production of "45 Minutes from Broadway" at the George M. Cohan Theater.

As politics became center stage in the Big Apple, the movers and shakers in the business world were feeling the impact of the fire that destroyed the Equitable Insurance building, the city's first skyscraper. Six men died in the fire including two firefighters but all of the important records and deeds and contracts, housed in safes and vaults inside the building, were preserved.

Though it was his home state, Roosevelt had suffered some recent political setbacks such as losing the temporary chairmanship of the state convention to James Sherman—Taft's vice president. And while early on, Roosevelt had not been in favor of primary elections, he had backed the proposal to have them in New York as a favor to then-governor Charles Evans Hughes who wanted them.

The day after the North Dakota loss, Roosevelt spoke to an overflow crowd of 3,000 at Carnegie Hall. Often shouting above the roar of the crowd, he laid out once again the principle on which his campaign was based. "The great fundamental issue now before the Republican Party and before our people can be stated briefly," he said. "It is: Are the American people fit to govern themselves, to control themselves? I believe they are. My opponents do not."[5]

New Yorkers would be voting in a primary election for the first time, and it was far more complicated than they had imagined. The ballot included candidates for just about all public offices from the state legislature to the presidency, from an assortment of political parties, plus delegate selections from specific districts as well as at-large delegates. The result was a ballot that was long and unwieldy. Roosevelt mocked the ballot in his campaign stops, rolling out a 14-foot replica of the ballot for his audiences to see at laugh at.

Before the election was even held, the Taft and Roosevelt forces were in court, accusing the other of fraud, bribery and other unsavory acts. Each side had hired private detectives to investigate, among other things, claims that the other side was going to stuff the ballot boxes with votes from people who didn't exist.

In addition to all of the allegations swirling about, some actual problems surfaced. In some districts, ballots did not arrive at polling places on time. In others districts, the ballots were damaged on arrival because they had been folded in such a way that the bottom parts had become detached, leaving some candidates' names on the floor of the polling places.

In the end, when the votes were counted, Roosevelt had suffered another stunning defeat. Taft was the winner with 66.4 percent to Roosevelt's 33.6 percent, a victory margin of 2-to-1 for the president. LaFollette received just a smattering of support. It was a complete reversal of what had occurred in North Dakota.

April would be a pivotal month for all of the candidates. Primaries were scheduled in Wisconsin on April 2, Illinois on April 9, Pennsylvania on April 13, Nebraska and Oregon on April 19 and Massachusetts on April 30. LaFollette was expected to be the easy winner in his home state of Wisconsin on April 2, giving him two wins in the first three primaries in which Roosevelt was a loser in all three. The rest of the elections took on added importance for both the president and the ex-president.

LaFollette took nothing for granted in his home state. "He faces his audience with flashing eye and a forty-man power energy. He convinces by the sheer force of eloquence with his vigorous speaking style—lots of arm waving and fist shaking."[6]

When the results were in, LaFollette as expected captured 73.2 percent of the vote, overwhelming both of his major opponents. This time, however,

Roosevelt, hat in one hand, pointing vigorously with the other hand, fires up a crowd in New Jersey in a 1912 campaign stop.

it was Roosevelt that took the real drubbing because of a fundamental mistake by his organization. He missed the filing deadline to be on the ballot. Taft got 26.1 percent while the colonel scored less than 1 percent—write-in votes.

It was on to Illinois on April 9, a state Roosevelt and his supporters felt was crucial to keep his campaign on track. He had made the decision that it was important for states to hold primaries, to "let the people rule," and now he had been defeated in the first three. Illinois would not be easy because the president was popular there and it was situated practically in LaFollette's backyard. The Wisconsin governor had already shown his prowess in Midwestern states.

There was another factor at play. States that were not holding presidential primaries—and there were 35 of them—were electing delegates to the national convention at their state conventions, and all indications were that Taft was doing well. The party bosses in many of those states owed their power and influence to the Republican machine—and that, by extension, meant Taft—and they were not about to relinquish it.

Illinois was in the midst of a political scandal that had been going on for three years. These were the days before senators were elected by popular vote. In 1909 the Illinois Legislature appointed Congressman William Lorimer to the Senate after four months of debate and 95 votes. He was in office less than a year when the *Chicago Tribune* broke a story in which a Democrat state legislator said he and several other legislators were each paid $1,000 to vote for Lorimer.

The senator vigorously denied the charges but the scandal persisted. In September 2010, Roosevelt was scheduled to speak at a Republican fundraiser in Chicago. When he learned Lorimer was not only going to be there but was to sit at the speaker's table with him, Roosevelt canceled his appearance. So those planning the dinner withdrew Lorimer's invitation after which Roosevelt agreed to come.[7]

The Senate conducted an investigation of the Lorimer appointment process and decided in March of 1911 not to expel him. The vote was 46–40. But hearings were reopened when more allegations of corruption surfaced. In July of 1912, the Senate expelled Lorimer by a vote of 55 to 28.[8]

The Senate investigation was in full swing as the Illinois primary approached on April 9. A year earlier, Taft and Roosevelt, still on reasonably good terms at that time, corresponded with one another about the damage the Lorimer scandal was doing to the Republican party and about what each of them, as president and ex-president, could do to hasten Lorimer's expulsion.[9]

But on the campaign trail, Roosevelt used whatever method he could to infer Taft's loyalty to Lorimer. In one speech, he reminded his Illinois audience that this was the land of Lincoln and found it shameful that Washington influences would tarnish that name. In another, he drew a comparison between corruption in Washington and shenanigans in Illinois.

His message resonated in Illinois. He won his first primary decisively, gaining 61.1 percent of the vote to 29.2 percent for Taft and 9.8 percent for LaFollette. "Suddenly, Roosevelt was on fire. Stimulated by adoring crowds and true believers, invigorated by the conviction that he was fighting liars and crooks, energized by themes of social justice and true democracy, he seemed to become young again on the campaign trail.... He believed in his cause and in himself."[10]

Lorimer, on the eve of his expulsion—and three months after the Illinois primary—defended himself on the floor of the Senate and castigated President Taft. Describing the dilemma he found himself in, Lorimer lamented, "Was ever mortal man more completely surrounded by conspiracy and intrigue?" Apparently unaware that Roosevelt and Taft had both sought his ouster, Lorimer referred to Roosevelt as "the custodian of all morality of the country, private and public."[11]

The next stop on the campaign trail was Pennsylvania on April 13. Sensing his boss was in political trouble and needing his comfort and support, Archie Butt, Taft's military aide, decided to cut short his vacation overseas and come home. On April 10, in Southhampton, he boarded the luxury ship *Titanic* to start his voyage home.

In Pennsylvania, Sen. Boise Penrose was a longtime political power broker who gained respect through the number of patronage jobs he controlled. His situation was much like that of Lorimer in Illinois in that there was always the air of corruption around him though he had never been convicted of anything. Unlike Lorimer, Penrose was never in danger of being expelled from the Senate. In fact, he held his seat for 24 years and was the state's longest serving senator.

But his reputation and his links to the Republican political machine fed neatly into Roosevelt's campaign rhetoric and he rode it to victory in Pennsylvania just as he had in Illinois. He received 59.7 percent to Taft's 40.3. LaFollette was not on the ballot.

On Monday morning, April 15, with much of America experiencing pleasant spring weather, baseball season getting under way and politics not yet hitting fever pitch in much of the nation, disturbing news came from across the Atlantic Ocean. The *Titanic*, carrying 2,300 passengers and crew, including Archie Butt, had hit an enormous iceberg. First reports were that the ship had sustained damage but was still afloat, thanks to how well it had been constructed to withstand the force of whatever might come its way.

Taft, concerned for the safety of his military aide and the others aboard, asked to be kept informed of the ship's fate throughout the day. By night time, having been assured that everything seemed to be on an even keel, he followed through on an invitation to the theater that night to see a performance of *Nobody's Widow*, a comedy at Poli's Theatre.[12]

The optimistic forecasts changed later that night when it was learned the *Titanic* had sunk. There were reports that hundreds of passengers, mostly women and children, had been lowered to lifeboats and were rescued. In the midst of the panic, confusion and frantic rescue efforts, there was no immediate information on names of those who had perished and those who had survived. Taft, fearing the worst, told White House telegraph operators to bring him the latest news throughout the night, regardless of the hour.

He held out slight hope that Butt would be among the survivors but he knew in his heart that Archie would see the disaster as a call to duty and part of that duty was to go down with the ship, if necessary. Tired and depressed, the president was already feeling the loss of the man who had been his aide, his confidante, the person who was always at his side, literally at official functions and figuratively when times were tough, when he needed a friend, when he needed someone in whom he could confide. And confide he did, on the golf course, at the retreat at Beverly, after bridge games when the other players had left and on the many rides along the Washington countryside that the president enjoyed for a few minutes of solitude away from the daily grind.

At about noon on Tuesday, *Titanic* ownership had compiled what it considered a fairly complete list of about 700 survivors. Archie Butt's name was not on the list. He had not only gone down with the ship but he had been on the ship because he felt the duty to cut his vacation short to come home and serve his commander in chief, the same position he had held during the last year of the Roosevelt administration. He had served two presidents and two presidents grieved.

Taft attended memorial services for Butt in Georgia but wept during his eulogy to him and was unable to finish. On April 19, a day on which primary elections were being held in Nebraska and Oregon, the White House released a eulogy Taft had written for public distribution. It said, "Major Archie Butt was my military aide. He was like a member of my family and I feel his loss as if he had been a younger brother. The chief trait of his character was loyalty to his ideals, his cloth and his friends. His character was a simple one in the sense that he was incapable of intrigue or insincerity. He was gentle and considerate to everyone, high and low. He never lost, under any condition, his sense of proper regard to what he considered the respect due to constituted authority. He was an earnest member of the Episcopal church and loved that communion. He was a soldier, every inch of him, a most competent, successful quartermaster and a devotee of his profession. After I heard that part of the ship's company had gone down, I gave up hope for the rescue of Major Butt unless by accident. I knew that he would certainly remain on the ship's deck until every duty had been performed and every sacrifice made that properly fell on one charged, as he would feel himself charged, with the responsibility for the rescue of others. He leaves the widest circle of friends whose memory of him is sweet in every particular."

Roosevelt was campaigning in western states when he learned the news of the *Titanic* going down. "Major Butt was the highest type of officer and gentleman," he said. "He met his end as an officer and gentleman should, giving up his own life that others might be saved. I and my family all loved him sincerely."

The political news continued to be bleak for President Taft. In Oregon, where Sen. Paul Bourne had been the champion of having a primary election in his state and advocated for them to be held nationwide, the Progressive movement was alive and well, and it showed at the polls. Roosevelt won with 40.2 percent of the vote. LaFollette, whose campaign always seemed to be down but not out, was second with 31.3 percent. Taft, for the second time, finished third—a close third but nonetheless third—with 28.5 percent.

Roosevelt scored a resounding victory in Nebraska, registering 58.7 percent to 21.5 percent for Taft and 17.1 percent for LaFollette.

After losing the first three primaries, Roosevelt had won four in a row—Illinois, Pennsylvania, Oregon and Nebraska—and his campaign appeared to be on the verge of steamrolling him into to victory at the Republican National Convention in Chicago on June 7.

But Taft was counterpunching in a much less colorful but effective means—winning many delegates in the 35 states that did not hold primaries but selected them at state conventions controlled by the party bosses who were, in many cases, controlled by the Taft forces in Washington.

Some of those state conventions turned into the political equivalent of bar room brawls. In Michigan, both Taft and Roosevelt backers challenged the credentials of each others' supporters to the point of physically blocking them from entering the convention center. Fist fights broke out inside and outside the arena. Inside, a county judge who was a Roosevelt supporter climbed up on the stage and to the podium in an attempt to restore order. A Taft backer came after him and threw him off the stage, causing serious injury.

A train carrying 200 Roosevelt delegates hit numerous delays and arrived at the convention five hours late. Roosevelt's people claimed Taft's surrogates were responsible for the late arrivals. In the end, Taft came out the victor. Roosevelt claimed he was the victim of fraud, that Taft had stolen the election from him. It would not be the last time he would make that assertion.

Taft knew he had to stop the Roosevelt bandwagon in the primaries and that led him to a most unusual decision. He would hit the road and take his case directly to the people prior to the April 30 Massachusetts primary—

unusual because the president disliked public speaking and was most uncomfortable doing it and, because incumbent presidents had rarely stepped away from the dignity of the White House to take part in good old-fashioned hardball campaigning.

Massachusetts represented what, in modern times, is called the "firewall"—the protection from letting a little fire become an out-of-control blaze. Taft was ready for the fight though he was to fight it with a heavy heart. He no longer had his military aide to pack his bags and be at his side.

He arrived in Massachusetts on April 25 and was energized by the large crowds who came to see him at every little town and hamlet, speaking in parks, church basements, school auditoriums and gymnasiums, all leading up to a major speech in Boston.

The president, who sometimes seemed unprepared as he rambled through long speeches, was now focused as he delivered carefully crafted remarks aimed at smacking down his nemesis. He told his audiences Roosevelt was fond of saying he would give them a square deal but what about giving a square deal to me, Taft asked.

In Boston, he provided a litany of instances in which Roosevelt had misquoted him or simply not told the truth. Taft had never said, as Roosevelt claimed, that America should be governed by a certain segment of the population as opposed to TR's position to "let the people rule." Letting the people rule, in Roosevelt's view, did not include women or other minorities, Taft asserted.

He assailed Roosevelt for claiming Taft supported Sen. Lorimer in Illinois, the man involved in the bribery scandal that led to his expulsion from the Senate. Taft produced the letter he had written to Roosevelt in which he outlined ideas on how to get Lorimer removed from office.

Taft's attack on his old friend was relentless—and documented. Roosevelt had assailed the president for his ill-fated attempt to get a reciprocity agreement with Canada. But Taft produced a letter, written by Roosevelt while the negotiations were going on, in which he praised the president for his efforts.

Taft, the old jurist, liked arguments augmented by evidence, and his hope was that Massachusetts voters would feel the same way. He rattled off eleven points, refuting claims made by Roosevelt with documentation for each, hoping voters would see the former president as a political opportunist who would say anything to get elected.

He concluded by telling his crowds that Roosevelt acted as if he was the only man capable of being president, the only man capable of carrying out the plans he had for the country. In seeking what amounted to a third term as president, Taft pointed out, Roosevelt was breaking precedent that had started as far back as George Washington, a precedent that Roosevelt himself had approved of when he declined to run for re-election in 1908.

The president said Roosevelt could not possibly accomplish in four years, all that he said he wanted to do. And since he believes he is the only one capable of doing the job, he must envision himself being president forever, said Taft.

Roosevelt countered with a speech in Boston the next night in which his vicious comments about Taft were met with hoots and hollers from an appreciative crowd. "He only discovered I was dangerous to the people when I discovered he was useless to the people," said Roosevelt.[13]

"This is our first presidential campaign under the preference primary plan. We hope it may be our last," the *New York Times* lamented. "The spectacle presented by the fierce fight for the nomination is one that must be amazing to foreigners. It is one that should bring a blush of shame to the cheek of every American."[14]

Taft's efforts in Massachusetts paid off, but just barely. He won the primary with 50.4 percent of the vote, edging out Roosevelt who had 48.2 percent. LaFollette was once again a non-factor with 1.2 percent. Despite the narrow victory, Taft was encouraged. A win is a win, regardless of the margin and besides, he had been receiving reports from his staff that he was piling up delegates in states that did not have primaries but prevailed in often raucous state conventions.

Roosevelt picked up primary wins in Maryland on May 5 and in California on May 14. Roosevelt's win in California was by a 2–1 margin, 54.6 percent to Taft's 27.3 percent, with the colonel getting a boost because of the support of his Progressive friend, Gov. Hiram Johnson, like Roosevelt, a flamboyant reformer. Elected governor in 1910, Johnson had overseen many changes in his state that Roosevelt wanted on a national level, such as primary elections, referendums and recall of elected officials.

Johnson had been one of the early Progressive leaders. He was one of the people in LaFollette's living room when the National Progressive organization was formed during the time when Roosevelt was not yet an announced candidate. Later, Johnson wanted to support Roosevelt but needed a reason to switch allegiance. LaFollette's shaky performance in Philadelphia provided the means he sought.

LaFollette picked up 18.1 percent in California. Had he not been in the race, Roosevelt's victory would have been even larger because he would have snared the Progressive vote that went to LaFollette.

The next primary was another crucial one, another firewall for Taft for it was in his home state of Ohio. The president hit the campaign trail as strenuously as he had in his winning campaign in Massachusetts. Roosevelt was extremely popular in Ohio. It was in Columbus that the colonel had delivered the clarion call of his campaign earlier that year, urging major reforms to let the people rule, including allowing the public to overrule unpopular court decisions.

California governor Hiram Johnson, studies some notes as he sits on a bench before a campaign appearance. An early apostle of Progressivism, Johnson was Roosevelt's running-mate on the Progressive ticket.

The campaign rhetoric was filled with personal jibes that had nothing to do with the many issues that had been debated. Taft called Roosevelt an egotist and a demagogue. Roosevelt's expressions were much more colorful and debasing. He referred to the president as a "puzzlewhit" in one speech and a "fat head" in another. LaFollette attacked them both but was far more critical of Roosevelt because of his belief that the colonel had stolen his thunder in becoming the darling of the Progressives and had probably prevented LaFollette from becoming president.

Roosevelt won Ohio in a heart-breaking defeat for Taft who got less than 40 percent of the vote compared to Roosevelt's 55.3 percent. A *Chicago Tribune* cartoon, drawn by John McCutcheon, embodied Taft's despair. It showed a man consoling the president, saying, "The Ohio result is a great compliment to you, Mr. President. The state loves you so well that they want you to live at home."

Roosevelt won the last two primaries, in New Jersey and South Dakota and was prepared to go to the convention in Chicago with tremendous momentum. After losing in the first three primaries, he won in nine out of the next 10, losing only in Massachusetts by about two percentage points.

TR's plan all along had been to use the primary elections as a way of driving a wedge into the machine politics of the Republican Party and to demonstrate the power of the people to determine who their leaders should be. And in that, he had proved his point. Of the 13 primaries held, Roosevelt had won nine, Taft won two and LaFollette won two.

But it was in the total popular vote in the 13 primaries where Roosevelt ruled. The totals: Roosevelt 1,214,969; Taft 865,835, LaFollette 327,357.

Despite the huge victory for Roosevelt in the popular vote, Taft held his own in state conventions and as the national convention neared, neither candidate had secured enough delegates to win the nomination. There were 254 contested delegates from the state conventions in which disputes as to the winners were would have to be determined by the Republican National Committee.

The bruising primary season was over and yet the fight for the Republican nomination for president had really just begun.

12

THE REPUBLICAN NATIONAL COMMITTEE

The long primary schedule began on March 19 in North Dakota and ended June 4 in South Dakota with 13 states participating. During that time, 35 other states elected delegates at state conventions. The result was, despite all the hoopla from Roosevelt and his supporters who were victors in nine of the 13 primaries, and the Taft forces, who worked diligently in relative obscurity to win scores of delegates at state conventions, neither man had enough support to win the nomination on the first ballot.

A total of 540 delegates were needed for the nomination. Prior to the convention, Roosevelt reportedly had 411; Taft had 201 but claimed another 166 "unpledged" who supported him. LaFollette had 36. Senator Albert Cummins of Iowa, who had not campaigned but was seen as a possible compromise candidate, had 10.

There were 254 contested delegates, almost half of what were needed to secure the nomination. It was the job of the Republican National Committee to rule on the political fate of those delegates. It began its deliberations on Thursday, June 6 and worked through Friday, June 14.

The irony of it all was striking. The primary election process was designed to give the people the opportunity to pick their leaders—to let the people rule, as Roosevelt was fond of saying. Yet, in the end, the decision was to be made by a handful of party leaders listening as both sides engaged in bickering, brokering and begging on behalf of their candidate. Taft had a decided advantage before the proceedings ever began. Of the 53-member committee, 39 were Taft delegates while only 14 supported Roosevelt. "The battle for control of the convention quickly became a toxic brew of public appeals, name calling, legal strategy, backstage intrigue, political maneuvering, threats and bribery."[1]

It was clear that whereas Roosevelt's strength was in the primaries, where his theatrics and histrionics played well to large audiences and, in the same settings, Taft was noticeably uncomfortable. But now, the comfort level and the momentum switched when the action moved inside. "When it came to political strategy and manipulation, it was soon evident that in addition to having a majority of members on the national committee, Taft's forces were tougher and more experienced. Their ranks were filled with veterans who knew the rules and knew how to make backroom deals."[2]

Also, Roosevelt had lost the support of some of his longtime allies such Henry Cabot Lodge, Henry Stimson and Elihu Root because of some of the extreme views, such as judicial recall, that he expressed in his speech in Columbus just before announcing his candidacy.

The Roosevelt forces had put together a strategy to take control of the committee, but it was doomed almost from the start. The plan was to convince a majority of committee members to support Roosevelt; to elect a temporary chairman who favored TR; and that the temporary chair would select the Credentials Committee which would support Roosevelt's delegate challenges. Failing any or all of that, they would take their fight to the floor of the convention.

The *Chicago Tribune* told its readers, "the fight has now reached a point where political strategy and manipulation is expected to count."[3]

If there was any expectation of courtesy and decorum, it was quickly quashed by supporters of both candidates making their way from one committee room to another, spreading rumors, whispering deals, offering promises and both sides offering bribes. "A smell of cocktails and whiskey was ubiquitous; a dense pall of tobacco smoke pervaded the committee rooms; and out of doors, the clang of brass bands drowned out even the incessant noise of the throngs. There was no night, for the myriads of electric lights made shadows but no darkness and you wondered when these strange creatures slept."[4]

The Roosevelt forces lost two early decisions. The first was their call for increased press access to the proceedings, for Roosevelt was the darling of the press and knew how to use his relationship with the newsmen to his advantage. But that motion failed 38–15—decisive enough to forecast tough times ahead.

Then Victor Rosewater, a slender 41-year-old Jewish man with boyish good looks who had succeeded his father as editor of the *Omaha Bee* in Nebraska, and who was a Taft delegate, was elected chairman of the Republican National Committee. It was another huge blow to Roosevelt and his people. Hopes for the nomination were slipping away from the colonel.

About the only chance he had was to win challenges on delegates that had been awarded to Taft. But TR's advisers made a tactical mistake that seriously hurt their chances to gain delegates. In an effort to roll the dice and see what happened, they filed challenges to 254 Taft delegates. Many of the

Missouri governor Herbert Hadley (right) shown with Montana governor Edwin Norris, was a Roosevelt supporter who was supposed to provoke a riot at the convention but couldn't bring himself to do it.

challenges had no merit and only served to sour the committee's attitude about the rest of them. After several days of hearing the challenges, the committee voted to seat all but a few Taft delegates.

The only option left was to take the most promising challenges to the Credentials Committee at the convention. But chances were slim that anything would change, given the committee was well aware of the shenanigans of the Roosevelt people in filing so many frivolous challenges.

Roosevelt's convention chairman and floor manager was Governor Herbert Hadley of Missouri, one of the seven governors who had signed the letter of support for TR that helped propel him into the race. Hadley was an honorable man, was loyal to Roosevelt and could be trusted. He had an air of chivalry and decency about him and was courteous in his dealings with others. Roosevelt liked him and appreciated his honesty.

Historians differ on Hadley's discussions with Roosevelt on delegate challenges. One version is that when Hadley suggested to the colonel that they had the best chance of winning 28 challenges. Roosevelt was incensed. Even if he won all 28, he said, it would not be nearly enough to make a difference. He told Hadley to challenge 100. Hadley privately thought that was a hopeless cause. He filed 72 challenges and lost them all.

Another version of the same discussion is that Hadley, trying to be realistic about their chances, suggested they challenge 24 Taft delegates. Roosevelt knew that would not be nearly enough to overturn the probable outcome, so he told Hadley to triple the number.

The two best challenges were on the seating of delegates from Texas and Washington, who were elected at their respective state conventions.

Roosevelt was said to be especially strong in the "lily white" areas of Texas whereas Taft was more popular in the black areas. Each side wanted its slate of delegates seated. Taft's people argued that their slate represented a much heavier populated area—and the committee agreed. Whereas Roosevelt expected to make a clean sweep and pick up all of Texas' 40 delegates, the committee awarded 34 to Taft and 6 to TR.

The Washington state convention, held in May, was a wild one. Roosevelt's people arrived weeks in advance and organized what they called an "advisory primary" which was good for show but had no legal standing. Roosevelt won it big, at least partly because Taft supporters boycotted it. It was up to the state party's Executive Committee at the state convention to sort it all out.

The Executive Committee anticipated a mob scene at the state convention and decided to distribute badges that would allow anyone wearing one to enter the convention arena. Taft supporters arrived en masse early to pick up their badges and get their seats inside. When Roosevelt's people arrived, armed guards prevented many of them from entering. So, foreshadowing

12. The Republican National Committee

what would happen months later at the national convention, the colonel's supporters left, went to a different hall, and elected their own slate of delegates, just as the Taft people had done in the main hall.

Officials at the RNC heard arguments from both sides and awarded all 14 delegate seats to Taft. Roosevelt's people said the outcome was worse than theft—it was treason.

Roosevelt kept track of the proceedings from Sagamore Hill, the name he had given to his spacious home in Oyster Bay, New York, where he and his family had lived since 1885.[5]

He was soon to realize that while he had prevailed in the primaries, Taft was now operating in an environment which he controlled. Roosevelt lost delegate challenges in Alabama, Washington, Indiana, Texas and California, some of which, based on the merits, should have gone to the colonel. After one such vote, Roosevelt angrily asserted men had "been sent to the penitentiary for less reprehensible election frauds."[6]

When the intense committee hearings concluded, Taft had been awarded 235 delegates to 19 for Roosevelt. The system had clearly worked in favor of the president but even if Roosevelt had secured 100 delegates instead of just 19, he still would have been short of what he needed for the nomination.

"Many of the cases that the Roosevelt supporters presented were flimsy and even the Roosevelt-leaning members of the committee voted against these contests. Four states—Arizona, California, Texas and Washington presented a better case for Roosevelt's claim of Taft's robbery of delegates." Even changes in those states would not have affected the outcome.[7]

Roosevelt was not about to give up, for that was not his nature. Every fiber of his being always called on him to fight to the end, and that is exactly what he intended to do. On Friday, June 14, he boarded a train for Chicago to take up the fight in person as the Republican National Convention was about to convene.

Word spread quickly that the colonel was on his way. Chicago was buzzing with excitement. Roosevelt had a presence about him—the wire-rimmed glasses, the moustache, the upper teeth that were so prominent when he smiled, the brisk, quick handshake and, of course, the personality that could change from a diplomat to a warrior in a matter of seconds. Those who knew him or only knew him by reputation could feel that presence in just anticipating his arrival.

That sense of presence sometimes provided the means for him to steal the spotlight from others who might have deserved it more. Sometimes, that was intentional, such as now when he wanted to pummel the image and reputation of Taft. Sometimes, it was unintended, as it was six years earlier when his fifth cousin, Franklin Delano Roosevelt, got married TR's niece, and the colonel walked the bride, Eleanor, down the aisle in the absence of her father who was deceased. Roosevelt was president at the time and while his intention in this instance was noble, his presence detracted from that of the bride on her special day.

William Allen White, a journalist from Kansas who was a friend of Roosevelt's, said it was hard to reconstruct the emotions of the time as Roosevelt headed to Chicago because of the mounting hatred between the two rival factions. He said Roosevelt was motivated to come by boiling passions within him. "Enmity to Taft certainly was one. The fear of defeat, which he did not take easily, was another. Rage, sheer animal rage at the indignity put upon him by the conservatives, and the contempt for him so evident in the course of the national committee, formed no small element, I think, in his decision."[8]

Presidential scholar Geoffrey Cohan wrote, "Every fiber in his body told Roosevelt to go to Chicago: his love of adventure, adulation and action; his belief in the righteousness of his cause; his anger at the men whom he felt were stealing the election, not just from him but from the public's will...."[9]

But it was even more than that, Cohan argued. It was "his crusading zeal; his passion for a good fight; the chance to hit and hit hard; and his unique ability to act as his own publicist, to create sensational headlines and a compelling narrative."[10]

When his train arrived in Chicago on Sunday, thousands of cheering people greeted him when he disembarked. The car carrying him and his wife Edith to the Congress Hotel had to move slowly to avoid hitting anyone in the throngs of people who lined the streets to get a glimpse of the colonel. Chicago police had to cordon off an area just to provide a way for him to get into the hotel where he was staying. He was to give a speech that night to rally his people, who really didn't need rallying. Thousands of leaflets had been distributed announcing that the colonel would speak that night, that "Colonel Roosevelt would walk on the waters of Lake Michigan at 7:30 p.m."[11]

Hours before Roosevelt arrived in Chicago, the LaSalle Street railroad station had a ballpark atmosphere as cheering fans awaited the arrival of their hero and, in the tumult, the sounds of bands could be heard along the platform. "Thousands of screaming men and women lined the streets as the former president rode in an open car to the Congress Hotel. So frenzied was the crowd in the lobby that it took a team of five men using 'football tactics' to propel Roosevelt to the elevator."[12]

The Roosevelts had a personal apartment as well as a private office with a reception room. In the hallway, a private detective who had served the family for years stood guard to ward off unwanted visitors. There were plenty of visitors whom the colonel welcomed, often emerging from his apartment or office into the reception room to greet well-wishers.

Meanwhile, he was receiving reports from young supporters, including

12. The Republican National Committee

some Roosevelt cousins, whose job it was to roam the halls on other floors of the hotel and make their way through the lobby and dining areas with the purpose of overhearing as many pertinent conversations as they could, and to report back to the colonel. They were thrilled to make the rounds and come back and provide information that might be helpful to the Roosevelt team.

One of them infiltrated a Taft campaign rally that he came across when he heard a bellhop running up and down the hotel corridors announcing it. When the bellhop shouted the rally announcement, the Roosevelt supporter cried out, "all postmasters welcome"—a reference to those who had their jobs through federal appointments.

Stump speeches, made spontaneously by supporters of both candidates, were heard throughout the hotel. Even when the colonel and his wife made it into the comfort of their hotel suite, the energy of the soul of the former president could not allow him to relax. He climbed onto a balcony outside of his room and waved to the crowds in the street and vowing to retrieve what had been stolen from him by the Republican National Committee.

The next day, instead of staying in the quiet of his room, crafting the speech that he would give that night—the last speech he would give in this long, bitter, grueling campaign, Roosevelt busied himself trying to line up last-minute support on the eve of the convention. He met with supporters to keep them revved up—although there was little need for that other than their need to see him and feel his fervor. He also met with Taft supporters who Roosevelt's aides thought might be swayed to the colonel's side. And of course he met with reporters because they were TR's outlets to the rest of the country. The day was filled with Roosevelt's "crowded hours."

As day turned into night, thousands of people started making their way to the venue in which Roosevelt would speak, a place aptly called The Auditorium, which held a little over 4,000 people. Patrons needed a ticket to get in. Chicago police were there in force to make sure no one without a ticket tried to sneak in or talk their way past security. Hundreds were turned away. Those who had tickets and were admitted had to sit for about two hours. An organist entertained them, playing "The Battle Hymn of the Republic" and popular patriotic songs. It wasn't long before the crowd was singing along.

Roosevelt walked briskly onto the stage, flashing that familiar toothy smile and waving his arms to the adoring throngs. Like a pulpit-pounding preacher, he stated his case. He was running, he said, because President Taft had abandoned the ship, forfeiting Progressive principles to serve the political bosses. He was involved in a tough fight, he said, because of the fraud of the Republican National Committee that awarded delegates to Taft that should have been in the Roosevelt column.

He appealed to the 30 or 40 delegates still supporting Governor LaFollette, claiming that he now was in the best position to promote the cause of the Progressives and turn it in to victory. Calling for LaFollette people to jump ship was a crowd pleaser to the colonel's legions of fans but Roosevelt had to know it was politically impossible to achieve. LaFollette was one of the most shrewd politicians in the country and remained incensed that Roosevelt had stolen his thunder. One way of keeping the colonel from getting the nomination was to stay in the race and not release any delegates pledged to him. LaFollette had no intention of dropping out.

The colonel would also have liked to snare the 10 delegates pledged to Sen. Albert Cummins of Iowa, a three-term governor who had been in the Senate since 1908 and would remain until his death in 1926. Cummins, who would serve at one time as president pro temp of the Senate, putting him third in line to the presidency, obviously had no chance for the nomination in 1912 but whose ego made him proud of the 10 delegates he had. The colonel knew that 10 more delegates probably was not going to make a difference but he needed every delegate he could get.

Another Roosevelt ploy that was going on even as he took the stage for his campaign speech was behind-the-scenes efforts to sway Negro delegates from southern states who favored Taft but were not legally bound to vote for him. They had been nominated at state conventions that Taft controlled while Roosevelt was traveling around gaining support in the 13 presidential primaries.

"The hopes of the Roosevelt managers to control the convention rest today more strongly than anything else on their hopes of winning over enough of the Taft negro delegates from the south to make up the deficit that still separates them from a majority," the *New York Times* reported. Black delegates later reported being offered bribes of up to $1,000, mostly from zealous Roosevelt supporters and done perhaps without the colonel's knowledge.[13]

Roosevelt did not disappoint his followers as he spoke for more than an hour on that hot Monday night, whipping the crowd into fits of hollers, chants and cheers as dozens of police officers watched to make sure things did not get out of hand. He often had to shout to make himself heard above the roar of the crowd and he loved every minute of it. He was in his element. "He poured himself out in one of his torrential speeches calculated to arouse the passions rather than the minds of his hearers ... the soul of sincerity and courage, impressing upon them that they were engaged in a most solemn cause and defying the opposition as if it were a legion of evil spirits."[14]

The former president ended by proclaiming a message that journalist White said "sizzled in the hearts of his audience."

"We stand at Armageddon," Roosevelt declared, "and we battle for the Lord!"

Roosevelt's rhetoric, oratory and theatrics, which came so naturally to him, thrilled the hearts of his supporters who were likely to stick with him to the end. But as the convention was about to begin, while the colonel was winning the emotional vote, Taft, the non-politician, and his supporters were methodically using traditional politics to secure the only thing that really mattered at the convention—committed delegates. "While President Taft slowly lost his hold on the American people, he gained proportionately with the Republican Machine. That Machine was composed of the regulars of the party, or the Conservatives, as they preferred to be called."[15]

Many of them were office holders or federal appointees who owed their jobs to patronage, as did those who worked under them. Their power, their influence and their quality of life were secure as long as nobody came along and rocked the boat.

On the eve of the convention, even the colonel's most ardent supporters were convinced the deck had been stacked against him, that he was the victim of outright fraud, and that he could not win the nomination. "Insiders knew that the convention itself—the fight over the temporary roll, over the permanent chairmanship, even over the credentials challenges—was theater, for effect, for public consumption."[16]

Some, like Governor Johnson of California, a Progressive stalwart who possessed the same kind of verve and nerve of Roosevelt, thought the Roosevelt forces should bolt the convention before it even started as a means of mass protest.

But the colonel thought it was important to stay, to fight the good fight as he had done all of his life, and to make sure every defeat he suffered on the convention floor would be publicized all over the country. In a strange twist to a strange convention that had not yet officially begun, Roosevelt wanted to stay to make sure Taft was nominated instead of a divided convention opting to nominate a compromise candidate. "If TR had walked out at that point (before the convention started), the convention might have named Missouri Gov. Herbert Hadley or Supreme Court justice and former New York governor Charles Evans Hughes as the candidate, making it much harder for TR to create a new party because the Republican candidate would be a reformer."[17]

The Roosevelt forces issued a statement to the press late Monday night. "We denounce the fraud by which the discredited majority of the Republican National Committee has made up a temporary roll of the national convention; and we deny the right of the committee to make a roll that might result in the nomination that is effected by dishonesty and trickery."[18]

It was signed by the chairmen of 13 Republican state committees: Pennsylvania (Henry Wasson); Ohio (Walter F. Brown); New Jersey (Borden Whiting); Kansas (William Allen White); California (Meyer Lisner); Nebraska

(R.B. Howell); South Dakota (Thomas Thorson); Minnesota (I.A. Caswell); Missouri (Thomas Niedeerhaus); North Carolina (Richmond Pearson); Oklahoma (George Priestley); West Virginia (William Seymour Edwards); and Michigan (Frank Knox).

13

The Unconventional Convention

"Would a candidate for president of the United States ever officially condone a riot on the floor of a national convention? Would a candidate ever actually ever seek to promote one? Should delegates to a convention be permitted to carry guns? Can supporters of a candidate try to buy delegate votes?"[1] These are all rhetorical questions involving the morality and decency expected when statesmen and political leaders gather to perform one of the most important duties in a democracy. The only reason why questions like these have any relevancy is because of what occurred in Chicago June 18–22, 1912, at the convention that split the Republican Party and left it bleeding.

The setting was the historic, sturdy, stoic Chicago Coliseum at 1513 S. Wabash Avenue, about a mile and a half south of Chicago's Loop, the business and commercial center of the Windy City. It was the largest venue of its kind in the city, stretching a full city block, and was the setting for the city's largest events, including five consecutive Republican conventions beginning in 1904.

Going into the convention, Roosevelt was "The Big Noise," as the *New York Times* referred to him, and he inspired big noise among his many followers. He won nine out of 13 primaries and appeared on the surface to have enough momentum to take over the convention. At least, that was the plan. But he did not have an effective organization. President Taft, for all his political frailties, had people working for his re-nomination who knew what they were doing.

The president had three secretaries in his first two years in office—men who handled much of his correspondence, worked within political circles to promote his programs and to make sure he was in the best possible position to succeed. Fred W. Carpenter served only for a short time and was replaced by Charles Norton, whose political instincts often antagonized those he was trying to woo. Charles Hilles, a former Treasury Department official, took over as secretary in 1911 and worked tirelessly behind the scenes to right the president's ship.

While Roosevelt was making speeches and making headlines, Hilles was corresponding and meeting with Republican Party leaders all over the country, lining up the only kind of support that really mattered—delegates. "While newspaper attention concentrated on Theodore Roosevelt and Robert LaFollette, Taft was on the way to locking up the Republican nomination by the end of 1911. Roosevelt's entry into the race in January of 1912 disrupted that scenario, but the organizational labors that Hilles expended during 1911 helped the president to withstand the challenge from Roosevelt in June 1912."[2]

Day One Tuesday

At noon on Tuesday, June 18, in the Chicago Coliseum packed with boisterous delegates and rimmed by armed police officers along the walls, Republican National Chairman Victor Rosewater of Omaha, (temporary chairman), called the convention to order, standing on a rostrum protected by barbed wire strung across it but hidden by red, white and blue bunting.

Immediately, Governor Hadley stood up and made a motion to replace 72 Taft delegates, who he claimed were elected by fraud, with 72 Roosevelt delegates. In making the motion, he had put into play the first of many ploys the Roosevelt forces planned to try to win the nomination. And, right on cue, the Roosevelt delegates in the crowd erupted in wild cheers.

Then James Watson of Indiana, a Taft delegate, rose and said the Hadley motion was out of order because the convention had no chairman and therefore could do no business. Rosewater allowed debate for about 40 minutes before ruling in favor of Watson, agreeing that Hadley's motion was out of order because there was no chairman. Roosevelt and his people had lost their first fight of the convention but it would not be the last.

As Rosewater prepared officially to rule against Hadley and the Roosevelt appeal, Sen. Boise Penrose of Pennsylvania gave him a word of warning: "Victor, as soon as you've made that decision, jump off the platform for someone is going to take a shot at you for sure."[3]

The Roosevelt people expected to lose because the Taft forces controlled the convention. But Roosevelt thought, with good reason, that the system was rigged if delegates whose legitimacy was being challenged were allowed to vote on that legitimacy. It was at this point that Roosevelt's men, by prearranged signal, were to start a riot in the convention hall to protest the unfairness of it all in a way that would be reported and photographed for the whole nation to see.

The signal would be Hadley, reacting to his motion being denied, turning

13. An Unconventional Convention

and shouting to the galleries about the injustice that had just been done. Then, the Rough Riders in the crowd and others from the Roosevelt camp would use their voices, their fists and their feet to create bedlam—"roughhouse tactics" was the term used when the demonstration was being planned.

As the hundreds of police on hand would converge on the rioters in an attempt to restore order, Roosevelt's supporters were to storm out of the convention hall to put an exclamation point on their protest. The plan "was as much theater as it was practical politics," as historian Geoffrey Cowan has written, but it never came about.[4]

When it came time for Hadley to shout his appeal, he decided against it, or in the view of the Roosevelt crowd, got cold feet—got cowardly, according to Gov. Johnson. Years later, Hadley, in recounting what happened, said he determined the rough stuff was not favored by a majority of the Roosevelt people, and that in fights with the hundreds of Chicago police, wielding their billy clubs, the delegates would have been "badly worsted."[5] "Hadley did his job as best he could but by nature, he wasn't cut out to be a street fighter. He stood on the platform protesting every inch of the proceedings. He was most courteous. Indeed he breathed an air of chivalry that was pleasant to the heart. He had a kindly, resonant voice. His elocution was polished, his gestures pleasant, his manner firm and determined."[6]

Elihu Root, a distinguished, well-respected statesman, had the job of trying to keep order at the Republican convention.

The Taft people then nominated New York senator Elihu Root as permanent chairman. Root had served in Roosevelt's cabinet as both secretary of war and secretary of state and was considered a statesman by politicians on both sides of the aisle. He had been a Roosevelt man until he became disenchanted with some of the colonel's Progressive ideas, particularly public recall of judges. As was often the case, and a concept that Taft could readily confirm, Roosevelt could turn on an old friend and be vicious if it suited his political purpose, and Root was no exception.

"In the past, Mr. Root has rendered distinguished service," said Roosevelt. "But in this context, Mr.

The convention hall was filled to the rafters with excited delegates and with hundreds of policemen who had to try to keep the activities peaceful.

Root has ranged himself against the men who stand for progressive principles.... He is put forward by the bosses and the representatives of special privilege."[7]

The political chess game continued and it was Roosevelt's move. His people nominated Wisconsin governor Francis McGovern. He was a Progressive in the mold of his fellow Wisconsin man, LaFollette. Roosevelt, who was monitoring everything from his hotel room as he received reports from the convention floor, hoped the nomination of McGovern might serve as a peace offering to LaFollette, who controlled 36 delegates, but that was not about to happen. The convention could take many twists and turns, but LaFollette helping Roosevelt in any way was not one of them. "Sen. LaFollette himself has no use for the colonel, who, his friends declared, used him as a stalking horse before he got into the fight himself, and then double-crossed him to make his own candidacy possible."[8]

LaFollette's floor manager, Walter Houser, rose to let delegates know the nomination was done without LaFollette's support. But McGovern did not resist. Demonstrations began in support of Taft, Roosevelt and McGovern and within minutes the cheering and shouting turned to pushing and shoving and fists flying. The pandemonium was such that it took three hours before

13. An Unconventional Convention

The name of Wisconsin governor Francis McGovern (right) shown here with Wyoming governor J.R. Carey, was placed in nomination as convention chairman as a ploy by Roosevelt forces to try to win over Senator LaFollette. It didn't work.

the votes were tallied. The final count: Root, 558, McGovern, 501. It was a narrow victory for Taft, just 18 above the delegate count he would need for the nomination. It was also another loss for Roosevelt. Had the 72 contested delegates not been allowed to vote, the outcome would have been different and might have provided some momentum for Roosevelt. In the end, if the momentum had shifted, it might have changed American history. But the Taft forces were not about to let that happen.

Announcement of the results created another period of boisterous bedlam in the coliseum. Cheers and jeers soon became finger pointing and jabbing and then punching and throwing one another to the ground and pouncing. Police moved in from all sides to break up the fighting and do what they could to restore order.

Root watched from his perch at the podium, literally and figuratively above the fray. He might very well have been the most intelligent man in the arena, a learned, erudite, distinguished conservative and a former secretary of war and secretary of state. His credentials to stand where he stood were impeccable. When he clicked the gavel to resume the business of the convention, it was if a father was summoning his naughty children and telling them enough is enough. "He looked down upon the sweating, wrathful faces in the pit where the delegates sat and swept his eyes around the vast horseshoe of spectators who jammed the gallery, sometimes crowding the police guards off their feet. But Root's hands did not tremble, his face did not flicker. He was master."[9]

It was in that setting that Root delivered the keynote address, succinctly outlining the Republican platform and espousing other principles of the party in strong, measured tones that brought order back to the floor. Taft's influence on the platform was obvious with its specific references to the judiciary and, in so doing, applying a slap of the hand to Roosevelt's views that sparked his political comeback.

The platform endorsed the independence of the courts, saying, "The Republican Party reaffirms its intentions at all times the authority and integrity of the courts, both state and federal, and it will ever insist that their powers to enforce their process and to protect life, liberty and property shall be preserved inviolate."

It also said that with the exception of rare circumstances, "we regard the recall of judges as unnecessary and unwise."

Roosevelt and Taft had profoundly different demeanors on the first day of the convention. Roosevelt monitored the activities from his hotel suite through telephone calls and messages relayed to him. Outside his room and in the halls and lobbies of the hotel, crowds gathered and gossiped as they awaited news from the convention hall. In the main lobby, a man with a megaphone received messages from the convention hall and shouted them to the crowds.

13. An Unconventional Convention

Meanwhile, President Taft and Nellie went to the ballgame where the Washington Nationals were playing the Philadelphia Athletics. The president received hearty applause from the crowd of 15,516 who spotted him as he made his way to his seat. Taft spoke briefly to the players before the game, congratulating them on their 16-game winning streak. Then he watched them win their 17th straight, scoring a run in the bottom of the ninth inning to win, 5–4. He did not seek nor did he receive any reports from what was happening at the convention a half-continent away. After the game, he was pleased to learn that Root had been elected chairman.

At Roosevelt's hotel suite that night, his supporters met to discuss their next move. The loyalty to the colonel still prevailed but some dissention was developing among the troops as to what they should do. Hadley stood on a chair and did his job. Mopping his brow to stop the flow of sweat, he gave a stirring speech urging the forces to keep up the fight.

His speech drew applause from many in the room, but Sen. Johnson was suspicious. There had been talk among some in the room of putting up a compromise candidate, someone other than Taft or Roosevelt who could win in the fall election, which, in their view, Taft could not. Hadley's name had come up in those conversations, and Senator Johnson wondered if Hadley was as loyal to Roosevelt as he had let on. So after Hadley spoke and the applause died down, Johnson asked him what he would do if the Roosevelt delegates walked out. Hadley said he didn't expect that to happen and if it did, he would have to determine what to do, depending on the situation. He then got down from his chair and walked out of the room.

Many in the room wanted to walk out of the convention. Some talked about starting a third party. Still others talked among themselves about coming up with a compromise candidate, thinking that if Roosevelt couldn't get the nomination, maybe someone else could, someone who, unlike Taft, in their view, could win in the fall election. As the meeting drew to a close, Roosevelt spoke. "The colonel was fighting mad after the day's reverses and that seemed merely to add to the sharpness of his speech. The meeting broke up with something like a revival of optimism. Though talk of a deadlock and a possible third candidate is again heard, delegates seemed determined to stick to the colonel for another round."[10]

Day Two

After Root gaveled the convention to order at noon on Wednesday, the beleaguered Hadley once again took up the fight for Roosevelt. He once again moved that the 72 contested delegates for Taft be replaced with

Roosevelt delegates. It was the same motion he had made the day before, only this time there was a permanent chairman which made all proceedings official.

And once again, Watson rose to object, saying the full convention had no knowledge of the delegate dispute and therefore could not vote on the matter fairly.

At that point, a couple of weird things happened in an already extremely strange convention. Someone got up and yelled, "Hadley for President," triggering a huge demonstration on the convention floor for the possible compromise candidate. While that was taking place, an attractive woman in a white dress in the gallery, and later identified as Mrs. W.A. Davis of Chicago, rose and unfurled a large poster of Roosevelt.

As attention was drawn to her, delegates encouraged her to come to the main floor where she walked up the long aisle to the platform, waving her poster and encouraging the crowd to cheer. Within moments, the demonstration for Hadley turned into an explosion of excitement for Roosevelt. She tried to speak but could not be heard over the din of the crowd. Suddenly, it had become a Roosevelt crowd, at least for the moment.

History has not recorded whether the demonstration for Hadley or the appearance of the woman in white for Roosevelt were spontaneous events or carefully planned diversions. In the meantime, Hadley and Watson had worked out a compromise on the seating of the contested delegates. Instead of putting it to a vote of the full convention, they recommended to let the Credentials Committee, which was to meet that night, settle it. But Hadley insisted that none of the contested delegates be appointed to the Credentials Committee because it would be like the accused being in a position to vote for their own acquittal. Root ruled there was nothing in the official rules of the convention that prevented contested delegates from serving so he allowed it. The full convention voted in favor of the compromise.

That night, after the convention had spent two days doing little more than demonstrating, fighting and arguing over procedural matters, the Roosevelt supporters were summoned to a meeting in his hotel suite. Various discussions took place as delegates gravitated into small groups and whispered among themselves about the same topics that had occupied them for days—sticking with TR, seeking a compromise candidate, walking out of the convention, starting a third party. All the voices in all the little circles of conversation created an unintelligible buzz throughout the room.

Amos Pinchot, Gifford's brother, who was in the room, said there was "a moment when the third party was born."[11]

It had been an idea that had floated like a balloon over Republican politics for several weeks but, according to Pinchot, it was at 2 a.m. on Thursday morning, June 21, that it all came together. It was then that Roosevelt emerged

13. An Unconventional Convention

from a room where he met with his closest advisers, including his two biggest financial backers, Frank Munsey and George Perkins.

He told his supporters that if the convention failed to purge the rolls of the fraudulent delegates, which was now in the hands of the Credentials Committee where the outcome was not in doubt, then the Republican Party was no longer worthy of him. For those who did not want to take on the next journey, he thanked them for their support and wished them well. He invited the others to join him in the formation of a third party. But he warned anyone who joined forces with Taft or chose to support a compromise candidate, he would make life miserable for them in their districts when they sought re-election.

"I went before the people and I won," said Roosevelt. "Now the National Committee and a portion of the convention ... are trying to cheat me out of the nomination. But it is not me they are cheating. It is the people, the rank and file of the Republican Party."[12]

He told them the deck was stacked because the convention allowed fraudulently elected delegates to serve on the Credentials Committee that was investigating the fraud. Therefore he asked any Roosevelt delegates on the committee to refuse to serve.

"If you want my advice," said Roosevelt, "I would advise that you place no further trust, I would advise that you waste no further time, I would advise that you do not permit yourselves to be committed in any way, shape or form by further association with these men as long as they retain control of the Republican convention."[13]

George Perkins was a New York millionaire and political kingmaker. His decision to financially back Roosevelt as a third-party candidate was a key factor for the colonel.

Day Three

As Chairman Root gaveled the convention to order at noon Thursday, delegates and visitors were talking about what they heard early that morning in the Roosevelt suite, or what they had been told by people who were there or what gossip mongers were peddling. The word was out that Roosevelt might bolt the convention and take many of his followers with him. The questions were many: Will he really do it? What effect will that have on the fall elections? What effect will it have on the livelihoods of many of those gathered in the arena, regardless of which candidate they supported? Will the Republican Party ever be the same again?

As it turned out, there would be much more time that day for that kind of talk. Within a minute or two after the Thursday session opened, Hadley called for a recess since the Credentials Committee had not yet reported its findings. Root called a recess until 4 o'clock that afternoon. But at 4 o'clock, the Credentials Committee was still out. Hadley rose again to make his motion and this time Root recessed the proceedings for the day.

The convention, with all its twists and turns, its personality clashes, its demonstrations and fist fights, its political wranglings, provided a fertile field for journalists from all over the nation who had come to Chicago to cover a nominating convention.

One who didn't have to travel was John Callan "Cal" O'Laughlin, a veteran newspaperman who had worked in the Washington bureau of the *New York Herald*, then served on the European staff of the Associated Press and then went to work for the *Chicago Tribune* and *Chicago Herald*. Roosevelt had developed tremendous rapport with the press throughout his political career and O'Laughlin was one of his biggest supporters. While working for the *Chicago Tribune*, he also moonlighted as the colonel's chief publicity man, churning out press releases every day shining the best possible light on TR. In his later years, O'Laughlin was the publisher of the *Army and Navy Journal*.

Samuel G. Blythe, who worked for many newspapers over his long career, was covering the convention for the *Richmond Times-Dispatch*. At the time of the convention, he was described by one admirer as "the greatest American correspondent, who knows intimately, more public men and politicians than any other writer of the present day." He was also an accomplished author whose books hit on a variety of subjects such as *The Fun of Getting Thin*, *The Fakers* and *The Making of a Newspaperman*.

A.J. Philpott, who later made a name for himself as an art critic, was in Chicago as a young political reporter for the *Boston Globe*.

Victor Rosewater, who was chairman of the Republican National Committee and temporary chairman of the convention, followed his father as publisher of the *Omaha Bee*, which would later be sold and merged into the *Omaha World-Herald*. He was not in Chicago as a newspaperman per se, but he was a Roosevelt man with a pen in his hand.

Frank Munsey made a fortune as a pulp fiction publisher who also owned 17 newspapers during the course of his career. He had known Roosevelt from the colonel's early political career in New York and was one of his chief financial backers when the colonel ran for his first full term for president in 1908. His role in Chicago in 1912 was as an adviser and as someone who still controlled the purse strings of Roosevelt's political career. If the colonel was to start a third party movement, it would not have been financially possible without the backing of Munsey.

William Allen White was the editor and publisher of the *Emporia Gazette* in Kansas and was a personal friend of Roosevelt. They had known each other for years, had dined together, campaigned together and trusted each other's judgment. Though he was a small town newspaper editor, his writings carried a lot of clout. His editorial, "What's the Matter With Kansas?" in which he identified reasons the state was not experiencing growth, was picked up by the Republican Party in the 1896 McKinley campaign and applied to the problems of the nation.

White had been elected a Republican national committeeman from Kansas which put him in touch regularly with GOP officials from throughout the country. In Chicago, he was heavily involved in the Roosevelt campaign but was also reporting on the convention for about 40 newspapers.[14]

Like most of the other correspondents, he went back to his hotel room every night, after the convention recessed, and banged out his stories on a manual typewriter, making several carbon copies. He filed some of his stories through Western Union, some through Postal Telegraph Company and about a dozen through separate filings. Papers in Milwaukee and Detroit got their reports via the mail.

With the ever-changing developments, members of the press found themselves scrambling in much the same manner as the people they were writing about.

Day Four

When Chairman Root gaveled the convention to order at noon on Friday, the first order of business was the long-awaited, yet predictable report from the Credentials Committee, whose members had been at work since Wednesday night with little sleep. Giving account for each state alphabetically, the outcomes were not in doubt.

It began with Alabama giving its support to Taft delegates. Then Arizona. Then Arkansas. With each state's report, the political shellacking was continuing. "Slowly, motion by motion, phase by phase, the steamroller crushed its way toward the nomination of Taft. Every time a motion was made by the Taft people, a thousand toots and imitation whistles of the steamroller engine pierced the air sharply.... Kipling said it of the American: His sense of humor saves him whole."[15]

Humorous, yes, but it was another audible burst of defiance. First, there was a chorus of boos as state by state, the Taft delegates were approved. The Roosevelt people, primed and ready to protest one more time, emphasized their feeling of being railroaded by shouting, "Toot, toot" and "Choo choo." Some even had pieces of sandpaper in each hand, which, when shuffled together, made the "choo choo" sound of a train. One man stood and shouted repeatedly, "All aboard."

As the convention had once again become a den of bedlam, Root called a recess, as he had done so many times since the convention began. Proceedings were to start Saturday morning with completion of recording the vote of the Credentials Committee.

Day Five

On Saturday, the roll call of the Credentials Committee resumed, complete with more jeers and "toot, toots" from the crowd, with the result, time after time favoring Taft, assuring him of the nomination, though it had been assured long before that by all the previous votes of the convention. In the end, all 72 of the contested delegates were awarded to Taft. "State after state was taken up in the fight over credentials, which was not really a fight any more. In each case the Taft men voted to sustain anything .The Roosevelt men mechanically and wearily voted the other way. The convention buzzed and hummed with conversation so during most of the time, the votes were inaudible."[16]

Though the outcome had seemingly been decided well in advance of Saturday's activities, there was reportedly still attempts at wheeling and dealing for delegates votes. There were several reports of black delegates from southern states who were willing to switch their allegiance from Taft to Roosevelt if the price was right. In one case, they had already been given a down payment and now were holding out for more. In any case, the black delegates were keeping the money they had already received. It is likely that any deals, especially ones involving bribery, were cooked up by Roosevelt surrogates and not by Roosevelt himself because the colonel steadfastly said he would buy no man's vote.[17]

There wasn't much business left for the delegates. The Committee on Rules and the Committee on Permanent Organization gave reports that were accepted with little fanfare and with silence from the Roosevelt delegates, just as they were instructed. Then, in an unusual and totally unparliamentary move, the convention agreed to allow Henry Allen, a Roosevelt delegate from Kansas, to read a message from the colonel. The Taft delegates did not object. They had won the battle and the war and nothing Roosevelt could say or do would change that. Chairman Root told Allen to proceed.

Allen solemnly read the colonel's words. "The convention has now declined to purge the roll of the fraudulent delegates placed thereon by the defunct National Committee, and the majority which thus endorsed fraud was made a majority only because it included fraudulent delegates themselves who all sat as judges on each other's cases. If these fraudulent votes had not thus been cast and counted, the convention would have been purged of their presence. This action makes the convention in no proper sense any longer a Republican convention representing the real Republican Party. Therefore I hope the men elected as Roosevelt delegates will now decline to vote on any matter before the convention. I do not release any delegate from his honorable obligation to vote for me if he votes at all, but under the actual conditions I hope that he will not vote at all. The convention as now composed has no claim to represent the voters of the Republican Party. It represents nothing but successful fraud in overriding the will of the rank and filed of the party. Any man nominated by the convention as now constituted would be merely the beneficiary of this successful fraud; it would be deeply discreditable to any man to accept the convention's nomination under these circumstances; and any man thus accepting it would have no claim to the support of any Republican on party grounds, and would have forfeited the right to ask the support of any honest man of any party on moral grounds."[18]

Roosevelt's words, though spoken by a surrogate, thrust a dagger into the chest of the convention, reducing its work to thievery and trivializing the pending nomination of the sitting president who not that long ago had been a friend, confidante and the man Roosevelt had made heir apparent to his "throne."

After reading Roosevelt's statement, Allen concluded with some words of his own. "Gentlemen, you accuse us of being radical," he said. "Let me tell you that no radical in the ranks of radicalism ever did so radical a thing as to come to a national convention of the great Republican Party and secure through fraud the nomination of a man whom they know could not be elected."[19]

So it was almost anticlimactic when, that night, Ohio Gov. Warren G. Harding placed Taft's name in nomination. At 9:28 he received the endorsement of the convention, but it was lukewarm, considering all the circumstances surrounding it. The vote of the convention was Taft 561; Roosevelt 107; LaFollette 41; Cummins 17; absent 6; Hughes 2; and not voting 344.

The Roosevelt dissidents who refused to vote, along with LaFollette and Cummins delegates who stayed loyal to their candidates, resulted in Taft gaining a first ballot victory by just 21 votes. The convention nominated James Sherman of New York as vice president. "A convention wherein the name of its candidate is received with jeers, hisses and taunts when he is proposed for nomination cannot be said to start out its campaign under the happiest auspices. That happened to Mr. Taft tonight, not only when Harding nominated him but every time his name was mentioned."[20]

Taft had his own assessment. He "had accomplished that which to me and to the country was the most important thing, to wit, the defeat of Theodore Roosevelt." With the colonel's loss, Taft said he had preserved "the regular organization of the party as a nucleus about which the conservative people who are in favor of maintaining constitutional government can gather."[21]

Root agreed. "The result of the convention was more important than the question of the election because it settled the critical question of 1912—whether the Republican Party should be seized and carried over to populism."[22]

Taft and Nellie spent a quiet evening in the White House as the convention wrapped up. Their son, Charlie, who was 14 hustled back and forth from the telegraph room, bringing in the latest news from the convention. After Taft was nominated and the polling of the individual states began, Charlie's smile grew broader as the night went on and Taft came closer and closer to securing the nomination. When the final tally was in, Taft and Nellie smiled at each other and sighed as if they had just overcome a family crisis. It was a far different reaction than four years earlier when Taft reacted with joy to his nomination and Nellie swelled with pride as her husband was on his way to achieving her goal for him. That was 1908. This was 1912.

The *New York Times* said the convention would go down in political history as one of the longest and most momentous. It concluded, "The Grand Old Party is, for the moment, smashed to pieces."[23]

Before the Taft conservative wing of the party could begin to contemplate how to pick up the pieces, Theodore Roosevelt and his legions of supporters were headed to Orchestra Hall, not far from the Coliseum. There, within hours of the end of the convention in which their party nominated their incumbent president, they began the work of forming a new political party.

14

The Democrats

Since 1860, only one Democrat had occupied the White House—Grover Cleveland, who accomplished it twice in non-consecutive terms in 1884 and 1892. The party of Lincoln had won with Lincoln in 1860, with Andrew Johnson in 1868, with Ulysses Grant in 1872, with Rutherford B. Hayes in 1876, with James Garfield in 1880, with Benjamin Harrison in 1888, William McKinley in 1896, Theodore Roosevelt in 1904 and William Howard Taft in 1908.

It was nine Republican presidents and just one Democrat in 52 years, a clear sign of the GOP being the dominant, united party that consistently met the approval of the American voter. On June 25, two days after the raucous Republican convention concluded in which the party was split wide open, Democrats opened their convention in Baltimore having their best chance in a generation to move back into the White House.

Three times in the past 20 years, they had nominated William Jennings Bryan, a great orator and considered by many as an oracle of Democratic principles. He was a well-known public speaker and a two-term member of the U.S. House of Representative from Nebraska.

At the Democratic National Convention in 1896, Bryan delivered an impassioned speech advocating a "free silver" standard for U.S. currency, proclaiming, "You shall not crucify mankind on a cross of gold." His speech captivated his audience and helped catapult him to the Democratic nomination. He lost to William McKinley and lost again to McKinley in 1900 and to Taft in 1908. He was considered one of the great statesmen of his party, and although he was not a candidate in 1912, he still had great influence on who the eventual candidate would be.

Going into the convention, the leading candidate for the nomination was James Beauchamp "Champ" Clark of Missouri, who had become Speaker of the House in 1911, uprooting Joe Cannon, the venerable Republican, when Democrats took control of the House in the mid-term elections.

He was described as a man with a commanding presence, someone who was not only persuasive but forceful, a good speaker, often witty but

"Champ" Clark was the early favorite to win the Democratic nomination and was said to be heartbroken when it slipped away from him.

who had a penchant to occasionally say things that got him into political hot water.

He told his biographers that as a young man, he read a book about Patrick Henry that inspired him to his chosen career. "That book determined me to be a lawyer and a congressman before I had ever seen a lawyer, a law book, a courthouse or a congressman," he said.[1]

Clark was a supporter of tariff reform who thought Taft's reforms had not gone far enough. He also favored a free-silver currency policy, as Bryan had advocated, as well as direct election of senators. He was the beneficiary of picking up delegate strength in the western part of the country that had previously gone with Bryan.

Another leading candidate was Thomas Woodrow Wilson, who went by "Woodrow," and whose background was totally the opposite of Clark's. Wilson, son of a southern Baptist preacher, grew up in the south but was educated at Princeton University where he later taught and still later became president of the institution. His first formal entry into politics was his election as governor of New Jersey, which set the stage for his presidential run.

Wilson believed protective tariffs favored special interests and hurt the national economy. He also favored strengthening anti-trust laws because he believed trusts allowed government-sanctioned advantages to special interests.

He was reserved by nature, was not given to flamboyancy, hyperbole or exaggeration which meant that he seemed very academic to some people, very mundane to others. If the race was to be between Clark and Wilson, it would match the conservative versus the progressive, respectfully.

In a letter to Nellie about a year before the conventions, Taft wrote about being at a meeting that Wilson attended but was not on the official program. The managers of the program feared that Wilson might be asked to say a few words, a request they knew he would gladly accept but would change the format of what they had planned.

"He is a good deal of a 'butter in,' wrote Taft, the context being that he liked to "butt in" even in situations where he was not invited. "They call him 'Dr. Syntax' and 'The Open Mouth' and 'I Would Run Wilson.' I was very much amused at the anxiety the old deacons manifested to get into a song, 'America' and the benediction to head him off."[2]

Other candidates with some support as they arrived in Baltimore included Ohio governor Judson Harmon, whose background included being a judge in Cincinnati in his younger days, similar to the resume of President Taft. Harmon served as attorney general in the administration of President Grover Cleveland. He came to the Baltimore convention as a favorite-son candidate from Ohio.

A fourth candidate with support was Congressman Oscar W. Underwood of Alabama, chairman of the House Ways and Means Committee. His backing came mainly from the southern bloc of delegates, which was sizeable and might be significant if the field of candidates narrowed.

At the Republican convention a week earlier, there was controversy but there were two main candidates with the winner being who ever received a majority of delegates' votes. While the outcome, Taft's victory, was scorned by Roosevelt backers and which led to the formation of a third party, the nomination, for better or worse, was achieved on the first ballot.

The Democrats operated under a different set of rules. Their candidate was required to get two-thirds approval in order to be the nominee. And that would be no easy task.

The elephant in the room all week was Bryan, who was not going to get the nomination, even as a compromise candidate after having lost three previous attempts. But because he had been a valiant, loyal Democrat who had accepted the call of his party three times, he was due the respect of his peers and his opinions still held sway. "Bryan was a curious figure in that convention. The 16 years that had elapsed since the boy orator of Platte stampeded the convention at Chicago had broadened his girth, thinned his hair and taken youth out of him."[3]

Early on at the convention, Bryan, now a delegate from Nebraska, offered a resolution repudiating any candidate who could be associated with what Bryan called "privilege hunting or favor seeking." He specifically named New York delegates Thomas Ryan and August Belmont, both of whom were Wall Street tycoons. Bryan demanded they be expelled from the convention, a ridiculous notion but one that set off a boisterous response in the galleries. Living up to his reputation, he delivered his message with the fervor of a preacher at a revival "and had enough fire in it to draw howling approval from the galleries. It was a ridiculous notion for delegates to consider but it played out as a dramatic moment in the newspapers." Nonetheless, after much cajoling, Bryan agreed to withdraw the name-calling from his resolution, which was then approved.[4]

Bryan, like Roosevelt, was flamboyant, opinionated, boisterous and belligerent who could raise the temperature of any room in which he was speaking. Unlike Roosevelt, he was a three-time loser in presidential races. Like Roosevelt, he would not have turned down another opportunity to run.

But observers believed he was past his prime. "His speech, which he intended to be a war hymn, had the sad cadence of a swan song, so much so that even those who were rejoicing in Bryan's defeat, could not help but sympathize with him."[5]

Clark was the frontrunner when the delegates arrived in Baltimore but made a tactical error as the convention started. He supported Alton B. Parker, a New York judge who was the unsuccessful Democratic candidate for president in 1904, for temporary chairman. Parker was known to have political connections with Tammany Hall, a New York political machine with a reputation for corruption. Bryan objected to Parker as temporary chair and lobbied in vain against him. But the linkage of Clark to Parker and the potential of Tammany Hall influence had an impact that would surface much later.

Similar to the Republican dynamic, Democrats were forming into two distinct factions, conservatives and progressives. Clark had always been part of the conservative wing while Wilson was a progressive who favored reforms much in the same way that Roosevelt did.

Despite Bryan's antics, the start of the convention seemed dull compared to previous conventions and particularly dull compared to the Republican shoot-out just a week earlier in Chicago. "The convention was unlike any national convention in 20 years. It was without snap and ginger, without inspiration, seemingly without a man or a cause to cheer for."[6]

When nominations began Thursday night, nobody could have conceived that the convention would go on for eight days and that it would take 46 ballots before a winner was determined. The nominating and seconding speeches were long and fairly predictable as the evening wore on. Wilson was last to be given his due and was nominated at 2:08 a.m. Friday morning.

14. The Democrats

The first balloting took place at 7 a.m.—hardly enough time for delegates to get much sleep or breakfast. There were no fisticuffs or riots on the convention floor, but eight candidates received votes with no one coming near the 726 needed for the two-thirds majority for nomination. Clark led with 440½ votes followed by 324 for Wilson, 148 for Harmon and 117½ for Underwood.

Also receiving smidgeons of support were Indiana governor Thomas Marshall, 31 votes; Connecticut governor Simeon Baldwin, 22 votes; New York governor William Sulzer, 2 votes; and Bryan 1 vote. Others whose names were placed in nomination but who received no support were Massachusetts governor Eugene Foss, Indiana senator John Kern (Bryan's running mate in 1908), Kentucky congressman Ollie James (who was elected permanent chairman of the convention), New York City mayor William Gaynor (also a friend of Tammany Hall) and Illinois senator J. Hamilton Lewis who had the distinction of having served two different states in Congress because previously he had been elected to Congress from Washington state.

Through the first nine ballots, the highest level Clark reached was 452 on the ninth ballot, a gain of just 11½ from the first ballot. Wilson peaked at 354 on the sixth ballot, 30 more than on the first ballot but less than half of what he needed for nomination. In fact, no candidate even got a majority until the 10th ballot when the New York delegation shifted its allegiance from Harmon to Clark. That pushed Clark to 556, about 200 short of what he needed for the nomination but more than 200 ahead of Wilson, his only real challenger.

In past conventions, when a candidate reached a majority, it started a bandwagon rolling to the nomination. But Clark's chances were actually hurt rather than helped when he got the majority vote, because the shift of New York delegates came from Tammany Hall and that incensed Bryan, the pious, passionate populist who had tacitly supported Clark but was suspicious of him for his support of Parker a few days earlier. With the movement of New York delegates to Clark, Bryan went on the offensive once again, publicly withdrawing his support for Clark and backing Wilson instead.

His support of Wilson had an impact. On the 14th ballot, his Nebraska delegation, which had been unanimous for Clark, went 13–6 for Wilson. As the delegates voted, ballot after ballot, Wilson's gains were minimal. By the 20th ballot, he had gained 30 delegates but was still trailing Clark by more than 100. About the only thing more relentless than the balloting itself was the intense lobbying of both Clark and Wilson supporters.

Governor Harmon became a non-factor when the New York delegation abandoned him on the 10th ballot. Congressman Underwood was not going to get the nomination but the Alabama politician had a loyal following. He received 117½ votes on the first ballot and by the 20th ballot, when the race was obviously between Clark and Wilson, Underwood's support had actually increased, with 121½ delegate votes.

Underwood's showing was significant for two reasons: underlings can exert tremendous influence because a shift of their delegates to one candidate or another can determine who the eventual winner will be. So, while candidates like Underwood may be 400 votes behind, they are in a position of having the upper hand in any deal making. Second, Underwood was a southerner and southern states made up about two-fifths of the overall voting bloc in the U.S. So Underwood's status would be important long after the convention was over.

Indiana was also an important state. One of its senators, John Kern, had been Bryan's running mate in 2008 and early on, was considered by some to be a potential presidential candidate in 2012. Indiana's governor, Thomas Marshall, was also highly thought of and, like Kern, was receiving votes for the nomination each time the roll was called.

After the 26th ballot on Saturday night with still no clear winner in sight, the convention was adjourned until Monday morning to give the weary delegates a day of rest. But there was no rest for the operatives of the candidates who worked diligently to come up with more delegate support for their men.

On Monday morning, a significant move came on the 30th ballot. Indiana switched its support from Clark to Wilson on the promise that if Wilson was the nominee, he would ask the convention to elect Governor Marshall as his running mate. Historians believe the deal was made without Wilson's knowledge because the professor, a stickler for propriety, would probably have nixed the deal.

With that deal in hand, Wilson overtook Clark, securing 460 dele-

Thomas Marshall was governor of Indiana who gained support for the Democratic presidential nomination. When Wilson supporters made a deal to have Marshall be Wilson's running mate, Indiana delegates switched their support to Wilson and helped him win the nomination.

gates to Clark's 455, both still far from the 726 needed for nomination. Significantly, Marshall, who had consistently received 30 delegate votes on ballot after ballot through the first 27 votes, received none on the 28th nor in any subsequent vote. It was on the 28th ballot that Wilson gained 30 delegates and started to gain the momentum he needed to receive the nomination.

The next day, on ballot 43, Illinois moved its 58 delegate votes from Clark to Wilson, giving the New Jersey governor the lead, and the stampede was on. The momentum that Clark could never achieve in the first week of the convention, was now fully on Wilson's side.

On the 46th ballot, Underwood released his delegates that had been loyal from the beginning, giving Wilson nearly 100 more votes and putting him over the top for the Democratic nomination.

William Allen White, the Kansas newspaperman who was a Republican national committeeman and a staunch Roosevelt backer, nonetheless reported on the Democratic convention for several newspapers, including his own. He watched as the Clark majority slowly started to crumble, eventually breaking his stronghold and, according to White, breaking his heart as well. White took some solace in the fact that Wilson was a progressive—a Democrat to be sure—but a progressive.

"What really was back of the [Clark] collapse?" he asked. "The instinct to climb on the bandwagon? The belief of these delegates who left Clark that the progressive cause was the righteous cause? Fear? It came to the same thing, that crystallization of the progressive elements of the Democratic convention which we had witnessed in the Republican convention."[7]

But White observed a big difference in the outcome of the hotly-contested Democratic and Republican conventions because Wilson faced no revolt when he took his nomination.

As White observed, "I heard no such deep and bitter damnation for the winner from his beaten opponents as I heard in Chicago when Taft won. I could see that Wilson would go before the country with his party phalanx behind him."[8]

Wilson's nomination had imme-

Woodrow Wilson, a lifelong educator and relative newcomer to politics, was nominated as Democratic candidate for president on the 46th ballot.

diate reverberations within the Republican Party and in particular, the campaigns of Taft and Roosevelt. The GOP had been split wide open at its convention and now the bleeding was beginning to show. Colorado governor Chase Osborn, who had been one of the seven governors who, months earlier, had signed the cooked-up letter urging the colonel to run, announced he was supporting Wilson. Osborn said with a progressive candidate now in the race, there was no need to start a third party.

The Minnesota Progressive League issued a statement saying it intended to support Wilson. Wilson's campaign reported receiving thousands of letters from Republicans all over the country supporting the Democratic candidate. Senator LaFollette, a man who knew how to carry a grudge and was still full of hate for Roosevelt, endorsed Wilson and vowed to travel across the country campaigning for him.

Roosevelt had a unique view of the circumstances. He told friends if the Democratic convention had been held first, and nominated Wilson, he probably would not have started a third party movement. But now there was no turning back. "It was quite out of the question," he said, "after having my men into the fight, that I should then abandon them."[9]

All political conventions have their share of ironies and the 1912 Democratic convention was no exception. "As a political scientist and reformer, Wilson actually opposed the two-thirds rule (for nomination), which he considered undemocratic. But that rule put him in power. Unlike TR, who won most of the Republican primaries, Wilson won only five of the 12 Democratic primaries."[10]

In a long letter to Nellie shortly after the Democratic convention, the president observed, "If I cannot win, I hope Wilson will and Roosevelt feels if he cannot win, he hopes Wilson will."[11]

A few days later, in another letter to his wife, he told of the concern of Hilles, his secretary, over the press coverage his opponents were receiving. "Hilles is sensitive because Wilson gets a column every day and so does Roosevelt on political subjects. And there is no news from me except that I played golf. It always makes me impatient as if I were running a P.T. Barnum show."[12]

There was a lot of politics brewing in August. Roosevelt's newly-formed Progressive Party, which met in a disorganized, frenzied session at Orchestra Hall in Chicago as the Republican convention was concluding, now was preparing to hold its own convention and formally nominate its own candidates.

And in Washington, as was the custom of the day, a delegation of Republicans was headed to the White House to officially notify Taft that he was their party's candidate after which Taft would give a speech formally accepting the nomination.

For his part, Wilson maintained the countenance that people had come to expect of him—passive acceptance—even with the achievement of a lifetime.

He told newsmen they probably have been surprised at his lack of emotion, "I have been afraid that you might get the impression that I was so self-confident and sure of the result that I took the steady increase in the vote for me complacently and as a matter of course," he said. "The fact is that this emotion has been too deep to come to the surface."[13]

15

The Progressives

The Roosevelt loyalists left the Chicago Coliseum and headed for Orchestra Hall to start the formation of a third party movement. Among them were George Perkins and Frank Munsey, two of the colonel's biggest financial backers; Senator Joseph Dixon, Frank Knox, an influential newspaper publisher who gained fame later on as Franklin D. Roosevelt's secretary of the Navy; Governor Walter R. Stubbs; Gifford and Amos Pinchot; James Garfield; and many who were denied credentials at the Republican convention including Mississippi delegates Perry Howard, Charles Banks, Willis Mollison Frank Swalm and Sidney Redmond, Howard's brother-in-law. The Mississippi men's loyalty would soon be shunned in a pivotal moment of the Progressive campaign.

Perhaps as significant as the hundreds who formed the Roosevelt brigade were the ones who didn't. Among them were Taft, of course, and Sherman, his running mate; and Elihu Root, the distinguished convention chairman who had served Roosevelt as his secretary of war and secretary of state; there was Robert LaFollette, the original Progressive who would go to his grave hating Roosevelt for stealing his thunder; there was Governor Chase Osborn of Michigan, who Roosevelt had called on early on to rally other governors to sign the letter urging him to seek the GOP nomination; and there was Governor Herbert Hadley of Missouri, Roosevelt's floor manager at the convention and one of seven governors who signed the letter.

California governor Hiram Johnson, who oversaw many Progressive reforms in his own state, presided over this group of renegades who were willing to desert the Republican Party—at the risk of decimating it—in order to form a new party and march to the tune of Theodore Roosevelt. Several men made short speeches in support of the cause. Then Roosevelt rose and after thunderous applause, the place grew relatively silent as the colonel spoke to them.

He said the issue before them was no longer just a question of Progressivism but a question of fundamental honesty and doing right. He told the crowd to go home, talk to their families and friends and come back in two months to nominate a candidate. "If you wish me to make the fight, I will make it, if only one state should support me. The only condition I impose is that you shall feel entirely free, when you come together, to substitute any other man in my place, if you deem it better for the movement, and in such case I will give him my heartiest support."[1]

Six weeks later, the Progressives returned to Chicago to get organized, draft a platform and nominate their candidate for president, although the latter was a foregone conclusion. The convention opened on August 5 and among the delegates were many women. One of the planks of the party platform was giving women the right to vote. "There was not a saloon keeper in the crowd. The delegates were younger and more earnest than the usual convention goers. Petticoats were everywhere. Hundreds of social workers, suffragettes and advocates of working girls' rights had enlisted in the new party."[2]

It was "a political organism the likes of which no one had ever experienced: equal parts party convention, public policy seminar, Protestant camp meeting and cult of personality. Even reporters and observers predisposed to be hostile to the event remarked on the earnest evangelical fervor that coursed through the thousands of delegates and spectators filling the Chicago Coliseum."[3]

The mood was festive. A banner above the speakers platform bore the words of Rudyard Kipling: "For theirs is neither East of West / Border, nor breed nor birth. / When two strong men stand face to face / Though they come from the ends of the earth."

Surrounding the banners were large portraits of George Washington, Thomas Jefferson, Abraham Lincoln, Andrew Jackson and Alexander Hamilton—principled men, all crusaders of sorts. "Throughout the proceedings, there was much enthusiasm but no battle. It was rather the gathering of several thousand very earnest men and women bent on consecrating themselves to a new cause which they believed to be the paramount cause for the political, economic and social welfare of the country."[4] "Fewer brass bands and floor bosses than usual populated the convention floor, replaced by more women, more young people and more intellectuals than anyone had ever seen at a political convention. Protestant hymns replaced sloganeering campaign marches."[5]

The exuberant men and women attending the convention wore red bandannas—symbols of unity with perhaps a hint of the Rough Rider mentality. The men wore the bandannas around their necks while the women had theirs around their wrists.

One of the chief topics of discussion—and dispute—harkened back to a belief Roosevelt had expressed early on, one that exposed a surprising personal attitude and yet a measure of political expediency. While Roosevelt stated publicly the importance to "let the people rule," as it turned out, it was not all people. In the past, he had said privately that "only certain people were fit for democracy" and pointed to the problems that would develop if Chinese and Japanese immigrants voted in large numbers in California of if ignorant people, such as negroes in the south, were given political authority.[6]

Now, at the Progressives convention, his personal views were becoming political reality. Roosevelt had declared the new party should have no negro delegates from the south. He believed they would alienate southern whites and sharpen their hostility to the blacks. Roosevelt rationalized, therefore, that the cause of the blacks would be better served if the southern whites were not agitated by the presence of blacks. "He had persuaded himself that true justice would only come to negro residents of the old Confederate states by enlisting the efforts of high-minded white men."[7]

Gordon Orme, a rich rice dealer from New Orleans and a Progressive activist, wrote a letter to his friend, John M. Parker, whose wealth came from cotton and who, eight years later would be elected governor of Louisiana. In the letter, Orme urged that the Progressive Party be a white man's party and that blacks could come to the convention for educational purposes only, but not as delegates.

Parker agreed with Orme. The two powerful southerners, with the support of others, helped make it part of the Progressive plan for the south. One of the others was Theodore Roosevelt, Jr., who was active in his father's campaign. He said, "We recognize that practically it would be impossible to work with the best elements of the community if they [blacks] were on the delegation.... The majority have no intelligence at all."[8]

It was a blatantly racist comment and it was assumed that the "we" he referred to was a reference to his father. The colonel did not believe the Progressive Party should be an all-white party because, from a purely political standpoint, he thought it would alienate black voters in the north whose support he needed, but he was adamant about having no black delegates.

Roosevelt made his views known in a letter he wrote on August 1 to Julian Harris of Georgia, a personal friend who represented Georgia on the Bull Moose Party National Committee. Roosevelt wrote, "I earnestly believe that by appealing to the best white men in the south, and by frankly putting the movement in their hands from the outset, we shall create a situation by which the colored men of the south will ultimately get justice."[9]

Redmond, Howard and other Mississippi blacks were stunned. They felt that the Republican Party had abandoned them two months earlier and now, Roosevelt was leaving them out in the cold. Howard wrote to Dixon, the colonel's campaign manager, asking in effect, where was the square deal for blacks. The *Jackson Daily News* did not mince words. Its headline, in all caps: "COL. ROOSEVELT THROWS NEGRO LEADERS OVERBOARD."

15. The Progressives

The Mississippi black leadership did not give in. They organized quickly, formed a bi-racial group to hold caucuses and elected a bi-racial slate of delegates to go to Chicago for the purpose of being seated at the convention. Meanwhile, the white Progressives had their own delegation headed for Chicago.

Pre-convention activities began Saturday, August 3, in the familiar surroundings of the Congress Hotel. The usual political talk filled the lobbies and the meeting rooms but there was a noticeable difference from other conventions. There was no suspense about who their candidate would be, but there was much suspense as to how the controversy over the elimination of southern black delegates would be resolved.

The convention's Provisional Committee met to go over provisions of the convention, usually a routine matter. But the colonel's edict regarding the black delegates dominated discussions inside the meeting room, while just outside the room, disenchanted, disenfranchised black men gathered.

Senator Dixon, Roosevelt's campaign manager, presided at the meeting. He discovered early on that the colonel's hold on white supporters from northern states was starting to fracture because of his disdain for black supporters in southern states. Dixon heard over and over again from white delegates in New England states that they prided themselves on their Christian values and sense of fairness and that they would be embarrassed to go home and face their neighbors if they supported denying the negroes their rights. The bickering among the committee members went on until about 10:30 p.m. when Dixon called a recess until Monday morning when Roosevelt was due to arrive in Chicago.

Redmond, Howard and others used Sunday to strategize and to lobby more delegates to their cause.

There were 5,000 enthusiastic, screaming supporters at the train station Monday morning when Roosevelt arrived in Chicago. Crowds lined the streets as he made his way to the hotel and was whisked up the several floors to his suite. Mississippi black delegates demanded to meet with him but he refused, sending word that they should read his letter to Julian Harris, which was widely published.

The Provisional Committee resumed its work at 10 a.m., and predictably, the arguments resumed from where they left off on Saturday. Dixon, bound by Roosevelt's wishes, offered a compromise. He suggested the all-white Mississippi delegation be seated and that Redmond's bi-racial delegation be denied delegate status but be awarded honorary certificates of admission. It was not an acceptable comprise to those who had traveled from Mississippi to Chicago to be active participants. The committee voted 22–12 to seat the all-white delegation.[10]

The next step was for it to go to the Credentials Committee which met

Crowds packed the streets of Chicago to greet Colonel Roosevelt as he arrives for the Progressive Party convention.

Monday night. The debate was as heated and as lengthy as it had been in the Provisional Committee, but in the end, at 3 a.m. Tuesday morning, after many weary members had left and gone to bed, the committee voted 17–16 in favor of the all-white Mississippi delegation.

Those supporting the bi-racial delegation refused to back down. Once again, they demanded to meet with Roosevelt and, if they were rebuffed again, they vowed to take their fight to the convention floor—and they had support of enough northern delegates to make it happen.

Roosevelt was persuaded to meet with them. The meeting was private, held on Tuesday morning before the start of the convention and there is no written record of what took place. What is known is that when the convention opened, the white delegation was seated. "Roosevelt held that a negro of good manners and education ought to be treated as a white man would be treated. He believed that if the southern whites would think as he did on this matter, they might quicker solve the negro question and establish human if not friendly relations with the blacks."[11]

Redmond and the others had put up a good fight. But they were in a bind. They had opposed Taft, they had left the Republican Party, they didn't have the strength to buck the system, so they were stuck.

15. The Progressives

Taft never expressed racial prejudice, at least publicly but dealing with racial equality proved to be a challenge in a manner he expressed in a letter to his wife. "I am having trouble finding places for intelligent negroes," he wrote. "The prejudice against them is so strong that it makes few places available, and yet I must do something for the race for they are entitled to recognition. Roosevelt has treated them so abominably that I feel more friendly toward them than ever and anxious to help."[12]

On Monday and Tuesday, the convention took care of its committee business, the routine and the not-so-routine. On Wednesday, Roosevelt made a triumphal entrance, coming on stage waving his red bandanna. A band played "The Battle Hymn of the Republic" and the crowd, brimming with excitement, rose as one and sang, "Mine eyes have seen the glory of the coming of the lord.... His truth is marching on."

Roosevelt purposely scheduled his speech before the platform was adopted because, in this carefully staged convention, he wanted to make sure the delegates knew exactly what he wanted in the platform before they voted on it.

His platform had not changed since he first espoused it in Columbus. Then it was called his "New Nationalism" speech. At the convention, it was his "Confession of Faith." It was a "let the people rule" platform calling for presidential primaries, direct election of senators, publication of campaign contributions, women's right to vote, end of child labor, a living wage, regulation of interstate corporations, graduated inheritance tax, workman's compensation and social insurance.

"You are taking a bold and greatly-needed step," he declared, "for the service of our beloved country. The old parties are husks, with no real soul within either, divided on artificial lines, boss-ridden and privileged-controlled, each a jumble of incongruous elements and neither daring to speak out wisely and fearlessly what should be said on the vital issues of the day."

It was as if he was reciting the national anthem of Progressivism and he delivered it with his characteristic flair—voice raised, hands waving, head shaking, teeth prominent—and the delegates were on the edge of their seats if not standing.

"Surely there was never a fight better worth making than the one in which we are engaged," the colonel said. "It matters little what befalls any one of us who for the time being stand in the forefront of the battle.... But win or lose, we shall not falter. Whatever fate may at the moment overtake any of us, the movement itself will not stop."

Assailing both the Republican and Democratic parties, he said the two had their differences but "they come together at once when the dominion of both is threatened by the supremacy of the people of the United States, now aroused to the need of a national alignment on the vital economical issues of this generation."

On the importance of presidential primaries, he said, "In the contest that culminated six weeks ago in this city, I speedily found out that my chance was at a minimum in any state where I could not get expression of the people themselves in the primaries. I found that if I could appeal to the rank and file of the Republican voters, I could generally win, whereas if I had to appeal to the political caste, which includes the most noisy defenders of the old system, I generally lost. The nomination of Mr. Taft in Chicago was a fraud upon the rank and file of the Republican Party. It was obtained only by defrauding the rank and file of the party of their right to express their choice...."

Regarding the rights of the working man, Roosevelt declared, "We hold that under no industrial order, in no commonwealth, in no trade, and in no establishment should industry be carried on under conditions inimical to the social welfare. The abnormal, ruthless, spendthrift industry or establishment tends to drag down all to the level of the least considerate." To that end, he called for healthy and safe working conditions for men and women, for a minimum wage that was fair and equitable, and working hours that were productive for the employer and reasonable for the workers."

The colonel offered words of support for the American farmer, saying, "Everything possible should be done to make life in the country profitable so as to be attractive from the economic standpoint and also to give an outlet among farming people for those forms of activity which now tend to make life in the cities especially desirable for ambitious men and women. There should be just the same chance to live as full, as well-rounded and as highly useful lives in the country as in the city."

Roosevelt touched on most areas of everyday life for Americans that would resonate with his supporters and in keeping with his overall theme of "let the people rule."

The one area of his speech that made even some of his staunchest backers cringe came in his blistering assault on the courts—and his solution. "The American people, and not the courts, are to determine their own fundamental policies," he said. "The people should have the power to deal with the effect of the acts of all their governmental agencies. This must be extended to include the effects of the judicial acts as well as the acts of the executive and legislative representatives of the people."

When Roosevelt talked about dealing with the "effect of the acts," he was promoting the notion of the public being able to overturn judicial decisions with which they disagreed and to even cast votes for the recall of judges. Of all of the colonel's Progressive proposals, his thoughts on reversing judicial decisions was by far the most controversial, the one where many Progressives as well as Republicans and Democrats felt he had gone too far.

After speaking for two hours, interrupted numerous times by cheers and applause, Roosevelt closed with an 80-word exclamation, with the rhythm and fervor of an evangelist's altar call and ending with the same line he shouted when he arrived in Chicago for the GOP convention. "Now you men, who in your turn, have come together to spend and be spent in the endless crusade against wrong, to you who face the future resolute and confident, to you who strive in the spirit of brotherhood for the betterment of our nation, to you who gird yourselves for this great new fight in the never-ending warfare for the good of humankind, I say in closing, we stand at Armageddon and we battle for the Lord."

Then Roosevelt was nominated, with Jane Addams, a leading women's rights advocate, giving the seconding speech. The colonel received the nomination by acclamation. Governor Johnson was chosen as his running mate.

The convention, which purposely had the atmosphere of a religious revival, ended in fitting form, with thousands of men and women singing the doxology: "Praise God from whom all blessings flow...." "We were mighty well pleased with ourselves, filled with a glowing sense of duty well done. We also believed we had seen a historic occasion, the birth of a party that was destined to rise and take in the country the place the Republican Party had occupied for 50 years."[13]

Many of the delegates, feeling that sense of history, gobbled up any mementoes they could get their hands on—badges, bandannas, photos of the colonel—knowing they would one day be family heirlooms, symbols not of a convention, but of a crusade. "We were indeed 'Christian solders, marching as to war'—and rather more than mildly mad."[14]

16

THE RESOLVE OF TAFT

It was customary in the era of Roosevelt and Taft for the nominee of the party to receive notification of the nomination by a special committee and then to formally accept the nomination either in writing or a speech or both.

President Taft received formal notification in August, proving that even a century ago, the wheels of government moved slowly. In his letter to convention chairman Root and the Notification Committee, he accepted the nomination with gratitude but said the convention exposed an issue that created a crisis in the life of the Republican Party.

Taft took the occasion to point out how the Republican Party and the country had avoided a potential disaster by not nominating Roosevelt. Among other things, said Taft, it protected the dignity of something close to his heart, the judiciary. He wrote, "A faction sought to force the party to violate a valuable and time-honored national tradition by entrusting the power of the presidency for more than two terms to one man, and that man, one whose recently avowed political views would have committed the party to radical proposals involving dangerous changes in our present constitutional form of representative government and our independent judiciary."[1]

Taft was also aware of the potential for a severely divided Republican Party and asserted, perhaps prematurely, that his nomination prevented that from happening.

"This occasion is appropriate for the expression of profound gratitude at the victory for the right which was won in Chicago. By that victory, the Republican Party was saved for future usefulness," he wrote.[2]

Taft continued his opportunity to snipe at Roosevelt. "We are living in an age in which by exaggeration of the defects of our present conditions, by false charges of responsibility for it against individuals and classes, by holding up to the feverish imagination of the less fortunate and the discontented, the possibilities of a millennium, a condition of popular unrest has been produced. New parties are being formed with the proposed purpose of satisfying this unrest by promising a panacea."[3]

16. The Resolve of Taft

He contended that the Progressives were better at pointing out problems than solutions and once again defended the independence of the judiciary. "Instead of giving us the benefit of any specific remedies for the hardships and evils of society they point out, they follow their urgent appeals for closer association of the people in legislation by an attempt to cultivate the hospitality of the people to the courts and to represent that they are in some form upholding injustice and are obstructing the popular will," he wrote.[4]

Taft realized that the political divide that was created by Roosevelt bolting the party probably would result in a Democratic victory in the fall election. But he was at peace with himself. He believed his victory over Roosevelt at the convention preserved the Republican Party, such as it was, and that might prove to be more important in the long run than any result in the November election. "Winning the nomination had been the all-important victory—and not simply because he had bested Roosevelt. He had long believed that a loss at the convention would have been regarded as a personal rejection whereas defeat in the fall election reflected a more general reverse for the party."[5]

He also believed it was undignified for an incumbent president to hit the campaign trail instead of tending to business in Washington. So while Roosevelt and Wilson were traveling all over the country sometimes making several speeches a day, the president was content to occasionally speak in Washington or from his summer home in Beverly, Massachusetts. The home was more of a retreat for Mrs. Taft than for the president, a place for her to get away from the torrid summer heat of Washington and to relax and enjoy the countryside. But nothing seemed to come easy for the Tafts in their White House years, and summer home in Beverly was no exception.

The Tafts had leased the 14-room cottage from Maria Evans, a recently-widowed socialite who was reputed to be one of the richest women in the world. It was an ideal location for the president, Nellie and two of their children. There were golf courses nearby and scenic country roads to drive on, fulfilling two of the president's favorite things to do. Mrs. Taft, still recovering from a stroke, enjoyed the time with her family. But Taft's presence in the community stirred excitement. Neighbors and tourists lined the streets around the home, hoping to get a glimpse of the president as he emerged from the house. Reporters, photographers and sight-seers, as well as the Secret Service, trampled on the property, killing the grass and often leaving trash on the premises.

After two summers of putting up with all the hoopla, Mrs. Evans had enough. She asked the first family to find another place to live. The Tafts left and found another suitable place in Beverly. In effect, Mrs. Evans had evicted the president of the United States.

Despite the onslaught of criticism, primarily from Roosevelt, Taft felt he had an honorable and admirable record in office, one that his surrogates could proudly proclaim as they campaigned in his stead across the land.

The nation had enjoyed four years of peace and prosperity. Taft had worked with Congress, as best he could, instead of waging war with it, and had managed to achieve several significant pieces of legislation. Amazingly in his four-year tenure, he was required to fill six vacancies on the Supreme Court, something no future president has had to do. Typical of the man who was once described as someone, if he was Pope, would have appointed some Protestants to the College of Cardinals, half of Taft's Supreme Court appointees were Democrats.

The president said the federal government could not "make the rain to fall or the sun to shine or the crops to grow," but it could wreak havoc on the economy if it instituted damaging policies and that his administration had kept the nation on an even keel. "The negative virtue of having taken no step to interfere with the coming of prosperity and the comfort of the people is one that ought highly to commend an administration, and the party responsible for it, as worthy of further continuance of power," he said.[6]

While Taft did his best to criticize Roosevelt on the issues, he did not hold back his personal contempt in long letters he wrote to his beloved Nellie when the two were separated. On August 26, he wrote to her that it was hard for him to realize that Roosevelt was the same man who had been his friend and who he had served so faithfully when the colonel was in the White House.

"I knew of course that his memory was defective about the things he did not want to remember, that he was so intense in his pugnaciousness and in making his enemy beware of him that he could think almost as he wished to think, but it is impossible to think of him as the fakir [sic], the juggler, the green goods man, the gold brick man that he has come to be," he wrote.[7]

Taft compared him to a leader of a religious cult who mesmerizes his followers with manipulation and deception. "He is seeking to make his followers Holy Rollers and I hope that the country is beginning to see this…, and that there is now going on a rapid disintegration … of the Jane Addams type, the fanatics and the dreamers and the enthusiasts and the politicians and the opportunists who joined Roosevelt."[8]

Despite the venom of his words, Taft told his wife he didn't hate Roosevelt but thought of him as he would think of a peculiar animal in a zoo, a one-of-a-kind species.

Writing like the even-tempered judge that was a hallmark of his career, Taft said, "The truth is my experience has been such that I do not have very much personal hostility to any of my enemies. Such a thing is not worth cultivating…. Life is too short to make that worthwhile, and I believe I have a clearer conception of what really contributes to the happiness of one than to permit him to take any pleasure in retaliation or revenge."[9]

16. The Resolve of Taft

Though Roosevelt's constant barrage of colorful criticism obviously irritated Taft, the former jovial jurist had shown over the years how he was able to brush off criticism as if it was dandruff on his lapel. Early in his administration Democrats on a congressional committee sought to rile him by dredging up a minor scandal that had occurred a decade earlier when he was in the State Department. "Taft said it reminded him of the man who was asked in a restaurant whether he wanted oxtail soup, which the waiter explained, was merely made from the tail of the ox. 'Neighbor,' the patron replied, 'don't you think that's going a hell of a long way back for soup?'"[10]

A potential scandal involving Woodrow Wilson was averted during the campaign. Wilson had a long, enduring relationship with Mary Hulbert Peck, a once well-to-do widow that began during his days at Princeton but had continued through each of Wilson's two marriages. Political opponents of Wilson's came across some correspondence that appeared to be love letters from Wilson to Mrs. Peck long after Wilson was married.

The Republican operatives had the opportunity to purchase the letters and use them to smear Wilson's glowing reputation as a decent, honorable man. Taft rejected the idea. So did Senator Dixon, Roosevelt's campaign manager. But Dixon then checked with his boss to make sure he had done the right thing.

Roosevelt assured him he had acted correctly. He said, "Nothing, no evidence would ever make the American people believe that a man like Woodrow Wilson, cast so perfectly as the apothecary's clerk, could ever play Romeo."[11]

Journalist William Allen White, who reportedly had seen the letters, agreed, describing Wilson as "grim visaged, dour, repressed and as gallant as a scarecrow."[12]

Taft had a lot of respect for Wilson, as he did most men, but he was not above making fun of him from time to time, telling Nellie he was known as "the open mouth" because of his penchant for speaking and repeating the story of how those in charge of public events would rush to the benediction before the professor had a chance to speak.[13]

Wilson showed he had a sense of humor from time to time. At a campaign speech at the Tremont Temple in Boston, he poked a little fun at the colonel. "Suppose you choose the leader of the third party as president," he said. "Don't you think he will be pretty lonely? Not that he'll mind it because I believe he finds himself rather good company." Later that night, Wilson returned to his hotel and discovered Taft was at a Chamber of Commerce dinner in the hotel's banquet hall. He had a message delivered to Taft that he would very much like to meet with him. The meeting took place at about midnight and was cordial—"delightful," Wilson told the press. He said he was fond of President Taft.[14]

Both men admitted the campaign was grueling and tiring. Meanwhile, Roosevelt continued wooing voters at frenetic speed as if hardly stopping to catch his breath.

A fourth candidate in the race was Socialist Eugene Debs of Indiana who had a relatively small but loyal following and was the only candidate who had served time in a federal prison.

Debs was a 57-year-old union organizer who espoused Christian principles in his quest for what he believed was best for the "brotherhood of man" while seemingly looking the other way when that quest caused violence in worker revolts across the country.

Debs was a founder of two powerful unions, the Industrial Workers of the World (IWW), sometimes called "Wobblies" and the American Railway Union. He was instrumental in helping many other unions grow and prosper.

Eugene Debs, Socialist Party candidate, made several runs for the presidency, failing each time but twice receiving more than 900,000 votes.

He was elected as a Democrat to the Indiana General Assembly in 1884 while working for several small unions. He rose to national prominence a year later when workers of the Pullman Palace Car Company, makers of the Pullman sleeper cars on trains, protested against their low wages and staged a work boycott—a wildcat strike. Debs supported the workers and moved in and signed them to memberships in his newly-formed American Railway Union.

The union organized a nationwide boycott against Pullman, affecting 250,000 workers in 27 states, paralyzing rail traffic west of the Mississippi River. One of the effects was stoppage of mail service. President Grover Cleveland called in the Army to take over the situation, leading to the end of the strike.

Debs was convicted on federal charges of denying a court injunction and served six months in a federal prison. During the strike and prior to his arrest, the *New York Times* referred to Debs as "a lawbreaker at large, an enemy of the human race."[15]

While he was in prison, Debs began reading about socialist principles and became a disciple of them. He came out of prison a dedicated Socialist and ran for president on the Socialist ticket in 1900, 1904, 1908, 1912 and in 1920. His reputation for endorsing violence, if necessary, in the quest for workers' rights, followed him into his political career but had begun to wane by 1912. "Debs' inclusion in the race did not mean that the Socialists were any more unified than their opponents.... For years, party members had debated whether Socialists should use violence to fight capitalism but by 1912, this was no longer a theoretical debate."[16]

Debs believed the capitalist system was out of touch with the needs of the working man. "To ensure more direct democracy, the Socialist platform proposed the abolition of the U.S. Senate, the elimination of the president's veto power and the removal of the Supreme Court's power to declare laws passed by Congress as unconstitutional."[17]

Roosevelt had no use for Debs or his followers "who by their public utterances and manifestoes and by the words and deeds of those associated with or subordinated to them, habitually appear as guilty of incitement to or apology for bloodshed and violence. If this does not constitute undesirable citizenship, then there can never be any undesirable citizens."[18]

17

MILWAUKEE

Theodore Roosevelt arose in Chicago on the morning of October 14, ignoring the fatigue that had set in and the hoarseness that was diminishing the thunder of his voice as he continued on his grueling, two-week, eight-state journey across the south and the Midwest.

He had started his campaign tour in August, not long after the end of the Progressive convention with a tour through New England states and then it was on to Missouri, Iowa, Minnesota, North Dakota, Montana, Washington, Oregon, Utah, Nevada and California. This latest campaign journey had taken him from Charleston, South Carolina to Atlanta to Chattanooga and then into the Midwest—Evansville, Indianapolis, Chicago, and then on to Michigan and Wisconsin.

So much had happened in Chicago in the past three months. It was here in July that he believed the Republican nomination had been stolen from him by the Taft forces; here that his supporters, on his command, had bolted out of the Republican National Convention, leaving the party in tatters; here that the Rooseveltians returned in August to form the Progressive Party, or Bull Moose Party as it came to be called. And now, here he was in October, back in the Windy City in the midst of the first serious challenge for the presidency by a third-party candidate in American history.

Like the old soldier that he fancied himself, the fight-to-the-end, never-say-die, spirit intact, the weary warrior was ready to battle another day. The cause and his duty to represent it superseded any other concerns he might have. And today, he was to venture into Wisconsin, the home state of Senator Robert LaFollette, "Fighting Bob," who had organized the Progressive movement and despised Roosevelt for laying back and then snatching the spotlight and running away with it. LaFollette easily defeated the colonel in Wisconsin's preferential presidential primary early in the year.

Wilson and Debs were also on the campaign trail but neither had the fortitude or the gumption to keep up with the colonel. At the end of September, Wilson went on an extensive tour of northwestern and Midwestern states.

Wilson, the son of a Baptist minister who grew up in the south, and with an academic and professional background that included being president of Princeton University, had a fascination with politics and wisdom that guided him. He was wise enough to figure out the geography of his political fortunes and knew he "had no hope of winning the Progressive West and no fear of losing the Solid South."[1]

Debs was also going around the country in another of his virtually hopeless campaigns but, like Roosevelt, had a cause and a message that he tried to hammer home where ever he went that was more important to him than individual glory. (On election day, he would finish fourth but received more than 900,000 votes.) "Since there was no radio or television, the candidates debated each other in the pages of the newspapers. Woodrow Wilson would make a speech one night, for example, and Roosevelt would read about it in the next day's paper, then refute it in his own speech that night."[2]

Roosevelt's schedule called for a stop in Racine and then on to Milwaukee for dinner with state and local dignitaries and a major speech at the city's civic auditorium that night. After the Racine stop, the Roosevelt entourage made its way to Milwaukee where the colonel dined at the Hotel Gilpatrick and readied himself for the four-block trip to the Milwaukee Auditorium (now the Milwaukee Theatre) where he would rally the faithful.

The Hotel Gilpatrick was not the most luxurious hotel in Milwaukee and did not have the ambiance that many people would feel fitting for a former president and presidential candidate. It was a five-story structure at the corner of Third Street and West Kilbourn Avenue in downtown Milwaukee. It had a stone façade and a large corner turret at the top which apparently was to give it an ornate look. A plain-looking "Hotel Gilpatrick" sign on the roof stole away the ornateness as well as a Scottish woolen mills store on the first floor. The building was originally the office of the Romadka Trunk Company. M.P. Gilpatrick purchased it in 1905 and converted it into a hotel which opened in 1907. "As no secret had been made of the plans of Col. Roosevelt, a crowd was in front of the hotel to see him leave for the Auditorium. When he came out, a cheer was set up, and he responded smilingly, raising his hat and bowing. Several persons pushed to the front to see him better or to try to shake his hand, as is usual. There were cries of encouragement from all sides."[3]

Roosevelt emerged from the hotel shortly before 8 p.m. and headed for his waiting vehicle. The crowd gathered along the streets and sidewalks and waited to get a glimpse of the man they so admired. The colonel acknowledged them with a tip of his hat and a wave and, noticing a news photographer nearby, turned and faced him so he could get a good image. (Even at a moment's notice, Roosevelt knew how to win the favor of the press.)

There had been no special arrangements made to protect Roosevelt though the colonel was known to carry a concealed pistol. Members of his traveling party included a cousin, Philip Roosevelt; Henry F. Cochems, the Bull Moose leader in Milwaukee; Albert H. Martin, one of his secretaries; and police captain A.O. Girard of Milwaukee. They were accompanying the colonel but they were not on guard.

When Roosevelt and his men crossed the sidewalk to the automobile, the colonel's companions stepped aside so that he could step into the vehicle. Martin was next in. There was another cheer from the crowd all around them and Roosevelt turned to face them, raising his hat once again, smiling.

John Schrank, a short man looking a little disheveled, standing at the edge of the sidewalk, pushed his way forward. No attention was paid to him because everyone seemed to be pushing forward to get as close to Roosevelt as they could. Roosevelt looked down at the little man and smiled. Schrank suddenly produced a .38 caliber pistol and fired point blank at the colonel.

He raised his pistol to fire again when Martin leaped forward and jumped on the assailant. He put his arm around Schrank's neck with one arm and used the other to disarm him.

"Col. Roosevelt had barely moved when the shot was fired and stood calmly looking on as if nothing had happened. Martin picked the man up as though he were a child and carried him the few feet which separated them from the car, almost to the side of the colonel. 'Here he is,' said Martin. "Look at him, colonel.'"[4]

The shooting and the disarming of Schrank all happened in a matter of seconds. When the crowd realized what had happened, many started screaming "lynch him" and "kill him." Roosevelt looked on, stunned by the turn of

John Schrank, a loner who dreamed President McKinley ordained him to kill Roosevelt, followed the colonel through several cities and shot him in Milwaukee.

events but showing no signs of pain or discomfort. As Martin and Capt. Girard wrestled with the assailant, the angry throngs moved in, creating the possibility of trampling him. It was Roosevelt, of all people, who shouted and waved his hands, motioning for the crowd to back off. The crowd at first was not disposed to heed his words, but at length fell back and permitted Mr. Martin and Capt. Girard to carry the man into the hotel. After a short struggle he gave up and was taken without resistance out of the reach of the crowd." "Are you hurt, colonel?" a hundred voices called out. "Oh, no," he responded with a smile. "Missed me that time. I'm not hurt a bit. I think we better be going on or we'll be late."[5]

No one, including Roosevelt, realized he had been shot. When the shooter was in police custody and a semblance of order had been restored, Roosevelt sat down in his vehicle with instructions to drive to the auditorium. After all, he reasoned, he had a speech to give and an audience was waiting for him.

The car had not gotten very far when John McGrath, another of Roosevelt's secretaries, looked at the colonel and noticed a hole in his overcoat.

"Col. Roosevelt looked down, saw the hole, then unbuttoned the big brown army coat which he was wearing and thrust his hand beneath it. When he withdrew it, his fingers were stained with blood. He was not at all dismayed. 'It looks as though I have been hit,'" he said, "'but I don't think it is anything serious.'"[6]

Dr. Scurry Terrell of Dallas, Texas, a throat specialist recruited by Roosevelt's aides to make sure the colonel didn't lose his speaking voice, had gotten into the car just before the group headed to the auditorium. He insisted Roosevelt return to the hotel but the colonel declined in forceful terms and they continued to short trip to the auditorium.[7]

The bullet entered Roosevelt's flesh under the right nipple but its force was deadened by the colonel's 50-page manuscript, folded in his breast pocket along with the case for his spectacles.

In a remarkable display of grit and endurance, Roosevelt spoke for 50 minutes. He began by telling his audience,: "Friends, I shall ask you to be as quiet as possible. I don't know whether you fully understand that I have just been shot." He unbuttoned his vest, showed his blood-stained shirt and said, "It takes more than that to kill a bull moose."

His voice was weak and his breath was short and, midway through, he seemed to slouch a little. But the colonel glared at his aides, standing nearby whenever they motioned to him to stop speaking or positioned themselves near him to catch him if he collapsed. "When asked how he could give a speech with a fresh bullet wound in his chest, Roosevelt later explained that after years of expecting an assassin, he hadn't been surprised. Like the frontiersmen and soldiers he admired, he was determined not to wilt under attack.

As he put it to his English friend, Sir Edward Grey, 'In the very unlikely event of the wound being mortal, I wished to die with my boots on.'"[8] "This extraordinary performance was most foolhardy, and some of his carping critics said that, as usual, Roosevelt wanted to be theatrical. But there was no such purpose in him. He felt to the depths of his soul that neither his safety nor that of any other individual counted in comparison with the triumph of the cause he was fighting for. "[9]

Immediately after his speech, Roosevelt was rushed to Emergency Hospital to have the wound examined and to have X-rays taken. But there was a delay because an X-ray machine had to be brought in from another hospital. The *New York Times* reported Roosevelt sat on the operating table talking politics with the physicians while they waited. Remarkably, after the X-rays, he was given the all-clear. Shortly after midnight, he was on his way to Chicago.

Doctors in Milwaukee gave out the following statement: "Col. Roosevelt is suffering from a superficial flesh wound in the right breast. There is no evidence of injury to the lungs. The bullet is probably somewhere in the chest wall. There is only one wound and no sign of injury to the lung. The bleeding is insignificant. The wound has been sterilized externally with gauze by Dr. R.G. Fayle, the consulting surgeon of the Emergency Hospital. The bullet passed through Col. Roosevelt's army overcoat and other clothing and through a manuscript and spectacle case in his breast pocket and its force was nearly spent before it penetrated the chest. The appearance of the wound also showed evidence of a much-spent bullet. Col. Roosevelt is not suffering from the shock and is in no pain. His condition is so good that surgeons did not object to his continuing his journey to Chicago in his private car. In Chicago, he will be placed under surgical care. The X-ray photograph has been finished and the colonel is feeling fine. He is seeing the newspaper men and presently will go to his [train] car to start for Chicago."[10] The statement was signed by Dr. F.I. Terrell, Dr. R.G. Fayle, Dr. Joseph Colt Bloodgood and Dr. F.A. Stratton.

But as the Roosevelt special train headed for Chicago, the engineer was ordered to stop. Doctors in Milwaukee discovered the bullet penetrated three inches of the abdominal wall and was more serious than at first thought as shown by an X-ray photo that had just been developed. It was finally decided at 12:45 a.m. that Col. Roosevelt should go on to Chicago and the train started up again. He convalesced in Chicago and then went home to Oyster Bay before returning to action with an address at Madison Square Garden in New York on Oct. 30. He carried the bullet inside him for the rest of his life.

Shrank, the assailant, was an unemployed New York saloon keeper. He told police he had a recurring dream in which President William McKinley, who was assassinated in 1901, rose in his coffin and glared at Roosevelt across from him and said, "This is my murderer and nobody else. Avenge my death." Shrank was obsessed with killing Roosevelt and his misplaced anger was further fueled by "King Roosevelt" wanting to serve a third term. He had tried to follow Roosevelt on the colonel's most recent campaign swing but was not able to position himself in other cities to fire a shot at him, until Milwaukee.

Schrank lived in a flophouse above a bar on Canal Street near Elizabeth Avenue in New York City. Ironically, the name of the building was the White House.

He purchased a revolver at a store on Broadway and bought a steamer ticket to Charleston, South Carolina where he intended to kill the Bull Moose. But because of huge crowds, he never got the chance. So he followed Roosevelt by boat, train and car as he tried to keep pace with the colonel's whistle-stop tour through the south and Midwest.

In 1914, Schrank pleaded guilty to the assassination attempt, was judged to be insane and was confined to the Central State Mental Hospital in Waupun, Wisconsin, where he remained until his death in 1943.

When Wilson learned of the shooting, he graciously announced that he would make no more speeches until Roosevelt recovered. Roosevelt insisted that was not necessary, saying a circumstance affecting him personally should not stop anyone from criticizing him politically. He said, "Whatever could with truth and propriety have been said against me and my cause before I was shot, can with equal truth and equal propriety be said against me now, and it so should be said; and the things that cannot be said now are merely the things that ought not to have been said before. This is not a contest about any man; it is a contest concerning principles."[11]

Taft was attending a banquet to honor the members of his cabinet at the Hotel Astor in New York when he was informed of the shooting. As dinner guests learned what happened, many scurried out of the room to telephones so they could spread the news. Taft, who never liked to speak spontaneously, was once again forced to face the press without preparation. He issued a short, terse statement of concern and sympathy. The next morning, he sent a telegraph to Roosevelt wishing him a speedy recovery.

Edith Roosevelt was also in New York City, attending a play, when she was informed that her husband had been shot. She headed for Chicago the next morning with two of her children to be at her husband's side, talk with doctors who were treating him and taking charge of who was allowed to visit him. The following Monday, he was taken by ambulance to his railroad car where he and his family traveled back to New York where he continued to recuperate.

Roosevelt was a lightning rod for attracting excitable people in his crowds, some who adored him, some who demonized him. As president, after McKinley was assassinated, he had Secret Service protection where ever he went but ex-presidents in those days had no such security. The colonel had to depend on his own security team as well as the revolver he often carried in his pocket for his own protection.

It had been a tumultuous month for the colonel. On September 13, in Reno, Nevada, a crowd at a train station pushed and shoved and jostled Roosevelt, separating him from his aides. Extending his arms, he pushed his way forward and made his way to his waiting automobile unscathed.

In Blackfoot, Idaho, his local escorts were "whooping cowboys and red-bandanna-toting Indians."[12] Once again, he was separated from his party but managed to get back with them uninjured.

In Pocatello, Idaho, the colonel spoke to a crowd that included a bunch of rambunctious school children whom he had to chide, as politely as he could, to settle down. When he finally began his speech, one of the children in the front row lunged forward and playfully grabbed his legs.

In Oakland, California, police received a threat on Roosevelt's life prior to him speaking there. His appearance went on without incident.

Roosevelt had a typical chippy reaction to the crowds he was drawing. "It's my past that brings them, not my future," he said.[13]

The election year was filled with tragedies and near-tragedies. Wilson experienced a couple of close calls. On one campaign trip, a freight car smashed into his Pullman, shattering the windows and narrowly missing him. He was shaken but was not injured. On another trip, while he was being driven home from a speaking engagement, his car hit a bump, jostling Wilson who incurred a cut on his head.[14]

Both Taft and Roosevelt suffered a deep personal loss in April when Archie Butt, who had served as military aide to both presidents, died in the sinking of the *Titanic*.

On October 30, James S. Sherman, Taft's vice president, who had been in ill health for years, died a week before the election. In addition to the personal loss, Sherman's death left Taft without a running mate, capping off a campaign season that had more downsides than upsides for the incumbent president.

Republicans scurried to try to fill the void left by Sherman's death on their now depleted ticket. It was decided that Nicholas Murray Butler, a longtime Republican from Sherman's home state of New York, would receive any electoral votes intended for Sherman, a strange solution to a strange set of circumstances.

Butler, 50, was president of Columbia University and was a well-known scholar, philosopher and author and loyal Republican, A brilliant student, he received his bachelor of arts from Columbia in 1882, his master's from the same school in 1883 and his doctorate in 1884. In 1885, he went overseas to continue his studies and spent time in Paris and Berlin.

17. Milwaukee

One of the Americans he met in his foreign travels was Elihu Root, the famous American statesman. They became lifelong friends. Back in the United States, Root introduced Butler to two of his friends, Theodore Roosevelt and William Howard Taft. Roosevelt is said to have been so struck by Butler's intelligence and academic achievements as student and professional that he referred to him at Nicholas "Miraculous" Butler.

Butler stayed active in Republican politics for many years to come, but in 1912, he was no more than a last-minute substitution on a team that was destined to lose.

18

VAST DIFFERENCES IN APPROACH

One of the intriguing aspects of the presidential campaign was that two of President Taft's opponents considered themselves "Progressives."

Roosevelt had stormed out of the Republican National Convention with his followers and, within weeks, formed a third party bearing the Progressive name as its title and loudly proclaiming its principles under the banner of what came to be called "The New Nationalism" as professed in the colonel's "Confession of Faith" speech in accepting the Progressive Party nomination.

Wilson, the wily professor, delivered his message of hope, fairness and prosperity as if each speech was a commencement address. His program for reform, later published in a collection of his speeches, came to be called "The New Freedom."

He was well aware of the difference in style between him and his rambunctious rival but neither he nor Roosevelt could have changed their styles any more than they could have changed their DNAs. But the response they were receiving on the campaign trail showed that whatever each of them was doing was working. "Privately, Wilson admitted that he often felt like a colorless schoolmaster next to the charismatic Roosevelt but people listened closely to his careful, elegantly-phrased speeches."[1]

Both Roosevelt and Wilson believed it was essential for the nation to strike a balance so that business and industry could prosper while still providing a good living wage for the working man, and do it in safe and healthy working conditions.

Wilson compared managing the economy to running a race; in order to keep up with the rapidly expanding economy, in his estimation, it was necessary to run the race twice as fast as had been the custom in recent years. And keeping pace meant adopting a special political philosophy. He wrote, "I am therefore forced to be a Progressive if, for no other reason, because we have not kept up with our changes of conditions, either in the economic field or in the political field. We have not kept our practices adjusted to the facts of the case, and until we do, and unless we do, the facts of the case will always have the better of the argument."[2]

Meanwhile, Taft, who abhorred campaigning, found it convenient to follow the road taken by many of his predecessors who deemed it unbecoming for an incumbent president to actively campaign. He stayed in Washington or at his retreat in Beverly, Massachusetts most of the time. But he maintained a philosophy of government that he had believed in for all of his professional career—a healthy respect for all three branches of government, with the intent of letting all three branches do their jobs. In all cases, the judiciary would be the impartial, non-political, final arbiter when no other solution could be reached.

His seemingly lackluster approach to governing, which infuriated Roosevelt, was contradicted by his cunning operatives who had the political savvy to win the nomination for their man, which also infuriated Roosevelt.

Taft's conservative platform called for retention of the protective tariff—meant to protect both the producer and the consumer; civil service protection to insure job security for deserving workers; conservation of natural resources, but without government intervention that Roosevelt supported; and restrictions on immigration in order to monitor it effectively.

The Republican Party platform stated succinctly, "The Republican tariff policy has been of the greatest benefit to the country, developing our resources, diversifying our industries and protecting our workmen against competition with cheaper labor abroad, thus establishing for our wage earners the American standard of living."

The Democrats' view of the tariff was starkly in contrast. "The high Republican tariff is the principal cause of the unequal distribution of wealth; it is a system of taxation which makes the rich richer and the poor poorer; under its operations, the American farmer and laboring man are the chief sufferers; it raises the costs of the necessities to them but does not protect their product or wages."

Taft was adamantly opposed to women's suffrage. Roosevelt made it one of the rallying points of his campaign, prompting well-known activist Jane Addams to give a seconding speech for him at the Progressive convention. Wilson thought the women's right to vote issue should be left up to individual states to decide.

As the political campaigns moved along and the candidates honed their messages as they spoke across the country, the differences between The New Nationalism and The New Freedom diminished as both espoused reforms that would be considered "liberal" generations later while the traditional Republicans stuck with conservative values.[3]

The biggest differences were on the role of the federal government in controlling business and industry. Roosevelt called for strict government control of monopolies. Wilson sought to break up all monopolies. Roosevelt saw differences between good and bad trusts. Wilson saw no good in trusts. Wilson believed government regulation wouldn't succeed in thwarting corporate power because corporations would still be able to exercise their power to control the supposed controller—the federal government.

Roosevelt believed in letting the people rule, at least in principle—it was the main theme of his Progressive movement. But he believed the government should be the trustee of the people, overseeing the economy and being ready to pounce on any business or industry, that, in the eyes of the government, had not acted in the public interest.

In his "Confession of Faith" address, when he accepted the Progressive Party's nomination for president, Roosevelt said, "We favor cooperation in business and ask only that it be carried on in a spirit of honesty and fairness. We are against crooked business, big or little; we are in favor of honest business, big or little. We propose to penalize conduct and not size. But all very big business, even though honestly conducted is fraught with such potentiality of menace that there should be a thoroughgoing governmental control over it, so that its efficiency in promoting prosperity at home and increasing the power of the nation in international commerce may be maintained, and, at the same time, fair play insured to the wage workers, the small business competitors, the investors and the general public. Wherever it is practicable, we propose to preserve competition; but where under modern conditions, competition has been eliminated and cannot be successfully restored, then the government must step in and itself supply the needed control on behalf of the people as a whole."[4]

Wilson's platform went further than calling for government control of monopolies; it sought to end them. "A private monopoly is indefensible and intolerable," the party platform said. "We therefore favor the vigorous enforcement of the criminal as well as the civil law against trusts and trust officials, and demand the enactment of such additional legislation as may be necessary to make it impossible for a private monopoly to exist in the United States."

The Socialists' belief was spelled out in unquestionable fashion in the first two sentences of their platform. "The Socialist Party declares that the capitalist system has outgrown its historical function and has become utterly incapable of meeting the problems now confronting society. We denounce this outgrown system as incompetent and corrupt and the source of unspeakable misery and suffering to the whole working class."

The platform proclaimed that the capitalist system was responsible for poverty, slums, child labor, insanity, crime and "much of the disease that afflicts mankind."

The Socialists called for, among other things, collective ownership and

18. Vast Differences in Approach

management of railroads, telegraph services and steamboat lines; government acquisition and control of grain elevators, stockyards and other food distribution centers; and collective ownership and management of the banking and currency system.

As election day came, there would be no more speeches, no more rambling train rides, no more shouting to be heard above the crowd noise, and no more pleading, plotting and pandering for votes. The boisterous former president, the cautious, judicious, politically savvy current president, the erudite college professor and the unabashed Socialist had all bared their souls to the people, each in their own special way.

Now it was time for American democracy to once again demonstrate its innate goodness, with the whole being far greater than the sum of its parts.

It was time for the voters to decide.

19

ELECTION DAY

On October 31, President Taft wrote a letter to Frank Jamison, an old friend in Cincinnati, who had written him a note of encouragement.

On White House stationery, Taft replied:

> My dear Frank,
>
> I want you to know that I greatly appreciate the kind words of your letter of Oct. 22. I am very hopeful of the outcome but if I am to be defeated, I can stand it because I shall have been an agent in preventing the return to the White House of the third termer whose candidacy I consider a genuine menace to the welfare of our country.

As the letter implies, Taft knew he was going to lose and seemed to be comfortable with that prospect because he had been imprisoned for four years in a job he didn't like. Still, the political instinct in him gave him great pleasure in seeing that Roosevelt would not succeed.

The next day, Taft kept a commitment to be interviewed by *New York World* reporter Louis Seibold. Taft was in a good mood and seemed to be at ease with the reality that his chance for re-election was small but again expressed the hope to finish ahead of Roosevelt. He said one of his weaknesses as president was not possessing "the genius of publicity" that Roosevelt obviously had. He said, "the training of a judge is something that leads you to depend upon the opinion published and the decree entered as speaking for themselves" instead of trying to embellish them or grandstand about them.[1]

Though Taft detested how the colonel had treated him during the campaign, he seemed cautious about how he wanted to describe him for publication. He asked to see a copy of Seibold's manuscript before it was published and, because of the president's stalling, deadlines passed and it never was published.[2]

On the same day the president wrote the note to his old friend in Ohio, Roosevelt, whose activities were curtailed by a bullet, came roaring back on the campaign trail with a rousing speech before thousands of supporters at Madison Square Garden in New York. His weeks of rest gave him a chance

19. Election Day

to regain his voice and he needed it as he rallied the troops in New York City. "We propose to lift the burden from the lowly and the weary, from the poor and the oppressed. We propose to stand for the sacred rights of childhood and womanhood. Nay, more, we propose to see that manhood is not crushed out of the men who toil, by excessive hours of labor, by underpayment, by injustice and oppression.... Surely there was never a fight better worth making than this."[3]

It was vintage Roosevelt and the crowd responded with cheers. When he was done, the colonel headed back to Oyster Bay where he would be with his wife and some of his children on election night.

On Monday, November 4, the day before the election and three weeks after the attempt on Roosevelt's life, Wilson was headed home to Princeton after giving a speech in Red Bank. It marked the end of a grueling campaign in which the old professor grew weary with all the travel but enjoyed the opportunity for speaking and engaging in stimulating discourse on the issues of the day.

Now, as he headed home, he looked forward to a restful night and preparing for whatever outcomes the next day would bring. It was after midnight, the road was dark and Wilson's chauffeur did not notice a bump in the road. His vehicle bounced, jolting Wilson upward. His head rammed into the roof of the car. The force was such that his glasses were knocked off his face, breaking one of the lenses, and his head was bleeding from a gash he received. They found a doctor who closed the wound on his head. Other than being startled and having the head injury, Wilson felt no ill effects from the incident but was sensitive to having his picture taken for a while.[4]

On election morning, Wilson slept later than usual which was his intent. When he arose, he had breakfast with his family and he told them wistfully that he had done his best during the long campaign and that now his fate was "on the knees of the gods."[5]

Just past 10 a.m., he went to the Chambers Street fire station to vote. Many reporters and photographers were there. Wilson took his place in line and joked with officials and the press. When his turn came, he gave his name and address and received his ballot. Before walking into the booth, he looked out a window and pointed out to his bodyguard the boarding house where he lived more than 30 years before as a college freshman. Much like Taft had never abandoned the jurist in his soul, regardless of his other life accomplishments—including being president of the United States—Wilson was an academic, and no matter what else happened in his life, he would always be a proud Princeton man.

Taft spent the first few days in November with Nellie in New York and then took a 28-hour train ride to Cincinnati, where his illustrious career had begun, and was still his voting district. He stayed at the home of his brother

Charles where, because of so many turns of events, so many clashes that continually slashed at his jovial personality, he could find some solace in friendly territory far away from the nerve center of Washington.

Similar to Wilson, Taft slept in on election day and then enjoyed a hearty breakfast with Charles and his family. At noon, he made a quick visit to the home of Congressman Nick Longworth, a flamboyant man with an unusual political pedigree who was in a tough re-election battle. He then headed to the polling place on Madison Road, where he had cast many ballots for many years, including four years ago in his first run for president.[6]

The president stood in line with the other voters, waiting for his turn to enter the voting booth, posing for photos and chatting cheerfully with others in line. His robust stature, both physically and politically, made him the center of attention in almost any place he entered, including his home polling place, amid friends, admirers and people he did not know who just wanted to get a glimpse of him. Taft voted and then returned to his brother's home where he would await the election returns that night.

Roosevelt got up on election morning and occupied himself by sorting through his mail, determining which letters required a response or acknowledgment and which could be tossed away. At noon, he ventured to his polling place at the Oyster Bay fire station and smiled broadly as a crowd cheered him upon his arrival. The colonel waved as he entered, flashed his familiar toothy smile, posed for photos and cast his ballot. Then he and his entourage returned to Oyster Bay. The colonel and Edith took a walk in the woods that

Nicholas Longworth had an unusual political circumstance in 1912. He was a Republican congressman from Ohio whom Taft supported, yet he was Roosevelt's son-in-law, married to the colonel's daughter, Alice.

19. Election Day

afternoon, as they had done on so many other afternoons, perhaps recalling the days when the colonel frolicked with the children and taught them outdoor skills in those same woods. Then they returned home and prepared once again for the outcome of the election.

Wilson was restless when he returned home from voting. In the afternoon, he took a stroll to some of his old haunts on the Princeton campus and town. He had spent most of his adult life at Princeton, as a student, as a professor and as its president. He knew the college campus well for he had designed part of it. He had accepted many challenges on that campus and many of them may have come to mind as he ambled along and looked around, perhaps forgetting, for the moment, the great challenges that might lie ahead.

While he was gone, a telegraph ticker was set up in the family home at 25 Cleveland Lane. The telephone rang constantly that afternoon and friends, supporters and aides popped in and out of the house with well wishes, observations and predictions.

After dinner, the family retired to a sitting room to try as best they could to relax. While others sat and chatted, Wilson stood before the hearth, waiting and contemplating what the evening would bring. To kill time, he took a book of Robert Browning poems and began reading them aloud. With book in hand, he was professorial as if he was reciting for a group of students. On this night, he was reciting for himself, attempting to stave off his anxiety. His daughter Nell kept slipping out of the room to take a look at the telegraph ticker.

At about 10 p.m., the silence of the night outside was broken by a shrill but familiar sound—the clanging of bells from Nassau Hill on campus. Ellen opened the front door and saw a crowd outside. Someone shouted, "He's elected, Mrs. Wilson." The latest returns on the teletype machine offered confirmation. Wilson hugged his family and began reading telegrams as they poured in. He was the president-elect of the United States, defeating a president and a former president and becoming only the second Democrat to be elected since before the Civil War.[7]

Wilson, ever the academician, read poetry aloud in his home while he awaited results on election night.

His victory had been expected because of the split in the Republican Party. But the margin of victory was staggering. He won 40 of the 48 states; Roosevelt won 6 states; and Taft, the incumbent president, won only two, Utah and Vermont. The electoral college results were equally stunning: Wilson 435, Roosevelt 88 and Taft 8. Wilson received nearly 6.3 million votes. Roosevelt received 4.1 million and Taft got about 3.5 million. Debs, who was never considered a serious contender, received more than 900,000 votes.

Wilson's electoral college margin was the largest in American history. Roosevelt's total was also the most ever for a third-party candidate as was Debs' total for a Socialist candidate. While Wilson's victory was substantial by any mathematical standard, it was also the beneficiary of the colonel's third party run. Roosevelt and Taft's totals in the popular vote surpassed Wilson's total.

Wilson, a native southerner, won all of the southern states. He was helped by Roosevelt alienating blacks in the south, confident he would make up the difference in the Midwest and west, which didn't happen.

Roosevelt won only three Midwestern states, Michigan, Minnesota and South Dakota and two in the west California and Washington. His only other victory was in Pennsylvania. The colonel's victory in California, by less than one percent, was aided in great part because of his running mate, Johnson, the governor of California.

Other states where the margin of victory was close were Idaho, Illinois and Wyoming, all won by Wilson by less than two percent margins, and Vermont, one of only two states won by Taft, which he carried by 1.91 percent.

The top ten states with the largest margins of victory, all won by Wilson, ranged from South Carolina where the margin was an astounding 93.3 percent to North Carolina at 30.9 percent. The other eight states were also in Wilson's solid south—Mississippi, Louisiana, Texas, Florida, Georgia, Alabama, Virginia and Arkansas.

Debs was never a serious contender and, while he did not win any states, made his presence known in several of them. In Florida, he received more votes than either Taft or Roosevelt. He finished ahead of Taft in Florida, Arizona, California, Louisiana, Mississippi and Nevada. He received more than 90,000 votes in Ohio, nearly 80,000 in California and Pennsylvania, more than 60,000 in New York and more than 40,000 in Washington and Oklahoma.

The president-elect received gracious telegrams from the president and the former president.

From President Taft in Cincinnati: "I cordially congratulate you on your election and extend to you my best wishes for a successful administration."

From Theodore Roosevelt in Oyster Bay: "The American people by a great plurality have conferred upon you the highest honor in their gift. I congratulate you thereon."[8]

19. Election Day

For Taft, election night, spent quietly at his brother's home in Cincinnati, was a somber contrast to the night of his nomination when his 14-year-old son Charlie cheerily kept his parents up to date on the balloting as they awaited the results in the White House.

Roosevelt, not accustomed to losing and stung by the margin of his loss, nonetheless took the time to talk to the press, many of them newsmen who had covered his activities for years. This was one of his shortest press conferences. He called them in, read the telegram he had sent to Wilson and said, "That is all."

A few weeks later, as the holiday season approached, a member of the press suggested to Wilson that this Christmas must be the happiest of his life. "My young friend," he replied, "evidently you have never been elected president of the United States."[9]

20

Retrospect

The 1912 Republican convention, along with the events that preceded it and the election that followed it, had impacts on American politics, some obvious, some not so obvious, for generations to come.

The election holds a distinction that will likely remain by itself in American history: As previously noted, it is the only time in which a president, a former president and a future president ran against each other. It was also the first and only time in American history that an American president, seeking re-election, finished third or that a third-party candidate finished second.

The personalities of the contenders offered Americans a choice between President Taft, the rotund, conservative judge who believed in the integrity of all three branches of government; Roosevelt, the former president, former Rough Rider, and leader of the Progressives, who believed that one of the roles of the executive branch was to use its vast powers to push through reforms; and Woodrow Wilson, the tall, slender, bespectacled professor, also a champion of progressive principles who benefited from the split in the Republican party.

A fourth candidate in the mix, Eugene Debs, the Socialist who had a history of promoting or condoning violence for the sake of strengthening workers' rights, received 900,000 votes. Eight years later, in another run for the presidency, he would again receive 900,000 votes, this time while in prison.

The election of 1912 provides many "what ifs." What if Roosevelt had won? Would the old Rough Rider, always eager for a fight, have hastened America's entry into World War I? If Taft had been the victor, would he have acquiesced to the will of Congress without imposing his own will? Would winning a second term have postponed or canceled his lifelong dream of being appointed to the Supreme Court? Would a Roosevelt victory have set in motion Taft's big fear—the colonel being elected to term after term until his death?

20. Retrospect

A crowd pushes toward the entrance to the Republican National Convention as police officers at the door try to keep order.

All of these fascinating scenarios, which can never be answered, are predicated by the campaigns leading up to the Republican national convention and the raucous outcome of it.

Presidential historian Lewis Gould writes, "The contest between Theodore Roosevelt and William Howard Taft for the Republican presidential nomination culminated in one of the most tumultuous and controversial national conventions in all of the nation's history. A key participant said of the scene in the Chicago Coliseum during those June days that, for the Republicans, 'a parting of the ways was imminent'—and so it proved."[1]

Gould says a popular story line of the convention is that Roosevelt was perhaps the most popular man in America in 1912—certainly more popular than Taft, that he had proven his appeal with the people by winning nine of 13 primaries, and that the nomination was stolen from him at the convention by conniving Taft forces who used deceit, bribery and whatever other means they had at their disposal to deny Roosevelt what he believed was rightfully his. So he formed a third party, dooming the Republicans in the fall election and creating a split between moderates and conservatives that has haunted the GOP ever since.

Gould argues that the adoration for Roosevelt and portrayal of him as the victim in 1912 misses another part of the narrative that is significant. "By giving Roosevelt the sole starring role in the saga, it depicts the political loser as the winner and thus understates Taft's skill as a party politician. That Roosevelt made a series of mistakes and unwise decisions gets overlooked."[2]

In 1911, while the colonel was flirting with party leaders and the public, hoping to be invited to the dance, Taft was busy polishing the dance floor. While Roosevelt was concocting a scheme in which Republican governors, at his behest, wrote and signed a letter urging him to run, Taft's secretary, Charles Hilles, a savvy political operative, was traveling across the country lining up delegates for Taft. He also stacked the Republican National Committee with Taft supporters just in case that would come into play –and it did.

Another factor was the role of Sen. Robert LaFollette of Wisconsin, the father of the Progressive movement, who also wanted to be president. LaFollette, perhaps the best orator of all the Republican hopefuls, and who is regarded by many historians as one of the nation's greatest senators, created his own campaign doomsday with the speech in Philadelphia in early 1912 before the Newspaper Publishers Association in which the exhausted candidate lost his place in his manuscript, repeated himself continually, rambled and berated the press—the very people to whom he was speaking as their guest.

His campaign never recovered, and when Roosevelt moved in to become the darling of the Progressives, LaFollette never forgave him. Though LaFollette did not want to support the conservative Taft, he adamantly refused to do anything to help Roosevelt even after his chances for the nomination were long gone. At the convention, in hopes of appeasing LaFollette, the colonel supported Gov. Francis McGovern of LaFollette's home state for temporary chairman. But LaFollette, who was a personal friend of McGovern, rejected his candidacy because of LaFollette's disdain for Roosevelt.

When the convention started, Roosevelt and his people were outmaneuvered at every turn. They lost every attempt at delegate challenges they mounted because Taft had established firewalls of protection on every committee that could potentially have helped Roosevelt.

Still another factor that helped derail a Roosevelt candidacy was his call for judicial recall—the right of the people to overturn judicial decisions with which they disagreed. It was not only the kind of thinking that infuriated Taft, whose passion was for the judiciary, but it also chased away many who backed Roosevelt, including the influential Elihu Root. "Roosevelt had entered the race late, never fully understood how the convention rules operated, and launched his candidacy on the vote-losing issue of judicial recall."[3]

When Roosevelt and his people bolted from the convention and formed their own party, they were obsessed with their cause and could not have foreseen the devastating split it would cause in the Republican Party—and for how long it would last. "Taft fared so poorly in the election that it was evident that the conservative wing of the Republican party was a distinct, almost negligible minority."4

There is a certain irony in that while the emergence of the Progressive Party left the Republican Party in tatters in 1912, the Progressive Party itself fizzled fairly soon although its principles remained an important part of the political spectrum. "The Progressive Party itself had a brief life. When TR refused to run again in 2016, he doomed the party to the dustbin of history. Still the platform of the Progressive Party and the causes it championed would endure."5

Historians and contemporaries of Roosevelt differ on whether Roosevelt's enormous ego, his obsession with being in the public eye, his theatrics and his desire to upend Taft motivated him to act, even at the expense of the Republican Party.

As much as Taft grew to despise his old friend, the president was careful about ascribing the colonel's motives. A week before the election, Louis Siebold of the *New York World* asked Taft if Roosevelt would have bolted the party and run as a Progressive if he had foreseen what Siebold called "the wrecking of the Republican Party." Taft replied, "I cannot tell. I do not think he went into it deliberately that way." But he said Roosevelt was not a planner but someone who "acts from day to day."6

Almost exactly 100 years after the election, the *Saturday Evening Post* speculated, "Roosevelt couldn't have known that his decision to run would put Wilson into the White House.... Nor could he know that, by splitting the progressive vote, he ended its power in the Republican Party."7

Roosevelt's friend and biographer, William Roscoe Thayer wrote that Roosevelt's principles were far more important to him than any personal glory he might have achieved in the Progressive movement. "If ambition, if envy, if a selfish desire to rule had been the motives which guided him," wrote Thayer, " he would have lain low in 1912."

Thayer said Roosevelt backers within the Republican Party assured him if he would step aside in 1912, he would be assured of the Republican nomination in 1916. "But he could not be tempted. He held that the cause was more important than the individual, and he followed this idea loyally, lead where it might."8

Historian Robert Novak said the Taft-Roosevelt schism "devitalized" the Republican Party and crippled it for at least the next 50 years.9

He points out that from the end of the Civil War through the start of the 20th century, the GOP was the dominant party, winning all but two presidential elections through 1908 with Grover Cleveland being the only Democrat to win, in 1884 and 1892. Republicans overcame splits within the party—the Stalwarts and the Half-Breeds, as one example—but there was never any serious damage. In 1896, William McKinley defeated William Jennings Bryan by the largest margin ever. Roosevelt inherited that loyalty of the American people when he ascended to the presidency upon the assassination of McKinley in 1901.

Bryan lost two other bids for the presidency, causing progressive Democrats to look for an alternative and many became Republicans, thus forming a liberal—or progressive—wing of the Republican Party. Though the progressives were the new guys on the block, by 1912 they had gained strength at about the same pace that Taft, the conservative, was losing favor within the party. "Actually, the party's conservative wing was not markedly superior in numbers to the progressive wing in 1912. On the contrary, Roosevelt was so much more clearly popular than President Taft within the party that the progressive wing was probably stronger under Roosevelt's leadership than the conservative wing under Taft."[10]

So while Wilson was the beneficiary of the divided Republican Party, the conservative wing of the GOP was not interested in trying to woo the Progressives back into their tent. "The conservatives who had stayed with Taft and the Republican Party actually were delighted that the party's left wing was no longer there to bother them."[11]

The party became one that could move to its right but not to its left. Republicans won presidential elections in 1920, 1924 and 1928, not because they had unified but because the nation turned to the GOP in the aftermath of World War I. But Democrats were slowly becoming the majority party in the country.

By 1932, with the nation plunged into a Depression during the administration of Herbert Hoover, the country turned to Democrat Franklin D. Roosevelt, a distant cousin of the colonel's, who endorsed a vigorous agenda that was similar in nature to the Progressive agenda of 1912. In the space of 20 years, the Republican Party had divided while the Democrats united.

"By 1940, the Republican situation was clear enough for realistic party leaders to see. Eight years of the New Deal had confirmed the Democratic Party, now clearly identified with a left-of-center ideology, as the nation's dominant party," much like the Republicans had been for 50 years after the Civil War.[12]

Democrats, riding the crest of FDR's New Deal, won the next five presidential elections while Republicans struggled to find an identity that would unify them—and make them competitive. Dwight Eisenhower broke the Democratic stronghold in 1952 but a divided Republican Party made for a contentious convention. Eisenhower, the World War II general who was so apolitical that both parties wooed him to be their candidate, won the nomination over Senator Robert Taft of Ohio—President Taft's son—who was known as both "Mr. Republican and "Mr. Conservative." In a strange political turn-about, just as Theodore Roosevelt had accused President Taft of stealing the nomination from him, 40 years later it was Taft's son accusing the Eisenhower forces of robbing him of the nomination.

The conservative wing of the party won the GOP nomination with Senator Barry Goldwater of Arizona in 1964 but he was defeated in a Lyndon Johnson landslide. The 1964 GOP convention in San Francisco had some of the same nastiness, name-calling and violent acts that permeated the 1912 convention and exposed, for a whole nation to see on television, the deep wounds still imbedded in the party politics.

As late as 2016, Donald Trump, a former Democrat now espousing conservative principles, was nominated at yet another deeply divided convention and went on to a controversial victory in November.

Not to be lost in the events of 1912 are the significant changes it ushered in with respect to the causes that were championed and how future political campaigns were to be waged. "A century further on, the election of 1912 is still recalled as one of the most stirring in American history.... In many ways, the election marked the birth of modern presidential politics, with direct primaries; a longer campaign season; more travel by the candidates; an expanded role for the press; and greater involvement of women."[13] "In some important respects, Theodore Roosevelt's third party had a lasting effect on American politics and policy. The Bull Moose campaign gave greater credibility to innovative ideas such as an eight-hour workday, a form of social security, a federal income tax and a federal inheritance tax."[14]

Some of his Square Deal ideas were included in the "New Deal" administration of his distant cousin, Franklin Delano Roosevelt who was elected as a Democrat 20 years after Theodore Roosevelt's third-party run. "The most direct impact of Roosevelt's campaign that year, however, was his role as a midwife in the birth of presidential primaries. Even though he didn't win the Republican nomination, his campaign transformed the presidential nominating process."[15]

The 1912 Republican convention has echoes that have lasted a century. It began with the parting of the ways of two old friends who came to Washington together, often walked to work together, enjoyed each other's successes together and eventually became teammates in a presidential administration. The rupture of that relationship, at first political but increasingly personal, became the catalyst for the political circus that dramatized the convention and overshadowed anything else that took place.

There have been many conventions since then that have had their share of drama, vindictiveness and controversy. New York governor Nelson Rockefeller, a liberal, was booed so loudly by conservatives that he could not continue his speech at the Republican convention of 1964 that nominated Barry Goldwater.

California governor Ronald Reagan challenged incumbent President Gerald Ford for the nomination in 1976. Texas billionaire Ross Perot offered a third-party challenge in 1992 and, strangely, accused his political opponents of trying to disrupt his daughter's wedding. But in each instance in which there was political intrigue, parallels are drawn to the convention of 1912 but none match it for outlandishness.

Perhaps, in retrospect, it is fitting to look beyond the headlines of 1912, beyond the bluster and determine the effects on society over the years. "How little has changed over the past century. During the election campaign of 1912, the major issues included the growing divide between rich and poor, the overwhelming influence exerted by the corporations in the political process, a feeling that the political system was broken and needed to be fixed and a split in the Republican Party. Sound familiar?"[16]

21

RECONCILIATION

The Blackstone Hotel in Chicago was majestic in its splendor and in the guests it housed and entertained. Built in 1910, the 21-story building was named for Timothy Blackstone, a millionaire who was the founder of the Union Stockyards, president of the Chicago and Alton Railroad and mayor of LaSalle, Illinois, a city far enough downstate as to not be considered a suburb. The Blackstone Theater, which was a part of the complex, was famous in its own right for its contributions to the Chicago social scene.

In years to come, the Blackstone would come to be known as the "hotel of presidents" because of the number of chief executives who stayed there. It even had a special room for presidents with hollowed out walls designed for the convenience of the Secret Service.[1]

Even in its infancy, the Blackstone became a setting for meetings involving influential people making significant decisions that would affect millions of people. In 1911, Julius Rosenwald, a philanthropist who was president of the Sears & Roebuck Company met with a group that included Booker T. Washington, an African American educator who was trying to raise money to build an institution of higher learning. The result of the meeting was a commitment to the construction of the Tuskegee Institute with Rosenwald becoming one of its first trustees. And Washington was the first African American to stay at the Blackstone.

In May of 1918, former president William Howard Taft was in the midst of a speaking tour in which he traveled by train from one city to another. He was no longer caught up in the trappings of politics, which he never liked, but had settled into the more comfortable role of educator, lecturer and statesman.

The world had changed dramatically since his presidency. He had been in effect ousted from the White House by his onetime good friend Theodore Roosevelt who had showered him with insults during a nasty, unforgiving campaign in 1912. In the end, Taft suffered the indignity of being an incumbent who finished third behind Democrat Woodrow Wilson and Roosevelt.

Presidents Roosevelt and Taft, standing proudly together after Taft's election in 1908, grew to despise each other during Taft's presidency, but reconciled years later in a chance meeting at a Chicago hotel.

21. Reconciliation

While Roosevelt still enjoyed a loyal following, he was also remembered as the turncoat who bolted the Republican Party, ran as a third-party candidate and left Taft in the dust of what was, at the time, a cruel destiny. Long gone were the days when the two young men, both new to Washington, walked to work together, sharing philosophic thoughts about books they were reading or the Washington political scene or just talking about their wives and children.

Now, America was engulfed in a world war. How would the world stage have changed if the results of the 1912 election been different? It is a question that surely crossed Taft's mind as the years went by but he was not one to dwell on the past. He had never really wanted to be president anyway, having his sights set instead on having a seat on the Supreme Court.

On the evening of May 26, 1918, Taft, now a law professor at Yale University, arrived in Chicago from St. Louis, where he had given a speech. He headed for the Blackstone at 8 p.m. where he would stay overnight.

The talk among Chicagoans on this day was the same as it was most everywhere, about the war and politics and the price of eggs. But for some, there was joy in the air because that afternoon, the Chicago Cubs had defeated John McGraw's New York Giants 5–1 behind the pitching of Hippo Vaughn, to climb within two games of the first place Giants.

Baseball was a wonderful diversion for the American public, a source of entertainment in which fans could forget about the war and other troubles for a couple of hours and root for their favorite teams. But there were reminders of war even in baseball. The Cubs, for instance, had acquired the great pitcher Grover Cleveland Alexander from the Philadelphia Phillies at the start of the season in a move Cub executives surely thought would bring them a championship. But now Alexander was a soldier in Germany, dashing any pennant hopes for the Cubs.[2]

Taft was an easily recognizable figure as he entered the lobby of the Blackstone. The former president had been a guest in the past and his characteristics hadn't changed—the great hulk of his body, the flowing white moustache and a certain grace in his gait that seemed to come naturally.

Hotel attendants took special notice of him on this night with a sense of anticipation about what might or might not happen in the next few minutes. For Colonel Roosevelt was in the house. The only two living former presidents were in the same place at the same time, purely by happenstance, and it was only fitting that Taft be informed of the occasion. Roosevelt was in the dining area alone, having a meal, Taft was told.

Without hesitation, he headed up the few steps to the dining room to get a glimpse of the man who was once his friend but had become his political assassin.

Taft surveyed the room full of people eating their dinners and engaging in chit-chat that created a buzzing that occurs when numerous conversations are taking place all at once, making them noisy but unintelligible. A blue-gray haze emanated toward the ceiling from the cigars and cigarettes of the patrons.

Taft spotted his old friend-turned-nemesis eating his dinner at a small table on the other side of the room. As he headed toward the table, the idle conversations of the other patrons began to subside as they saw what was about to happen.

The colonel had his head down, preoccupied for the moment with his meal. Then he looked up and saw Taft approaching his table. "He stiffened in surprise, then flung his napkin down and rose. He met Mr. Taft's handshake with one that equaled it. Mr. Taft's left hand flew to the colonel's shoulder, a gesture which the colonel returned."[3]

The dining room quieted as patrons watched almost in awe at the unexpected reunion of the two former presidents. They continued to shake hands vigorously as they talked and slapped each other on the back. "The crowd went wild and a cheer went up that startled them. They looked at each other and smiled and bowed to the other diners."[4]

Then, at Roosevelt's invitation, Taft sat down and joined him and the two men talked for about a half-hour. Roosevelt continued to eat his dinner as they talked, sometimes flashing that toothy grin that was so familiar to so many and once or twice pounding the table to make a point. For his part, Taft from time to time leaned forward toward the colonel to punctuate his sentence. Roosevelt's laugh was hearty and could be heard across the room. Taft was more apt to smile, chuckle and sometimes even giggle but was quieter and more stoic than the colonel.

At 9 o'clock, Roosevelt rose and said his good-byes, explaining he had to catch a train to Des Moines where he would be speaking the next day. Taft retired to his room for the night. Neither chose to share with the press much about what they talked about.

Roosevelt said it was good to see Taft and that he was looking "bully." Taft said their conversation was on "general things" and that he was glad to see Roosevelt looking well after a recent illness.

The *New York Times* reflected on the unusual reunion. "The temperamental differences between the two men reached a climax six years ago in the temporary wreck of the Republican Party and the reconciliation occurred not six blocks from the coliseum, the scene of the convention of 1912."[5]

Nine months later, in the early morning hours of January 6, 1919, Roosevelt died at his home in Oyster Bay. He was 60 years old. In Washington, Vice President Thomas Marshall said, "Death had to take him sleeping, for if Roosevelt had been awake, there would have been a fight."

Taft was among 500 guests invited to the colonel's funeral, a private

21. Reconciliation

service that was to include Roosevelt's oldest and dearest friends. Their meeting at the Blackstone seemed to have completed the circle that had begun so long ago when the two were young up-and-comers in Washington.

Two years later, President Warren Harding appointed Taft as chief justice of the United States. When he was elected president in 1908, Taft achieved his wife's dream for him and for herself. With his appointment to the high court, he had risen to the dream he always had for himself.

In 1922, George H. Lorimer, publisher of the *Saturday Evening Post*, came into possession of letters Roosevelt had sent to President Taft during the bitter campaign of 1912. The letters represented a treasure of documentation of the political war between the two men. Naturally, Lorimer wanted to publish the letters but, as a courtesy, wrote to now-Chief Justice Taft informing him of the recently found letters.

On October 10, 1922, Taft wrote back to Lorimer, saying, "I now cherish no ill will at all toward Theodore Roosevelt. There were times when I perhaps could not have said so, especially when his action seemed to require me to leave the White House to go out onto the stump to rebut his charges. But all that has gone into the past, and in his silence and inability to answer, I do not wish to appear to be reviving the discussion." Lorimer granted Taft's request to not publish the material.

Taft served as chief justice for nine years before retiring in 1930. He may have remembered his lament 17 years earlier, when he was president, that he wished justices would retire when they knew they were at the end of the road, instead of dying on the job, forcing presidents to offer hurried, sometimes disingenuous off-the-cuff words of tribute. Taft died a month after his retirement.

His letter of resignation to President Herbert Hoover, dated February 3, 1930, was in typical Taft style. Instead of providing any retrospect on his illustrious career which was coming to an end, Taft focused on the present and on what he thought he was entitled to for those years of service.

My dear Mr. President,

I am desirous of accepting the privilege and benefits which the Act of March 1, 1929, chapter 419, 45 Stat. 1422 accords to judges of the United States who have held commissions as such judges for at least 10 years, whether continuously or otherwise, and have attained the age of 70 years; and to that end I hereby resign my commission and office as Chief Justice of the United States.

From 1892 to 1900, I held a commission as a circuit judge for the Sixth Circuit of the United States and from 1921 to the present time I have held a commission and served as Chief Justice of the United States, making a total of more than ten years under the two commissions; and I now have attained the age of more than 70 years. Thus the conditions named in the statute are all present. This resignation is intended to take effect immediately upon its acceptance by you. With great respect, I am very truly yours, William H. Taft.

Upon his death, Will Rogers, the noted humorist, paid tribute to Taft, writing, "It's great to be great but it's greater to be human. We are parting with 300 pounds of solid charity to everyone, and love and affection for all his fellow men."[6]

The Taft-Roosevelt-Wilson era in American politics is filled with factual oddities. Roosevelt was the man who craved public office. His successor led a life in which public office seemed to crave him. In the 1912 election, Wilson, a former educator, defeated both Roosevelt and Taft. The defeated president then accepted a teaching position. Pundits pointed out that the professor had become a president while the president had become a professor.

Another oddity occurred in the Taft family legacy. While William Howard Taft had never sought public office until he ran for president, his descendants had no qualms about running for office. A son, Charles P. Taft, II, was elected mayor of Cincinnati. Another son, Robert A. Taft, Sr., was a longtime senator from Ohio who sought the Republican presidential nomination three times. The president's grandson, Robert A. Taft, Jr., son of the senator, was also a U.S. senator from Ohio. A great grandson of the president, Robert A. Taft, III, was governor of Ohio from 1999 to 2007.

Another oddity occurred 40 years after the 1912 convention in which Roosevelt believed Taft and his people stole the nomination from him. In 1952, Senator Robert A. Taft, Sr., the president's eldest son, who was known as "Mr. Republican" and represented the conservative wing of the party, sought the Republican nomination for the third and last time. In a convention in which there were many delegate challenges, the nomination went to Dwight D. Eisenhower, an Army general and war hero, who was a political moderate. This time it was the Taft forces claiming the nomination had been stolen from them. There were no guns in the convention hall and no fist fights in the aisles, but it was clear that the divisions within the Republican Party, so brazenly on display in 1912, still managed to climb back into the political spotlight.

Epilogue

Woodrow Wilson served two terms as president, led the nation through World War I and worked tirelessly and, in the end, unsuccessfully, to create a League of Nations whose purpose would be to help prevent another world war.

He suffered a stroke during his second term that limited his ability to serve. His second wife, Edith, is said to have made many executive decisions for him in an effort to hide the seriousness of his illness from the public and public officials. His illness also prevented him from running for a third term, a prospect he had contemplated.

Out of office, in 1921, he opened a law office in Washington with former Secretary of State Bainbridge Colby but found the work unsatisfying. The office closed in 1922. Wilson wrote extensively and had several works published on American history and on foreign affairs.

Despite his poor health, he hinted at seeking the Democratic nomination for president in 1924 but it was not to be. He died on February 3, 1924 at the age of 67.

President Theodore Roosevelt was seen as the Progressive candidate for president in 1916 but turned down the nomination and instead supported the Republican candidate, Supreme Court Justice Charles Evans Hughes, the former governor of New York.

After losing the presidential election in 1912, the colonel once again became an explorer, a habit that defined how he lived and thrived—having no time to waste on regrets. He and a party of about 20 went on a dangerous excursion in South America, traveling on the Paraguay River through unexplored areas of Central Brazil. "The peril of being swept over the falls was always imminent and, as the trail that constituted their portages had to be cut through the matted forest, their labors were increased."[1]

At one point, Roosevelt became deathly ill and could not continue. He urged his companions to move on, to leave him to die but they refused. In a few days, his strength returned enough so that he could resume the journey but lingering ailments from the Brazilian adventure stayed with him for the rest of his life.

During his political retirement, Roosevelt was involved in two lawsuits

Roosevelt is shown during a 1912 campaign rally in Oyster Bay, where he had lived since 1885 and where he died in 1919.

in which he fought as vigorously to preserve his reputation as he would have on any battlefield or political crisis. Both involved libel suits, one brought against him and one he initiated. In October of 1912, less than a month before the election, George Newett, publisher of a trade journal, wrote that Roosevelt was a liar who cursed a lot and was frequently drunk. Roosevelt, of course, was accustomed to blasphemy for political purposes but he was incensed at the accusation of drunkenness, fearing that was rumor that could stick if it went unchallenged.

The colonel and his legal team produced 40 witnesses who had known Roosevelt for all or most of his adult life and had never seen him drunk. As the evidence and testimony piled up, Newett admitted his report was based totally on hearsay and apologized to Roosevelt. The colonel sought no damages, saying he received what he wanted most—his reputation back intact.

In the other libel suit, Roosevelt was the defendant. He supported Harvey Hinman, the Progressive candidate for governor of New York in 1914. During the campaign, Roosevelt alleged that William Barnes, who controlled the Republican machine in the state, had engaged in illegal activities and had even worked with Democrats to line his own pocket. Barnes sued. In court, Roosevelt and his lawyers proved Barnes had profited from illegal campaign advertising and conspired illegally to have his way on legislation and elections. A jury ruled in favor of Roosevelt.

A last defining moment for Roosevelt came in 1917 after America's entry into World War I. The colonel, now 59 years old, petitioned President Wilson to allow him to lead a regiment of soldiers on the front lines overseas. Wilson declined, saying it was a military decision rather than anything personal. Roosevelt's reaction: It was personal.

His old friend Elihu Root told him, "Theodore, if you will promise to die there, Wilson will give you any commission you want, tomorrow."[2]

Some Progressives wanted him to be their candidate in 1920. While the colonel rarely turned down an opportunity to fight for what he believed was right, his health was failing and it is doubtful he would have accepted a candidacy. He never got the opportunity for he died in his sleep in January of 1919.

William Howard Taft, whose career was shaped more by public office seeking him rather than the other way around, became a professor of law and legal history at the Yale University Law School and also earned an income through making speeches and writing magazine articles. In 1916, his work *The Chief Magistrate and his Powers* was published. He served as chairman of the American Bar Association and the American Red Cross.

While he was president, he was chairman of the Lincoln Memorial Commission, the organization responsible for overseeing the construction and maintenance of the Lincoln Memorial. When he was out of office and Democrats tried to remove him from the commission, Taft reportedly said, "Unlike losing the presidency, this one would hurt." He was retained.[3]

Taft broke from many Republicans in backing President Wilson on America's entry into World War I and also the proposed League of Nations.

In 1921, President Warren Harding gave him the opportunity to fulfill a lifetime ambition by appointing him chief justice of the United States. He held that position until ill health prompted him to resign in 1930, not long before his death.. For Taft, his days on the high court were the most fulfilling days of his public career. "The truth is," he wrote after his first four years on the court—matching his time as president, "that in my present life, I don't remember that I ever was president." He was said to be amused one day as he walked to the Supreme Court building when a youngster approached him and said, "I know who you are. You used to be Calvin Coolidge."[4]

Eugene Debs continued promoting his Socialist agenda but his political popularity peaked in 1912 when he received 900,000 votes, 5.9 percent of the total vote. He ran for president again in 1920, his fifth and final time and got less than 4 percent, perhaps because he was serving a prison term. He had been convicted of violating the Sedition Act in 1918 for denouncing America's participation in World War I and sentenced to ten years in prison. President Warren Harding commuted Debs' sentence in 1921. He died in 1926.

Robert LaFollette, one of the earliest proponents of Progressivism, and who detested Roosevelt for taking the limelight away from him, remained in the Senate until his death in 1925, He was an outspoken opponent of America's entry into World War I and of the League of Nations. In 1924, LaFollette tried to resurrect the Progressive movement by running for president as a Progressive but finished a distant third in a race won by Republican Calvin Coolidge.

LaFollette is regarded as one of the Senate's most influential members whose legacy has been recognized long after his death. In 1957, a Senate committee named him as one of the five greatest senators along with Henry Clay, Daniel Webster, John Calhoun and Robert Taft (son of President Taft). In 1982, in a survey of American historians, LaFollette and Henry Clay were rated as the greatest senators.

Elihu Root, who was chairman of the Republican National Convention, was a distinguished statesman who served his country in a number of capacities. He served as secretary of war for two presidents, McKinley and Roosevelt and also served as Roosevelt's secretary of state. In 1912, the year he chaired the convention, he was serving as a U.S. senator from New York. That was also the year he was awarded the Nobel Peace Prize for his work in attempting to bring world powers together to keep the peace.

In 1916, when he was 71 years old, he received 103 votes on the first ballot for the presidential nomination eventually won by Charles Evans Hughes.

Epilogue

In 1917, President Woodrow Wilson sent Root to Russia to try to establish an alliance with the new revolutionary government that had formed there. He served as president of the Carnegie Endowment for International Peace from 1910 to 1925. At the start of World War I, Root was against Wilson's policy of neutrality but supported him when the U.S. entered the war.

He was the founding chairman of the Council on Foreign Relations which was formed in New York in 1918 and still exists today. He supported the League of Nations, which never came to be, and served on a commission which created the Permanent Court of International Justice. Root died in 1937 in New York City at the age of 91.

Like Root, Charles Evans Hughes was a distinguished statesman who served in many roles in government and the judiciary. He was governor of New York and had just been appointed to the Supreme Court by President Taft when he sought Roosevelt's help in accomplishing one more thing before leaving state government. Roosevelt had just returned from his safari after leaving office and was itching to get back into political forays. Hughes wanted New York to adopt the direct primary system for elections and enlisted Roosevelt's help to make it happen. Their efforts failed but the experience enhanced their respect for one another.

Hughes served as governor from 1907 to 1910 when he was appointed to the Supreme Court. He served as an associate justice on the court but resigned in 1916 when the Republican Party nominated him as its candidate for president. He received the endorsement of both Taft and Roosevelt and by the Progressive Party. But California Gov. Hiram Johnson believed Hughes had slighted him by missing an appointment with him and refused to endorse Hughes. He lost the election to President Woodrow Wilson by 23 electoral votes, including California's 13, which was the decisive factor.

Hughes chose not to seek the nomination in 1920 but his departure from public service was short-lived. In 1921, he became President Warren Harding's secretary of state and remained in that position under President Calvin Coolidge after Harding's death. He returned to private life in 1925 and rejoined his law firm in New York. In the next five years, he argued more than 50 cases before the Supreme Court.

In 1930, President Herbert Hoover appointed Hughes as chief justice of the United States. He replaced former President William Howard Taft who had appointed Hughes to the court 20 years earlier. He served in that capacity until his retirement in 1941. He died on August 27, 1948 at the age of 86.

Gifford Pinchot was the first director of the United States Forest Service, a department created by President Theodore Roosevelt. Both men had a passion for conservation of the nation's lands. It was the dismissal of Pinchot in the Taft administration over a policy dispute that helped trigger Roosevelt's wrath for Taft and his entry into the 1912 presidential race.

Pinchot remained active in conservation and founded the National Conservation Commission which he headed from 1910 to 1925. He supported Roosevelt's bid for the presidency in 1912 and ran unsuccessfully on the Progressive ticket for the U.S. Senate from Pennsylvania in 1914.

Pinchot returned to the Republican Party and was elected governor of Pennsylvania in 1923. At that time, Pennsylvania governors were prohibited from running for a second consecutive term. In 1926, he made a second try to win a U.S. Senate seat but lost in the Republican primary.

Four years later, Pinchot ran again for governor and won in a contentious election in which he claimed he was the victim of vote fraud. After much legal wrangling, the state Supreme Court ruled Pinchot as the winner. In 1934, having completed his term as governor, Pinchot made a third try for the U.S. Senate, once again losing in the primary. His final campaign, in 1938, was an unsuccessful attempt for a third term as governor. He died on October 4, 1946 at the age of 81.

Richard Ballinger was mayor of Seattle when President Roosevelt appointed him as commissioner of the General Land Office, a position he held from 1907 to 1908 when Roosevelt left office. In 1909, President Taft appointed Ballinger as secretary of the interior, replacing James R. Garfield, a Roosevelt appointee. He became involved in a huge political battle when he took actions to rescind Roosevelt policies regarding government control of public lands. Roosevelt's motive was to keep large corporations from purchasing lands and ruining conservation of them.

The Taft administration believed the government abused its power by controlling land use. That rift and other issues led to the dismissal of Forestry Chief Gifford Pinchot and resulted in a congressional investigation, instigated by Pinchot, of previous land deals Ballinger had made that supposedly benefited Ballinger's friends. Ballinger was exonerated of any wrong doing but his reputation in Washington had been sullied. He returned to Seattle and resumed his law practice. He died on June 6, 1922, at the age of 63.

Joe Cannon, "Uncle Joe" as he was known, the iron-fisted speaker of the House of Representatives who disliked Roosevelt's arrogance and Taft's timidness, is considered by historians to be one of the most dominant House speakers in history. He served 46 non-consecutive years in the House, beginning in 1873 and ending in 1923.

Cannon still holds the record as the longest serving Republican congressman. His portrait graced the cover of *Time* magazine's first edition on March 23, 1923. He died in 1936 at his home in Danville, Illinois, at the age of 90.

Jonathan Bourne, the Oregon Progressive who advocated primary elections and tried to persuade Roosevelt to run in 1908, had been elected to the Senate through a direct primary system in 1906, lost the Republican primary in 1912 and ran unsuccessfully as a third party candidate. He served as president of the National Republican Progressive League and worked in the newspaper industry until his death in 1940 at the age of 85.

Joseph M. Dixon, the senator from Montana who was Roosevelt's campaign manager at the GOP convention and chaired the National Progressive Convention that nominated Roosevelt, lost his bid for re-election later that year. He returned to Montana and looked after his business interests. In 1920, he was elected governor, defeating Democratic candidate Burton K. Wheeler. He lost his bid for re-election in 1924. In 1928, he ran for the U.S. Senate, this time losing to Wheeler. In 1929, President Herbert Hoover appointed him first assistant secretary of the interior, a position he held until 1933 when Hoover left office. He returned to Montana and died May 22, 1934, at the age of 66.

Perry Howard and Sidney Redmond, black activists from Mississippi whose credentials were denied at the Republican convention and then were shunned by Roosevelt when he banned southern blacks from being Progressive delegates, both led productive lives well beyond 1912.

Redmond became a bank president and real estate developer who at one time owned nearly 100 homes and was considered one of the wealthiest black men in the United States. When he died in 1948, his estate was valued at $604,000 which would be about $20 million in today's dollars.[5]

Howard remained active in Republican politics for the rest of his life but was criticized by many influential blacks for being more interested in personal gain than in the success of the black movement. By 1924, he was elected as a Republican national committeeman from Mississippi and was appointed as a special assistant to Harry Daugherty, President Harding's attorney general. He reportedly used his influence to get federal jobs for many of his cronies and was indicted but never convicted for selling some of those jobs. Through it all, his law firm, Cobb, Howard & Hayes, remained one of the leading black law firms in Washington. He died on February 1, 1961.[6]

Theodore Roosevelt, Jr., who, in his father's 1912 Progressive campaign dismissed southern blacks, saying "the majority have no intelligence at all" had a change of heart in his later years. He served in France in the war and, upon his return to the states, helped form the American Legion, an organization to support troops returning home. He considered the American Legion a brotherhood that should not be segregated, a view not shared by the majority of Legion members. He was active in civil rights activities for the rest of his life, serving on the board of Howard College and being elected to the board of the National Association for the Advancement of Colored People (NAACP).

He tried his hand at politics, serving in the New York Legislature and running unsuccessfully for governor in 1924. In 1929, President Herbert

Hoover appointed him as governor of Puerto Rico and three years later appointed him as governor-general of the Philippines, the same post Taft had held a generation earlier.

Where Roosevelt, Jr., really proved to be his father's son was in the military where he served as a battalion commander in France in World War I and earned the Medal of Honor for his bravery as a general leading troops on the beaches of Normandy on D-Day, June 6, 1944. At age 56, he was the oldest soldier at Normandy. He died of a heart attack there about a month after the invasion, on July 12, 1944.

Herbert S. Hadley, the affable Missouri governor who was floor manager for Roosevelt at the Republican convention, chose not to join the Progressive movement and remained with the Republican Party. The former attorney general of Missouri served one term as governor, leaving office in 1913. He never ran for elective office again. When he left office, he resumed his law practice. In 1917, he moved to Colorado and was a law professor at the University of Colorado for six years. He returned to his home state in 1923 to become chancellor of Washington University in St. Louis, a position he held until his death in 1927.

Hiram Johnson, the flamboyant California governor, early proponent of Progressivism and Roosevelt's running mate on the Progressive ticket, served six years as governor and then was elected to the United States Senate in 1917. After Roosevelt's death in 1919, many Progressives believed Johnson was the natural national Progressive leader and urged him to run for president in 1920. He did—but as a Republican. He sought the GOP nomination but lost to fellow U.S. Sen. Warren Harding of Ohio. Johnson declined to be considered as a vice presidential nominee. In addition to his choice to run as a Republican, another unusual factor in Johnson's campaign was his lack of support from Roosevelt's family. They supported General Leonard Wood, one of the colonel's best friends dating back to their Spanish American War days.[7]

Johnson sought the GOP nomination again in 1924 but was stymied when he lost the California primary to President Calvin Coolidge, who had been Harding's vice president and took office upon Harding's death. Johnson remained in the Senate for almost 30 years and died in 1945 at the age of 78.

One of the reforms he championed as governor of California—the recall of public officials—became a focal point nearly a century later when voters ousted California governor Gray Davis in 2003. That launched the political career of the man elected to replace Davis, body builder and movie star Arnold Schwarzenegger.

Charles D. Hilles, President Taft's secretary who worked tirelessly to raise money and round up delegates in Taft's re-nomination battle with Roosevelt, did not get actively involved in national politics until he was 42 years old. He was an Ohio native who was financial officer and superintendent of the Boys Industrial School of Ohio for 22 years and then moved to New York to become superintendent and then president of the New York Juvenile Asylum.

His administrative skills drew the attention of the Taft administration and he was appointed assistant secretary of the treasury in 1909. Two years later, Taft hired him as his personal secretary where, among other things, he oversaw Taft's fight against Roosevelt for the nomination.

Hilles continued his late-blooming political career as chairman of the Republican National Committee from 1912 to 1916 and was a New York delegate to the Republican National Convention for five straight conventions from 1916 to 1932 and again in 1940. He died in New York in 1949 at the age of 82.

Chase Osborn, the Michigan governor who got six other governors to sign a letter of support for Roosevelt—at Roosevelt's request—served two years as governor, from 1911 to 1913, and did not seek re-election. In 1915, he tried to regain the governorship but lost to his successor, Woodbridge Ferris. In 1918, Osborn lost in the Republican primary in his quest for a U.S. Senate seat.

Despite not being in public office, Osborn was highly respected in the Republican Party. In 1928, his name was placed in nomination to be Herbert Hoover's running mate on the GOP presidential ticket but lost to Charles Curtis. He made one more try for the U.S. Senate in 1930 but lost in the primary.

Osborn had an unusual personal life. In 1924, he hired a woman named Stellanova Brunt as his researcher and secretary. Seven years later, Osborn and his wife Lillian legally adopted Stellanova, who was 37, and she changed her last time to that of her adoptive parents. In his later years, after Lillian Osborn died, she became his fulltime nurse. Osborn arranged to have the adoption annulled. In April of 1949, the two were married. He was 89. She was 54. Two days after the marriage, Osborn died.

Frank Knox, the newspaper publisher who fought with Roosevelt as a member of the Rough Riders in the Spanish American War and later backed him in his third-party bid for the presidency, has the distinction of also serving President Franklin D. Roosevelt.

Knox was one of the Republicans who walked out of the 1912 convention and joined the Progressive movement for Roosevelt. But after that, he returned to the Republican Party and was an influential newspaper publisher for many years. He founded the *Manchester Leader* in New Hampshire which later became the *New Hampshire Union Leader*, an influential newspaper that was (and is) politically conservative. In 1930, Knox became co-owner of the *Chicago Daily News*.

He remained active in Republican politics and was the Republican candidate for vice president in 1936 with Governor Alf Landon of Kansas leading the ticket. They lost in a landslide to FDR who was elected to a second term. In 1940, when Roosevelt was trying to develop bi-partisan support for his foreign policy, he appointed Knox secretary of the Navy. Knox became an influential figure in the war effort in World War II and was a strong proponent of incarcerating Japanese Americans. He died while still in office in Washington on April 28, 1944, at the age of 70.

George Perkins was a millionaire banker who agreed to finance Roosevelt's 1912 Progressive presidential campaign, sealing the colonel's decision to run. Perkins joined the Progressive movement in 1910 and, because of his wealth and influence, became its national chairman. When Roosevelt declined to be the Progressive candidate in 1916, Perkins supported Charles Evans Hughes, the Republican candidate. Historians believe that contributed to the steady decline of the Progressive Party.

As a businessman and financier, Perkins believed in cooperation rather than competition among the nation's big businesses, putting him at odds with many Progressives who believed in the benefits of trust busting. Perkins used his influence in many positive civic efforts, including the raising of $200,000 to help the stability of the Young Men's Christian Association. He died in New York in 1920 at the age of 58.

John M. Parker was a Louisiana politician and a supporter of Roosevelt who believed Roosevelt should exclude southern blacks from being delegates to the Progressive national convention. Parker was a Progressive in a staunchly Democratic state and that hurt his own political ambitions. He ran for governor as a Progressive in 1916 and lost to a Democrat. He ran again in 1920, this time as a Democrat, and won. He served one term before retiring. Parker died in 1939 at the age of 76.

James Beauchamp "Champ" Clark of Missouri, succeeded "Uncle Joe" Cannon as speaker of the House and was the leading candidate for the Democratic nomination for president going into the convention of 1912. The GOP had already nominated Taft for a second term and Roosevelt and his supporters were mounting a challenge on the soon-to-be-formed Progressive or "Bull Moose" ticket. But Clark lost the nomination on the 46th ballot to Woodrow Wilson and never sought higher office again.

He remained as House speaker until 1919 and was outspoken on many issues. When President Taft was trying to gain approval for a reciprocity agreement with Canada, Clark gave a speech on the House floor supporting it but implying it would be almost like the U.S. annexing its neighbor to the north. Canadians rejected the agreement. Clark was also an opponent of the Federal Reserve Bank and of the U.S. entry into World War I. He was a victim of Republican landslide elections in 1920, losing his House seat. He died in March of 1921 on the day before he was to leave office.

Epilogue 187

U.S. Sen. Albert Cummins of Iowa, whose name was placed in nomination for president at the Republican convention in 1912, along with Taft, Roosevelt and LaFollette, had been Iowa governor from 1902 to 1908 and served in the Senate from 1908 to 1926. He received 10 delegate votes in 1912. He sought the nomination again in 1916 and finished fifth among 12 candidates on the first ballot.

Supreme Court Justice Charles Evans Hughes won the nomination but lost to Woodrow Wilson in the general election. In 1926, Cummins sought re-election to the Senate but was defeated in the Republican primary and died a month later. While in the Senate, he served as president pro tempore from 1919 to 1925, making him third in line for the presidency.

Henry Allen, who read Roosevelt's statement to delegates after the colonel lost the Republican nomination in 1912, was a publisher of several newspapers, including the *Wichita Daily Beacon* in Kansas. He stayed active in Republican politics and was elected Kansas governor in 1919 and re-elected in 1921. He did not seek a third term. In 1929, he was appointed to fill a vacancy in the U.S. Senate and served for two years.

Nicholas Murray Butler, who, for five days in 1912, was President Taft's running mate, remained as president of Columbia University until 1945—a 43-year tenure. During his time, the university's enrollment rose from 4,000 to 34,000 and became one of the most distinguished schools in the country.

He was a delegate to every Republican convention from 1886 to 1936 and was an adviser to seven presidents. In 1916, he actively supported Elihu Root as a candidate for the Republican nomination eventually won by Hughes. He sought the nomination for himself in 1920, losing to Warren Harding, and in 1928, losing to Herbert Hoover.

He remained active in scholarly and literary circles and served on the Pulitzer Prize board. Always self-confident and effusive, in 1941 he persuaded other Pulitzer jurors to reverse their decision to award the prize for literary fiction to Ernest Hemingway for *For Whom the Bell Tolls* because he found it offensive. No prize for fiction was awarded that year. Butler died in 1947 at the age of 85.

Thomas Marshall, the Indiana governor who became Woodrow Wilson's running mate as a result of a deal made the Democratic convention to secure Indiana's delegates for Wilson, served two terms as vice president was not popular with the Wilson inner circle and was often left out of decision-making. In fact, when Wilson became seriously ill, his family did not keep Marshall informed of the president's condition because they did not want him to try to take over.

When he completed his two terms as vice president, Marshall returned to Indiana where he opened a law firm. He wrote several books and a memoir. He died in 1925 at the age of 71.

Marshall was known around Washington for his quick wit. As vice president, one day when he was presiding over the Senate, there was a great debate going on about the American economy. Marshall broke the tension by uttering, "What this country needs is a good five-cent cigar."

Appendix A: 1912 Republican Primary Results

Date	State	Taft	Roosevelt	LaFollette
March 19	North Dakota	3.1%	39.7%	57.2%
March 26	New York	66.4%	33.6%	0%
April 2	Wisconsin	26.1%	0.3%	73.2%
April 9	Illinois	29.2%	61.1%	9.8%
April 13	Pennsylvania	40.3%	59.7%	0%
April 19	Nebraska	21.5%	58.7%	17.1%
April 19	Oregon	28.5%	40.2%	31.3%
April 30	Massachusetts	50.4%	48.3%	1.2%
May 5	Maryland	47.2%	52.8%	0%
May 14	California	27.3%	54.6%	18.1%
May 21	Ohio	39.5%	55.3%	5.2&
May 28	New Jersey	40.5%	56.3%	3.2%
June 4	South Dakota	28.9%	55.2%	15.9%

Appendix B: 1912 Democratic Party Platform (Summary)

We, the representatives of the Democratic Party of the United States, in national convention assembled, reaffirm our devotion of Democratic government formulated by Thomas Jefferson and enforced by a long and illustrious line of Democratic presidents.

Tariff Reform

We declare it to be a fundamental principle of the Democratic Party that the federal government, under the Constitution, has no right or power to collect tariff duties except for the purpose of revenue and we demand that the collection of such taxes shall be limited to the necessities of government honestly and economically administered.

The Republican tariff is the principal cause of the unequal distribution of wealth; it is a system of taxation which makes the rich richer and the poor poorer; under its operations, the American farmer and laboring man are the chief sufferers; it raises the cost of the necessaries of life to them but does not protect their product or wages. The farmer sells largely in free markets and buys almost entirely in protective markets. In the most highly protected industries, such as cotton and wool, and steel and iron, the wages of the laborers are the lowest paid in any of our industries. We denounce the Republican pretense on that subject and assert that American wages are established by competitive conditions and not by the tariff.

We favor the immediate downward revision of the existing high and in many cases prohibitive tariff duties, insisting that material reductions be speedily made upon the necessaries of life. Articles entering into competition with trust-controlled products and articles of American manufacture which are sold abroad more cheaply than at home should be put upon the free list.

We recognize that our system of tariff taxation is intimately connected with the business of the country and we favor the ultimate attainment of the principles we advocate by legislation that will not injure or destroy legitimate industry.

We denounce the action of President Taft in vetoing the bills to reduce the tariff in the cotton, woolen, metals and chemicals schedules and the farmers free bill, all of which were designed to give immediate relief to the masses from the exactions of the trusts.

The Republican Party, while promising tariff revision, has shown by its tariff legislation that such revision is not to be in the people's interest, and having been faithless to its pledges of 1908, it should not longer enjoy the confidence of the nation. We appeal to the American people to support us in our demand for a tariff for revenue only.

High Cost of Living

The high cost of living is a serious problem in every American home. The Republican Party, in its platform, attempts to escape from responsibility for present conditions by denying that they are due to a protective tariff. We take issue with them on this subject and charge that excessive prices result in a large measure from the high tariff laws enacted and maintained by the Republican Party and from trusts and commercial conspiracies fostered and encouraged by such laws, and we assert that no substantial relief can be secured for the people until import duties on the necessaries of life are materially reduced and these criminal conspiracies broken up.

Anti-Trust Law

A private monopoly is indefensible and intolerable. We therefore favor the vigorous enforcement of the criminal as well as the civil law against trusts and trust officials and demand that enactment of such additional legislation as may be necessary to make it impossible for a private monopoly to exist in the United States. We demand enactment of such additional legislation as may be necessary to make it impossible for a private monopoly to exist in the United States.

States Rights

Believing that the most efficient results under our system of government are to be attained by the full exercise by the states of their reserved sovereign powers, we denounce as usurpation the efforts of our opponents to deprive the states of any of the rights reserved to them.

Direct Election of Senators

We support the proposed constitutional amendment.

Federal Income Tax

We support the proposed constitutional amendment.

Presidential Primary

We direct the National Committee to incorporate in the call for the next nominating convention a requirement that all expressions of preference for presidential candidates shall be given and the selection of delegates and alternates made through a primary election conducted by the party organizations in each state.

Campaign Contributions

We pledge the Democratic Party to the enactment of a law prohibiting any corporation from contributing to a campaign fund and any individual from contributing any amount above a reasonable maximum.

Term of President

We favor a single presidential term and to that end urge the adoption of an amendment to the Constitution making the president of the United State ineligible to re-election and we pledge the candidates to this convention to this principle.

Democratic Congress

We call the attention of the patriotic citizens of our country to its record of efficiency, economy and constructive legislation.

Republican Extravagance

We denounce the profligate waste of money wrung from the people by the oppressive taxation through the lavish appropriations of recent Republican congresses which have kept taxes high and reduced the purchasing power of the people's toil.

Railroads, Express Companies, Telegraph and Telephone Lines

We favor the efficient supervision and rate regulation of railroads, express companies, telegraph and telephone lines engaged in interstate commerce. We favor such legislation as will effectively prohibit the railroads, express, telegraph and telephone companies from engaging in business which brings them into competition with their shippers or patrons; also legislation preventing the over-issue of stocks and bonds.

Banking Legislation

We oppose the so-called Aldrich Bill or the establishment of a central bank; and we believe our country will be largely freed from panics and subsequent unemployment and business depression by such a systematic revision of our banking laws as will render temporary relief in localities where such relief is needed, with protection from control of dominion by what is known as the money trust.

Rural Credits

We recommend that an investigation of agricultural credit societies in foreign countries be made so that it may be ascertained whether a system of rural credits may be devised suitable to conditions in the United States; and we also favor legislation permitting national banks to loan a reasonable proportion of their funds on real estate security.

Waterways

We renew the declaration in our last platform relating to the conservation of our natural resources and the development of our waterways. We hold that the control of the Mississippi River is a national problem. The preservation of the depths of its waters for the purpose of navigation, the building of levees to maintain the integrity of its channel and the prevention of the overflow of the land and its consequent devastation, resulting in the interruption of interstate commerce, the disorganization of the mail service and the enormous loss of life and property impose an obligation which alone can be discharged by the general government.

Post Roads

We favor national aid to state and local authorities in the construction and maintenance of post roads.

Rights of Labor

We pledge the Democratic Party to the enactment of a law creating a Department of Labor, represented separately in the president's cabinet in which department shall be included the subject of mines and mining. We pledge the Democratic Party, so far as the federal jurisdiction extends, to an employees compensation law providing adequate indemnity for injury to body or loss of life.

Conservation

We believe in the conservation and the development, for the use of all the people, of the natural resources of the country. Our forests, our sources of water supply, our arable and our mineral lands, our navigable streams and all the other natural resources with which our country has been so lavishly endowed, constitute the foundation of our national wealth.

Agriculture

We believe in encouraging the development of a modern system of agriculture and a systematic effort to improve the conditions of trade in farm products so as to benefit both consumer and producer. And, as an efficient means to this end, we favor the enactment by Congress of legislation that will suppress the pernicious practice of gambling in agricultural products by organized exchanges or others.

Merchant Marine

We believe in fostering, by constitutional regulation of commerce, the growth of a merchant marine, which shall develop and strengthen the commercial ties which bind us to our sister republics of the south, but without imposing additional burdens upon the people and without bounties or subsidies from the public treasury. We favor the exemption from tolls of American ships engaged in coastwise trade passing through the Panama Canal. We also favor legislation forbidding the use of the Panama Canal by ships owned or controlled by railroad carriers engaged in transportation competitive with the canal.

Pure Food and Public Health

We reaffirm our previous declarations advocating the union and strengthening of the various governmental agencies relating to pure foods, quarantine, vital statistics and human health.

Civil Service Law

The law pertaining to civil service should be honestly and rigidly enforced, to the end that merit and ability shall be the standard of appointment and promotion, rather than service rendered to a political party.

The Philippines

We reaffirm the position thrice announced by the democracy in national convention assembled against a policy of imperialism and colonial exploitation in the Philippines or elsewhere. In recognizing the independence of the Philippines, our government should retain such land as may be necessary for coaling stations and naval bases.

Arizona and New Mexico

We welcome Arizona and New Mexico to the sisterhood of states and heartily congratulate them upon their auspicious beginnings of great and glorious careers.

Alaska

We demand for the people of Alaska the full enjoyment of the rights and privileges of a territorial form of government and we believe that the officials appointed to administer the government of all our territories and the District of Columbia should be qualified by previous bona fide residence.

The Russian Treaty

We commend the patriotism of the Democratic members of the Senate and House of Representatives which compelled the termination of the Russian Treaty of 1832 and we pledge ourselves anew to preserve the sacred rights of American citizenship at home and abroad.

Parcels Post and Rural Delivery

We favor the establishment of a parcels post or postal express and also the extension of the rural delivery system as rapidly as practicable.

Panama Canal Exposition

We hereby express our deep interest in the great Panama Canal Exposition to be held in San Francisco in 1915, and favor such encouragement as can be properly given.

Protection of National Uniform

We commend to the several states the adoption of a law making it an offense for the proprietors of places of public amusement and entertainment to discriminate against the uniform of the United States, similar to the law passed by Congress applicable to the District of Columbia and the territories in 1911.

Rule of the People

We direct attention to the fact that the Democratic Party's demand for a return to the rule of the people expressed in the national platform four years ago has now become the accepted doctrine of a large majority of the electors. We again remind the country that only by a large exercise of the reserved power of the people can they protect themselves from the misuse of delegated power and the usurpation of government instrumentalities by special interests. For this reason, the national convention insisted on the overthrow of Cannonism and the inauguration of a system by which United States senators could be elected by direct vote.

Appendix C: 1912 Republican Party Platform (Summary)

The Republican Party, assembled by its representatives in national convention, declares its unchanging faith in government of the people, by the people, for the people. We renew our allegiance to the principles of the Republican Party and our devotion to the cause of Republican institutions established by the fathers.

The Courts

The Republican Party reaffirms its intention to uphold at all times the authority and integrity of the courts, both state and federal, and it will ever insist that their powers to enforce their process and to protect life, liberty and property shall be preserved inviolate.

Monopoly and Privilege

The Republican Party is opposed to special privilege and monopoly. It placed upon the statute book the Interstate Commerce Act of 1887 and the important amendments thereto, and the Anti-Trust Act of 1890 and it has consistently and successfully enforced the provisions of these laws. It will take no backward step to permit the re-establishment in any degree of conditions which were intolerable.

Federal Trade Commission

In the enforcement and administration of federal laws governing interstate commerce and enterprises impressed with a public use engaged therein, there is much that may be committed to a federal trade commission, thus placing in the hands of an administrative board many of the functions now necessarily exercised by the courts. This will promote promptness in the administration of the law and avoid delays and technicalities incident to court procedure.

The Tariff

We reaffirm our belief in a protective tariff. The Republican tariff policy has been of the greatest benefit to the country, developing our resources, diversifying our industries, and protecting our workmen against competition with cheaper labor abroad, thus establishing for our wage earners the American standard of living. We hold that the import duties should be high enough, while yielding a sufficient revenue, to protect adequately American industries and wages.

Cost of Living

The steadily increasing cost of living has become a matter not only of national but of worldwide concern. The Republican Party will support a prompt scientific inquiry into the causes which are operative, both in the United States and elsewhere, to increase the cost of living. When the exact facts are known, it will take the necessary steps to remove any abuses that may be found to exist, in order that the cost of the food, clothing and shelter of the people may in no way be unduly or artificially increased.

Banking and Currency

The Republican Party has also stood for a sound currency and for safe banking methods. It is responsible for the resumption of specific payments and for the establishment of the gold standard. It is committed to the progressive development of our banking a currency systems. Our banking arrangements today need further revision to meet the requirements of current conditions. We need measures that will prevent the recurrence of money panics and financial disturbances and which will promote the prosperity of business and the welfare of labor by producing constant employment. It is of great importance to the social and economic welfare of this country that its farmers have facilities for borrowing easily and cheaply they need to increase the productivity of their land.

The Civil Service

We reaffirm our adherence to the principle of appointment to public office based on proved fitness and tenure during good behavior and efficiency. We favor legislation to make possible the equitable retirement of disabled and superannuated members of the Civil Service in order that a higher standard of efficiency may be maintained. We favor the amendment of the Federal Employers Liability Law so as to extend its provisions to all government employees as well as to provide a more liberal scale of compensation for injury and death.

Campaign Contributions

We favor such additional legislation as may be necessary more effectually to prohibit corporations from contributing funds, directly or indirectly, to campaigns for the nomination or election of the president, the vice president, senators and representatives in Congress.

Conservation Policy

We rejoice in the success of the distinctive Republican policy of the conservation of our natural resources, for their use by the people without waste and without monopoly. We pledge ourselves to a continuance of such a policy. We favor such fair and reasonable rules and regulations as will not discourage or interfere with actual bona fide home-seekers, prospectors and miners in the acquisition of public lands under existing laws.

Parcels Post

In the interest of the general public and particularly of the agricultural or rural communities, we favor legislation looking to the establishment, under proper regulations, of a parcels post, the postal rates to be graduated under a zone system in proportion to the length of carriage.

Protection of American Citizenship

We approve the action taken by the president and the Congress to secure with Russia as with other countries, a treaty that will recognize the absolute right of expatriation and that will prevent all discrimination of whatever kind between American citizens, whether native born or aliens and regardless of race, religion or previous political allegiance. The right of asylum is a precious possession of the people of the United States and it is to be neither surrendered nor restricted.

The Navy

We believe in the maintenance of an adequate navy for the national defense and we condemn the action of the Democratic House of Representatives in refusing to authorize the construction of additional ships.

Merchant Marine

We believe that one of the country's most urgent needs is a revived merchant marine. There should be American ships, and plenty of them, to make use of the great American inter-oceanic canal now nearing completion.

Flood Prevention in the Mississippi Valley

The Mississippi River is the nation's drainage ditch. Its flood waters, gathered from 31 states and the Dominion of Canada, constitute an overpowering force which breaks the levees and pours its torrents over many millions of acres of the richest land in the union, stopping mails, impeding commerce, and causing great loss of life and property. These floods are national in scope, and the disasters they produce seriously affect the general welfare. The states unaided cannot cope with this giant problem; hence; hence, we believe the federal government should assume a fair proportion of the burden of its control, so as to prevent the disasters from recurring floods.

Reclamation

We favor the continuance of the policy of the government with regard to the reclamation of arid lands; and, for the encouragement of the speedy settlement and improvement of such lands, we favor an amendment to the law that will reasonably extend the time within which the cost of any reclamation project may be repaid by the land owners under it.

Rivers and Harbors

We favor a liberal and systematic policy for the improvement of our rivers and harbors. Such improvements should be made upon expert information and after a careful comparison of cost and prospective benefits.

Alaska

We favor a liberal policy toward Alaska to promote the development of the great resources of that district, with such safeguards as will prevent waste and monopoly. We favor the opening of the coal lands to development through a law leasing the lands on such terms as will invite development and will provide fuel for the navy and the commerce of the Pacific Ocean while retaining the title of the United States to prevent monopoly.

Philippine Policy

The Philippine policy of the Republican Party has been and is inspired by the belief that our duty toward the Filipino people is a national obligation which should remain entirely free from partisan politics.

Immigration

We pledge the Republican Party to the enactment of appropriate laws to give relief from the constantly growing evil of induced or undesirable immigration, which is inimical to the progress and welfare of the people of the United States.

Safety at Sea

We favor the speedy enactment of law to provide that seamen shall not be compelled to endure involuntary servitude, and that life and property at sea shall be safeguarded by the ample equipment of vessels with life-saving appliances and with full complements of skilled, able-bodied seamen to operate them.

Republican Accomplishment

The approaching completion of the Panama Canal, the establishment of a Bureau of Mines, the institution of postal savings banks, the increased provision made in 1912 for the aged and infirm soldiers and sailors of the Republic and for their widows, and the vigorous administration of laws relating to pure food and drugs, all mark the successful progress of Republican administration and are additional evidences of its effectiveness.

Economy and Efficiency in Government

We commend the earnest effort of the Republican administration to secure greater economy and increased efficiency in the conduct of government business.

Civic Duty

We call upon the people to quicken their interest in public affairs, to condemn and punish lynchings and other forms of lawlessness and to strengthen in all possible ways a respect for law and observance of it.

Arizona and New Mexico

We congratulate the people of Arizona and New Mexico upon the admission of those states, thus merging in the union in final and enduring form the last remaining portion of our continental territory.

Republican Administration

We challenge successful criticism of the 16 years of Republican administration under Presidents McKinley, Roosevelt and Taft.

Appendix D: 1912 Progressive Party Platform (Summary)

The conscience of the people, in a time of grave national problems, has called into being a new party, born of the nation's sense of justice. We of the Progressive Party here dedicate ourselves to the fulfillment of the duty laid upon us by our fathers to maintain the government of the people, by the people and for the people whose foundations they laid.

We hold with Thomas Jefferson and Abraham Lincoln that the people are the masters of their Constitution, to fulfill its purposes and to safeguard it from those who, by perversion of its intent, would convert it into an instrument of injustice. In accordance with the needs of each generation, the people must use their sovereign powers to establish and maintain equal opportunity and industrial justice, to secure which this government was founded and without which no republic can endure.

The country belongs to the people who inhabit it. Its resources, its businesses, its institutions and its laws should be utilized, maintained or altered in whatever manner will best promote the general interest.

The Old Parties

Political parties exist to secure responsible government and to execute the will of the people. The deliberate betrayal of its trust by the Republican Party, the fatal incapacity of the Democratic Party to deal with the new issues of the new time, have compelled the people to forge a new instrument of government through which to give effect to their will in laws and institutions. Unhampered by tradition, uncorrupted by power, undismayed by the magnitude of the task, the new party offers itself as the instrument of the people to sweep away old abuses, to build a new and nobler commonwealth.

A Covenant with the People

This declaration is our covenant with the people, and we hereby bind the party and its candidates in state and nation to the pledges made herein.

The Rule of the People

The National Progressive Party, committed to the principles of government by a self-controlled democracy expressing its will through representation of the people, pledges to secure each alterations in the fundamental law of the several states and the United States as shall insure the representative character of the government.

In particular, the party declares for direct primaries for the nomination of state and national offices, for nationwide preferential primaries for candidates for the presidency, for direct election of United States senators by the people and we urge on the states the policy of the short ballot, with responsibility to the people secured by the initiative, referendum and recall.

Amendment of Constitution

The Progressive Party, believing that a free people should have the power from time to time to amend their fundamental law so as to adapt it progressively to the changing needs of the people, pledges itself to provide a more easy and expeditious method of amending the federal Constitution.

Nation and State

Up to the limit of the Constitution, and later by amendment to the Constitution, if found necessary, we advocate bringing under effective national jurisdiction those problems which have expanded beyond reach of the individual states. The extreme insistence of states' rights by the Democratic Party in the Baltimore platform demonstrates anew its inability to understand the world into which it has survived or to administer the affairs of a union of states which have in all essential respects become one people.

Equal Suffrage

The Progressive Party, believing that no people can justly claim to be a true democracy which denies political rights on account of sex, pledges itself to the task of securing equal suffrage to men and women alike.

Corrupt Practices

We pledge our party to legislation that will compel strict limitation of all campaign contributions and expenditures and detailed publicity of both before as well as after primaries and elections.

Publicity and Public Service

We pledge our party to legislation compelling the registration of lobbyists, publicity of committee hearings except on foreign affairs, and recording of all votes in committee; and forbidding federal appointees from holding office in state or national political organizations or taking part as officers or delegates in political conventions for the nomination of elective state or national officials.

The Courts

The Progressive Party demands such restriction of the power of the courts as shall leave to the people the ultimate authority to determine fundamental questions of social welfare and public policy. To secure this end, it pledges itself to provide:

> That when an act, passed under the police power of the state, is held unconstitutional under the state constitution by the courts, the people, after an ample interval for deliberation, shall have an opportunity to vote on the question whether they desire the act to become law, notwithstanding such decision.
>
> That every decision of the highest appellate court of a state declaring an act of the Legislature unconstitutional on the ground of its violation of the federal Constitution, shall be subject to the same review by the Supreme Court of the United States as is now accorded to decisions sustaining such legislation.

Administration of Justice

The Progressive Party, in order to secure to the people a better administration of justice and by that means to bring about a more general respect for the law and the courts, pledges itself to work unceasingly for the reform of legal procedures and judicial methods.

Social and Industrial Justice

The supreme duty of the nation is the conservation of human resources through an enlightened measure of social and industrial justice. We pledge ourselves to work unceasingly in state and nation for:

> Prevention of industrial accidents and occupational diseases.
> Establishing minimum health and safety standards in workplaces.
> Prohibition of child labor.
> General prohibition of night work for women and establishment of an eight-hour day for women and young persons.
> One day's rest in seven for all wage workers.
> The eight-hour day in continuous 24-hour industries.
> The abolition of the convict contract labor system.
> Publicity as to wages, hours and conditions of labor; full reports on industrial accidents and injuries.
> Standards of compensation for deaths by industrial accident and injury and trade disease.

The protection of home life against the hazards of sickness, irregular and old age through the adoption of a system of social insurance adapted to American use.

The development of a creative labor power of America by lifting the last load of illiteracy from American youth and establishing continuation schools for industrial education under public control and encouraging agricultural education.

The establishment of industrial research laboratories for the benefit of American producers.

We favor the organization of the workers, men and women, as a means of protecting their interests.

Department of Labor

We pledge our party to establish a department of labor with a seat in the cabinet.

Country life

We pledge our party to foster the development of agricultural credit and cooperation, the teaching of agriculture in schools, agricultural college extension, the use of mechanical power on the farms, and to re-establish the Country Life Commission.

High Cost of Living

The high cost of living is due partly to worldwide and partly to local causes, partly to natural and partly to artificial causes. The measures proposed in this platform on various subjects such as the tariff, the trusts and conservation will of themselves remove the artificial causes.

Health

We favor the union of all of the existing agencies of the federal government dealing with the public health into a single national health service.

Business

We demand that the test of true prosperity shall be the benefits conferred thereby on all the citizens, not confined to individuals or classes, and that the test of corporate efficiency shall be the ability to better serve the public; that those who profit by control of business affairs shall justify that profit and that control by sharing with the public the fruits thereof. We therefore demand a strong national regulation of interstate corporations.

Patents

We pledge ourselves to the enactment of a patent law which will make it impossible for patents to be suppressed or used against the public welfare in the interests of injurious monopolies.

Currency

We believe there is urgent imperative need for prompt legislation for the improvement of our national currency system. We are opposed to the so-called Aldrich currency bill because its provisions would place our currency and credit system in private hands, not subject to effective public control.

Commercial Development

The time has come when the federal government should cooperate with manufacturers and producers in extending our foreign commerce. To this end, we demand adequate appropriations from Congress and the appointments of diplomats and consular offices solely with a view toward their social fitness and worth, and not in consideration of political expediency.

Conservation

The natural resources of the nation must be promptly developed and generously used to supply the people's needs but we cannot safely allow them to be wasted, exploited, monopolized or controlled against the general good.

We pledge our party to protect the national forests without hindering their legitimate use for the benefit of the people.

Agricultural lands in the national forests are, and should remain, open to the genuine settler.

We pledge our party to require reasonable compensation to the public for water power rights hereafter granted by the public,

We pledge legislation to lease the public grazing lands under equitable provisions.

Good Roads

We recognize the vital importance of good roads and pledge our party to foster their extension in every proper way and favor the early construction of national highways.

Alaska

The coal and other natural resources of Alaska should be opened to development at once. They are owned by the people of the United States and are safe from monopoly, waste or destruction only while so owned.

Waterways

It is a national obligation to develop our rivers, and especially the Mississippi and its tributaries, without delay, under a general comprehensive plan covering each river system from its source to its mouth, designed to secure its highest usefulness for navigation, irrigation, domestic supply, water power and the prevention of floods.

Panama Canal

The Panama Canal, built and paid for by the American people, must be used primarily for their benefit.

We demand that the canal shall be so operated as to break the transportation monopoly now held and misused by the transcontinental railroads by maintaining sea competition with them,

Tariff

We demand tariff revision because the present tariff is unjust to the people of the United States. Fair dealing requires and immediate downward revision wherein duties are shown to be unjust or excessive.

Inheritance and Income Tax

We believe in a graduated inheritance tax as a national means of equalizing the obligation of holders of property to government. We favor the ratification of the pending amendment to the Constitution giving the government the power to levy an income tax.

Peace and National Defense

We pledge the party to use its best endeavors to substitute judicial and other peaceful means of settling international differences. We favor an international agreement for the limitation of naval forces.

Treaty Rights

No treaty should receive the sanction of our government which discriminates between American citizens because of birthplace, race or religion or does not recognize the absolute right of expatriation.

The Immigrant

We favor governmental action to encourage the distribution of immigrants away from the congested cities, to rigidly supervise all private agencies dealing with them and to promote their assimilation, education and advancement.

Pensions

We pledge ourselves to a wise and just policy of pensioning American soldiers and sailors and their widows and children and to ex–Confederate soldiers, sailors and their widows and children.

Parcel Post

We pledge our party to the immediate creation of a parcel post with rates proportionate to distance and service.

Civil Service

We condemn the violations of the Civil Service law under the present administration. We demand legislation that will bring under the competitive system postmasters and all other non-political officers an insist on continuous service during good behavior and efficiency.

APPENDIX E: 1912 SOCIALIST PARTY PLATFORM (SUMMARY)

The Socialist Party declares that the capitalist system has outgrown its historical function and has become utterly incapable of meeting the problems now confronting society. We denounce this outgrown system as incompetent and corrupt and the source of unspeakable misery and suffering to the whole working class.

As measures calculated to strengthen the working class in its fight for the realization of its ultimate aim, the cooperative commonwealth, and to increase its power against capitalist oppression, we advocate and pledge ourselves and elected officers to the following program:

Collective Ownership

1. The collective ownership and democratic management of railroads, wire and wireless telegraphs and telephones, express service, steamboat lines and all other social means of transportation and communication and of all large scale industries.

2. The immediate acquirement by the municipalities, the states or the federal government of all grain elevators, stock yards, storage warehouses and other distributing agencies in order to reduce the present extortionate cost of living.

3. The extension of the public domain to include mines, quarries, oil wells, forests and water power.

4. The further conservation and development of natural resources for the use and benefit of all the people.

5. The collective ownership of land wherever practicable, and in cases where such ownership is impractical, the appropriation by taxation of the annual rental value of all the land held for speculation and exploitation.

6. The collective ownership and democratic management of the banking and currency system.

Unemployment

The immediate government relief of the unemployed by the extension of all useful public works in jobs of not more than eight hours a day and for not less than prevailing union wages.

Industrial Demands

The conservation of human resources, particularly of the lives and well-being of the workers and their families:

1. By shortening the workday in keeping with the increased productiveness and machinery.
2. By securing for every worker a rest period of not less than a day and a half each week.
3. By securing a more effective inspection of workshops, factories and mines.

Political Demands

1. The absolute freedom of the press, speech and assemblage.
2. The adoption of a graduated income tax and the extension of inheritance taxes, graduated in proportion to the value of the estate and to nearness of kin—the proceeds of these taxes to be employed in the socialization of industry.
3. The abolition of the monopoly ownership of patents and the substitution of collective ownership, with direct reward to inventors by premiums or royalties.
4. Unrestricted and equal suffrage for men and women.
5. The adoption of the initiative, referendum and recall and of proportional representation nationally as well as locally.
6. The abolition of the Senate and of the veto power of the president.
7. The election of the president and the vice president by direct election of the people.
8. The abolition of the power usurped by the Supreme Court of the United States to pass upon the constitutionality of the legislation enacted by Congress; national laws to be repealed only by act of Congress or by a referendum vote of the whole people.
9. Abolition of the present restrictions upon the amendment of the Constitution so that instrument maybe made amendable by a majority of the voters in a majority of the states.
10. The granting of the right of suffrage in the District of Columbia with representation in Congress and a democratic form of municipal government for purely local affairs.
11. The extension of United States government to all United States territories.

12. The enactment of further measures for the conservation of health; the creation of an independent bureau of health with such restrictions as will secure full liberty to all schools of practice.

13. The enactment of further measures for general education and particularly for vocational education in useful pursuits. The Bureau of Education to be made a Department.

14. The separation of the present Bureau of Labor from the Department of Commerce and Labor and its elevation to the rank of a Department.

15. Abolition of all federal district courts and the United States Circuit Court of Appeals. State courts to have jurisdiction in all cases arising between citizens of several states and foreign corporations. The election of all judges for short terms.

16. The immediate curbing of the power of the courts to issue injunctions.

17. The free administration of the law.

18. The calling of a convention for the revision of the Constitution of the United States.

Such measures of relief as we may be able to force from capitalism are but a preparation of the workers to seize the whole powers of government, in order that they may thereby lay hold of the whole system of socialized industry and thus come to their rightful inheritance.

Appendix F: Presidential Assassinations and Assassination Attempts

1865—President Abraham Lincoln was shot and killed at Ford's Theater in Washington by John Wilkes Booth, an actor and Confederate sympathizer in a plot involving four other conspirators who sought to kill several government officials. Booth was caught 12 days after Lincoln's death and was shot and killed. The four conspirators were hanged.

1881—President James A. Garfield, who had been in office for just four months, was shot at a railroad station in Washington and died eleven weeks later. The assassin was Charles Guiteau, a spurned government office seeker who blamed the president for his troubles. Guiteau was convicted and sentenced to death by hanging.

1901—President William McKinley was shot while he was attending the Pan American Exposition in Buffalo, New York. He died eight days later. The killer was Leon Czolgosz an anarchist who believed he was doing the right thing for the country. Czolgosz was convicted about two weeks after McKinley's death and was electrocuted a few weeks after that.

1912—Former president Theodore Roosevelt, who became president when McKinley was assassinated, was the victim of a would-be assassin when he was shot in Milwaukee while campaigning as a Bull Moose candidate for president. He survived. The shooter, John Schrank, said he had a dream in which McKinley rose in his coffin and told him to kill Roosevelt. Schrank was committed to a mental institution where he died 30 years later.

1933—President-elect Franklin D. Roosevelt escaped injury when a gunman fired five shots at him as he sat in a car on the streets of Miami. Chicago Mayor Anton Cermak, standing next to Roosevelt, was killed. The gunman, Giuseppe Zangara was arrested, pleaded guilty to the crime and was electrocuted about a month later.

1950—Two Puerto Rican nationalists tried to storm the Blair House, where President Truman was staying while the White House was being remodeled. A White House police officer as well as one of the attackers were killed. Truman was uninjured. The other attacker was sentenced to death but Truman commuted the sentence to life in prison. He was freed after serving 30 years.

1963—President John F. Kennedy was assassinated as he rode in a motorcade in Dallas. Texas Gov. John Connally was wounded but survived. The killer, Lee Harvey Oswald, shot and killed a Dallas policeman, J.D. Tippett, later in the day. Oswald was captured in a theater later in the day. Two days later, when Oswald was being transferred out of the Dallas jail, he was shot and killed by a bystander, Jack Ruby, a Dallas nightclub owner. Ruby was sentenced to life in prison.

1972—Alabama Gov. George Wallace, seeking the Democratic presidential nomination, was shot while campaigning at a shopping center in Laurel, Maryland. He survived but was paralyzed and was confined to a wheelchair for the rest of his life. The shooter, Arthur Bremer, was seeking publicity and fame and had considered trying to kill President Richard Nixon or George McGovern, another Democratic candidate. He served 35 years in prison and was paroled in 2007.

1975—President Gerald Ford was the target of assassins twice in a three-week period, both in California but in unrelated incidents. In one, Lynette "Squeaky" Fromme, a member of the notorious cult of madman Charles Manson, drew a gun but was stopped by a Secret Service agent before she could get off a shot in Sacramento, California. Seventeen days later, in San Francisco, Sara Jane Moore fired at Ford but missed as a bystander grabbed her arm and helped subdue her. Both Fromme and Moore were convicted in separate trials. Fromme served 34 years in prison. Moore served 32.

1981—President Ronald Reagan was shot as he emerged from a Washington hotel after giving a speech. Three other people were wounded including press secretary James Brady who was paralyzed for life. Reagan underwent surgery and spent several days in the hospital before resuming a full schedule. The shooter, John Hinckley, Jr., was obsessed with actress Jodie Foster, whom he did not know, and wanted to do something to try to impress her. He was confined to a mental institution.

Chapter Notes

Introduction

1. Geoffrey Cowan. "Riots, Guns, Bribes: TR's Contested Convention." *The Atlantic*, April 23, 2016.
2. *New Day*. CNN television broadcast, March 16, 2016.
3. Trump acceptance speech, July 21, 2016.
4. Tim Bryan. "Trump Is the Reincarnation of Teddy Roosevelt." *Lexington Libertarian*, January 5, 2017.
5. *The Daily Mail*, December 9, 2016.
6. "Lessons from 1912: Why Trumpmania Probably Won't Last." *Politico*, March 31, 2016.
7. Robert Novak. *The Agony of the GOP 1964* (New York: Macmillan, 1965), p. 17.
8. *Ibid*.
9. Thomas Patterson. "Teddy Roosevelt Failed to Save the GOP from Its Crazies." *Politico*, December 13, 2013.
10. *Ibid*.
11. William Roscoe Thayer. *Theodore Roosevelt: An Intimate Biography* (New York: William Roscoe Thayer, 1919) 157.

Chapter 1

1. The ad ran only once on television before it was pulled because it was considered too offensive. But it has been shown often in newscasts and in documentaries about campaigns and campaign advertising.
2. David Keirsey and Ray Choiniere. *The Unfolding of Character in the 40 Presidents of the United States* (New York: Prometheus Nemesis Company, 2002), p. 44.
3. Gerard Helferich. *Theodore Roosevelt and the Assassin: Madness, Vengeance and the Campaign of 1912* (Guilford, CT: Lyons Press, 2013) pp. 28–29.
4. Cowan. *Let the People Rule*, p. 13.
5. *Ibid*., p. 24.
6. William Allen White. *The Autobiography of the William Allen White* (New York: Macmillan, 1946), p. 445.
7. Thayer. *Theodore Roosevelt: An Intimate Biography*, 272.
8. Doris Kearns Goodwin. *The Bully Pulpit: Theodore Roosevelt, William Howard Taft and the Golden Age of Journalism* (New York: Simon & Schuster, 2013), p. xiv.
9. The passage, one of Roosevelt's most famous and eloquent deliveries, was buried deep in a long speech he gave in Paris on one of the many foreign trips he took when he was out of office.

Chapter 2

1. Nicholas Leman. "Progress's Pilgrims." *The New Yorker*, November 18, 2013.
2. www.ushistory.or/us/36.asp.
3. H. Roger Grant. "Review." *Journal of American History*, 2011, p. 544.
4. Thayer. *Theodore Roosevelt: An Intimate Biography*, p. 213.
5. White. *The Autobiography of William Allen White*, p. 428.
6. *Ibid*.
7. Lincoln Steffens. *The Same of the Cities* (New York: McClure, Phillips & Co., 1904), p. 27.
8. Ida Tarbell. *History of Standard Oil Company* (New York: McClure, Phillips & Co., 1908), p. 44.

9. Ray Stannard Baker, "The Right to Work." *McClure's*, January 1903.
10. Upton Sinclair. *The Jungle* (New York: Doubleday, Jabber & Co., 1906), p. 144.
11. *Ibid.*
12. Goodwin. *The Bully Pulpit: Theodore Roosevelt, William Howard Taft and the Golden Age of Journalism*, p. xii.
13. White. *The Autobiography of William Allen White*, p. 428.
14. *Denver Post*, April 27, 2012.
15. www.history.com/topics/titanic.
16. Roosevelt was the youngest president to take office at age 42. John F. Kennedy was the youngest elected president at age 43. Roosevelt's presidency began as the result of an assassination; Kennedy's ended by his assassination.
17. Robert Novak. *The Agony of the GOP 1964* (New York: Macmillan, 1965), pp. 16–17.
18. *Ibid.*

Chapter 3

1. Goodwin, *The Bully Pulpit*, p. 14.
2. "Cameron, Fritchie Are Luminaries of Era." *Lancaster Intelligencer Journal*, February 7, 2011.
3. Gordon Leidner. "Lincoln Outfoxed Seward for Nomination." *Washington Times*, August 10, 1996.
4. Lincoln appointed his Republican rivals to cabinet positions: Seward as secretary of state; Cameron as secretary of war; Chase as secretary of treasury; and Bates as attorney general.
5. ushistory.org/gop/origins.htm.
6. Lawrence D. Longley and Neal R. Peirce. *The Electoral College Primer* (New Haven: Yale University Press, 1996), pp. 28–29.
7. *Ibid.*
8. Goodwin. *The Bully Pulpit*, pp. 15–17.
9. *Ibid.*

Chapter 4

1. Theodore Roosevelt. *Theodore Roosevelt: An Autobiography* (New York: Charles Scribner's Sons, 1913), p. 7.
2. *Ibid.*, p. 9.
3. Roosevelt. *Theodore Roosevelt: An Autobiography*, p. 94.
4. *Ibid.*
5. Goodwin. *The Bully Pulpit*, p. 135.
6. *Ibid.*, 136.
7. *Ibid.*, 263.
8. "William Taft: Life Before the Presidency." millercenter.org/president/biography/taft-life-before-the-presidency.
9. Stephen Hess. "Big Bill Taft." *A Sense of History: The Best Writing from the Pages of American Heritage* (New York: American Heritage Press, Inc., 1985) p. 572.
10. *Ibid.*, p. 570.
11. *Ibid.*, p. 571.
12. www.let.rug.nl/usa/biographies/william-howard-taft/.
13. Ira Smith and Alex Morris. *Dear Mr. President: The Story of 50 Years in the White House Mail Room* (New York: Julian Messner, 1949), pp. 66–69.
14. Information on Taft's attempt at dieting are included in an article by Deborah Levine, a professor at Providence College for *The Annals of Internal Medicine* as reported in the *New York Daily News*, October 15, 2013.
15. Goodwin. *The Bully Pulpit*, p. 570.
16. Hess. "Big Bill Taft," p. 574.

Chapter 5

1. Goodwin. *The Bully Pulpit*, pp 280–281.
2. Elting E. Morrison. *The Letters of Theodore Roosevelt, Vol. III* (Cambridge: Harvard University Press, 1951).
3. Roosevelt. *Theodore Roosevelt: An Autobiography*, p. 408.
4. "Theodore Roosevelt: Domestic Affairs." http//millercenter.org/president/biography/Roosevelt-domestic-affairs.
5. "Theodore Roosevelt: Foreign Affairs." http//millercenter.org/president/biography/Roosevelt-foreign-affairs.
6. *Ibid.*
7. Thayer. *Theodore Roosevelt: An Intimate Biography*, p. 308.

Chapter 6

1. Archibald Butt. *Taft and Roosevelt: The Intimate Letters of Archie Butt, Military Aide, Volume II* (Garden City: Doubleday, Doran & Co., 1930), letter of August 17, 1910, 481.
2. *Ibid.*
3. *Ibid.*
4. Letter of May 28, 1911, 662.
5. Letter of July 5, 1910, 433.
6. Letter of August 20, 1910, 492.

7. Letter of November 25, 1910, 564.
8. Letter of February 23, 1912, 847.
9. Letter of February 27,1912, 851–852.

Chapter 7

1. Thayer. *Theodore Roosevelt: An Intimate Biography*, p. 338.
2. "Joe Cannon Dies in Danville at 90; 46 Years in House." *New York Times*, November 13, 1926.
3. Goodwin. *The Bully Pulpit*, p. 588.
4. *Ibid.*
5. Thayer. *Theodore Roosevelt: An Intimate Biography*, p. 339.
6. *New York Evening Post*, April 10, 1909.
7. *American Heritage Pictorial History of Presidents of the United States* (New York: American Heritage, 1968), p. 562.
8. Henry Beach Needham. "Why Roosevelt Opposes Taft." *Saturday Evening Post*, May 4, 1912.
9. *Ibid.*
10. Goodwin. *The Bully Pulpit*, 602.
11. Thayer. *Theodore Roosevelt: An Intimate Biography*, pp. 340–341.
12. *Ibid.*, p. 57.
13. Goodwin. *The Bully Pulpit*, p. 606.
14. *Ibid.*, p. 609.
15. *Collier's*, November 13, 1909.
16. Lewis L.Gould. *My Dearest Nellie: The Letters of William Howard Taft to Helen Herron Taft, 1901–1912* (Lawrence: University Press of Kansas, 2011), p. 73.
17. Butt. *Taft and Roosevelt: The Intimate Letters of Archie Butt, Military Aide, Volume 2*, p. 472.
18. Glavis was eventually rehired by the Interior Department and continued his career as an investigator. Ballinger returned to Seattle and resumed his law practice, never holding a federal office again. Pinchot remained active in Republican politics and served two terms as governor of Pennsylvania.
19. Needham. "Why Roosevelt Opposes Taft." *Saturday Evening Post*, May 4, 1912.
20. *Ibid.*
21. Theodore Roosevelt. *The Autobiography of Theodore Roosevelt* (New York: Macmillan, 1913), p. 409.
22. Butt. *Taft and Roosevelt: The Intimate Letters of Archie Butt, Military Aide*, p. 484.
23. "New Nationalism" speech. August 31, 1910, in Osawatomie, Kansas.
24. Goodwin. *The Bully Pulpit*, p. 668.
25. Gould. *My Dearest Nellie*, p. 101.
26. *Ibid.*
27. Hess. "Big Bill Taft," 579.

Chapter 8

1. Mari Jo Buhle, Paul Buhle and Harvey Kaye. *The American Radical* (New York: Routledge, 1994), p. 17.
2. "The Career of Robert M. Lafollette: Turning Points in Wisconsin History." Wisconsin Historical Society, Nov. 12, 2014.
3. Buhle, Buhle and Kay. *The American Radical*, p. 18.
4. Roosevelt mentioned LaFollette and "The Wisconsin Idea" in his Charter of Democracy speech delivered in Columbus, Ohio, February 22, 1912.
5. White. *The Autobiography of William Allen White*, p. 427.
6. Cowan. *Let the People Rule*, p. 45.
7. Gould. *My Dearest Nellie*, p. 149.
8. *Ibid.*, p. 155.

Chapter 9

1. Goodwin. *The Bully Pulpit*, pp. 672–673.
2. *New York World*, January 23, 1912.
3. Goodwin. *The Bully Pulpit*, pp. 674–675.
4. *New York Times*, February 3, 1912.
5. White. *The Autobiography of William Allen White*, p. 449.
6. *Ibid.*
7. Thayer. *Theodore Roosevelt: An Intimate Biography*, pp. 348–349.
8. *Ibid.*
9. *Ibid.*
10. Charter of Democracy speech delivered in Columbus, Ohio, February 22, 1912.
11. *Ibid.*
12. *Ibid.*
13. William Schambra. "The Saviors of the Constitution." *National Affairs*, Winter 2012.
14. Cowan. *Let the People Rule*, p. 27.
15. *Ibid.*
16. Butt. *Taft and Roosevelt: The Intimate Letters of Archie Butt*, pp. 846–847.
17. *New York Sun*, February 22, 1912
18. White. *The Autobiography of William Allen White*, p. 456.
19. *St. Louis Republic*, February 22, 1912.
20. *New York Tribune*, February 22, 1912.

21. Roosevelt's penchant for speaking out, sometimes controversially, and being confident the public would be on his side, was similar to the campaign Donald Trump ran in 2015 and 2016 when he defied "political correctness," spoke frankly and often profanely and was elected president after a highly volatile campaign.
22. Goodwin. *The Bully Pulpit*, p. 682.

Chapter 10

1. Cowan. *Let the People Rule*, pp. 42–44.
2. *Ibid.*
3. *Ibid.*, pp. 39–40.
4. *Ibid.*, p. 85.
5. Thayer. *Theodore Roosevelt: An Intimate Biography*, p. 342.
6. Cowan. "Riots, Guns, Bribes: TR's Contested Convention." *The Atlantic*, April 23, 2016.

Chapter 11

1. Cowan,. *Let the People Rule*, p. 90.
2. *New York Times*, March 20, 1912.
3. *Washington Post*, March 20, 1912.
4. Geoffrey Cowan. "Teddy Roosevelt Defends Presidential Primary." *New Republic*, February 1, 2016.
5. Roosevelt speech. Carnegie Hall, New York, March 25, 1912.
6. E.L. Philipp. *Milwaukee Sentinel*, as quoted on Wisconsin Public Radio, April 4, 2016.
7. David W. Scott. "Lincoln and Lorimer: How Illinois Politics Helped Change the Way of Choosing Senators." Presentation to Evanston Historical Society, 2002.
8. The Lorimer scandal in Illinois is believed to be a catalyst for the 17th amendment to the Constitution calling for the popular election of United States senators.
9. Goodwin. *The Bully Pulpit*, p. 689.
10. Cowan. *Let the People Rule*, p. 117.
11. *Grand Forks Evening Times*, July 12, 1912.
12. Goodwin. *The Bully Pulpit*, p. 691.
13. *Ibid.*, 694.
14. *New York Times*, April 27, 1912.

Chapter 12

1. Cowan. *Let the People Rule*, 184.
2. *Ibid.*
3. *Chicago Tribune*, June 6, 1912.
4. Thayer. *Theodore Roosevelt: An Intimate Biography*, p. 358.
5. Sagamore Hill was Roosevelt's home from 1885 until his death in 1919. In 1883, he purchased 155 acres of land in Oyster Bay, on Long Island, New York. He sold 60 acres to relatives and planned to use the remaining 95 acres to build a home he would call Leeholm, for he and his wife, Alice, with plenty of room for the big family they planned to have. Alice died while giving birth to a daughter, also named Alice, on February 14, 1884. Roosevelt decided to continue with construction of the home but renamed it Sagamore Hill in honor of an Indian chief who had reportedly lived on the land in the 17th century. Roosevelt married Edith Carow in 1886. They raised Alice as well as children born from their marriage and never moved from Sagamore Hill.
6. Goodwin. *The Bully Pulpit*, p. 699.
7. Lewis Gould. "Why TR Lost the Republican Nomination in 1912." *History News Network*, April 30, 2008.
8. White. *The Autobiography of William Allen White*, p. 464.
9. Cowan. *Let the People Rule*, p. 196.
10. *Ibid.*
11. White. *The Autobiography of William Allen White*, p. 464.
12. Goodwin. *The Bully Pulpit*, p. 701.
13. *New York Times*, June 16, 1912.
14. Thayer. *Theodore Roosevelt: An Intimate Biography*, p. 364.
15. *Ibid.*
16. Cowan. *Let the People Rule*, pp. 215–216.
17. *Ibid.*
18. *New York Times*, June 18, 1912.

Chapter 13

1. Cowan. "Riots, Guns, Bribes: TR's Contested Convention." *The Atlantic*, April 23, 2016.
2. Gould. *My Dearest Nellie*, p. 150.
3. Jeffrey Lord. "The GOP and the Ghost of the 1912 Convention." *Conservative Review*, December 14, 2015.
4. Cowan. *Let the People Rule*, p. 218.
5. *Ibid.*, 220.
6. White. *The Autobiography of William Allen White*, p. 467.
7. Cowan. *Let the People Rule*, p. 221
8. *New York Times*, June 19, 1912.

9. White. *The Autobiography of William Allen White*, p. 470.
10. *New York Times*, June 19, 1912.
11. Goodwin. *The Bully Pulpit*, p. 708.
12. *New York Times*, June 20, 1912.
13. *New York Times*, June 21, 1912.
14. There is a vast difference today in the relationship of the press and politicians than there was in 1912. There was a cadre of journalists in 1912 who not only supported Roosevelt but, in some cases, worked for him such as O'Laughlin of the *Chicago Tribune*; Munsey, the publisher and financier; and White, the Kansas newspaperman and Republican national committeemen. Those kinds of relationships are considered conflicts of interest in today's journalism.
15. White. *The Autobiography of William Allen White*, pp. 471–472.
16. *New York Times*, June 23, 1912.
17. Detailed accounts of the last minute bribery attempts can be found in Cowan. *Let the People Rule*, pp. 146–147.
18. Roosevelt's message is included in the official record of the 1912 Republican convention and is widely quoted in many publications.
19. 15th Republican National Convention (New York, 1912), 333–335.
20. *New York Times*, June 23, 1912.
21. Shambra. "The Saviors of the Constitution." Issue 10, Winter 2012.
22. *Ibid.*
23. *New York Times*, June 23, 1912.

Chapter 14

1. "Historic Missourians." State Historical Society of Missouri.
2. Gould. *My Dearest Nellie*, p. 181.
3. White. *The Autobiography of William Allen White*, p. 478.
4. *Ibid.*
5. *New York Times*, June 26, 1912.
6. *Ibid.*
7. White. *The Autobiography of William Allen White*, pp. 480–481.
8. *Ibid.*
9. Goodwin. *The Bully Pulpit*, p. 714.
10. Cowan. *Let the People Rule*, p. 5.
11. Gould. *My Dearest Nellie*, pp. 270–271.
12. *Ibid.*
13. Goodwin. *The Bully Pulpit*, p. 713.

Chapter 15

1. Thayer. *Roosevelt: An Intimate Biography*, p. 372.
2. Goodwin. *The Bully Pulpit*, pp. 718–719.
3. "The Progressives." http://ehistory.osu.edu/exhibitions/1912/content/Progressive Party.
4. Thayer. *Roosevelt: An Intimate Biography*, p. 373.
5. "The Progressives." http://ehistory.osu.edu/exhibitions/1912/content/Progressive Party.
6. Cowan. *Let the People Rule*, p. 43.
7. Goodwin. *The Bully Pulpit*, p. 719.
8. Cowan. *Let the People Rule*, p. 257.
9. *Ibid.*, 265.
10. Thayer. *Roosevelt: An Intimate Biography*, p. 282.
11. A remarkably similar circumstance occurred 52 years later at the 1964 Democratic National Convention in Atlantic City. For many years, blacks in Mississippi had been treated as second class citizens by a white majority population that, among other injustices, had prevented them from registering to vote and to exclude them for participating in county and state conventions. In 1964, assisted by white civil rights activists from the north, blacks organized, held their own statewide convention, and elected a bi-racial delegation to participate in the Democrat convention. They took a bus to Atlantic City and demanded to be seated in place of the all-white Mississippi delegation. They expected support from President Lyndon Johnson, who, earlier that year, had signed the historic Civil Rights bill. But Johnson wanted no trouble at the convention. He had FBI agents dispatched to tap phone lines and spy on the blacks and assigned Minnesota senator Hubert Humphrey, a vice presidential hopeful, to work out a compromise with the blacks. Johnson knew that if the all-white Mississippi delegation was unseated, the delegations from Louisiana, Alabama, Georgia and other states would probably walk out in protest and perhaps stay away on election day in November as well. Also, Johnson did not want the controversy to boil over onto the convention floor where it would be viewed by millions on television. In the end, with many other Johnson

cronies taking part, the blacks were told what the compromise would be—that they would not be seated but that a few of them would be seated as honorary, non-voting delegates—a solution totally unacceptable to the blacks but one in which they were forced to accept.

12. Gould. *My Dearest Nellie*, p. 265
13. White. *The Autobiography of William Allen White*, p. 484.
14. *Ibid.*

Chapter 16

1. Letter from William Howard Taft accepting the Republican nomination for president, August 5, 1912.
2. *Ibid.*
3. *Ibid.*
4. *Ibid.*
5. Goodwin. *The Bully Pulpit*, pp. 728–729.
6. *Ibid.*, p. 725.
7. Gould. *My Dearest Nellie*, pp. 289–290.
8. *Ibid.*
9. *Ibid.*
10. Hess. "Big Bill Taft," p. 578.
11. White. *The Autobiography of William Allen White*, p. 493.
12. *Ibid.*
13. Gould. *My Dearest Nellie*, p. 181.
14. Goodwin. *The Bully Pulpit*, p. 728.
15. *New York Times*, July 9, 1894.
16. Brett Flehinger. *The 1912 Election and the Power of Progressivism: A Brief History With Document* (New York: Bedford/St. Martin's, 2003), p. 18.
17. Goodwin. *The Bully Pulpit*, p. 731.
18. Roosevelt. *The Autobiography of Theodore Roosevelt*, p. 503.

Chapter 17

1. Gerard Helferich. *Theodore Roosevelt and the Assassin: Madness, Vengeance and the Campaign of 1912* (Guilford, CT: Lyons Press, 2013), P. 41.
2. *Ibid.*
3. "Maniac in Milwaukee Shoots Col. Roosevelt; He Ignores Wound, Speaks an Hour, Goes to Hospital." *New York Times*, October 15, 1912.
4. *Ibid.*
5. *Ibid.*
6. *Ibid.*
7. The attempt on Roosevelt's life was similar to an incident on March 30, 1981, when President Ronald Reagan was shot by John Hinckley as the president, in office for two months, emerged from a hotel (Washington Hilton) and was about to get into a waiting vehicle. As in the case with Roosevelt, it was not immediately determined that he had been shot. His press secretary, James Brady, was wounded and was paralyzed for the rest of his life. Two other persons, including a Washington D.C. police officer were also wounded.
8. Patricia O'Toole. "The Speech That Saved Teddy Roosevelt's Life." *Smithsonian*, November 2012.
9. Thayer. *Theodore Roosevelt: An Intimate Biography*, p. 279.
10. Characteristically and therefore not surprisingly, even with a bullet in him, the colonel was engaging the press.
11. Thayer. *Theodore Roosevelt: An Intimate Biography*, p. 285.
12. Helferich. *Theodore Roosevelt and the Assassin*, p. 49.
13. *Ibid.*
14. David Traxel. *Crusader Nation: The United States in Peace and the Great War* (New York: Vintage Press, 2006), 37.

Chapter 18

1. Woodrow Wilson: Campaigns and Elections. https://millercenter.org/president/Wilson/campaigns-and-elections.
2. "What Is Progress?" Woodrow Wilson campaign speech, First Principle Series, The Heritage Foundation.
3. Many of the progressive principles of 1912 were evident in President Franklin D. Roosevelt's "New Deal" 20 years later.
4. Roosevelt "Confession of Faith" speech, Progressive National Convention, August 1912.

Chapter 19

1. Goodwin. *The Bully Pulpit*, P. 736.
2. *Ibid.*
3. *Ibid.*
4. A. Scott Berg. *Wilson* (New York: G.P. Putnam's Sons, 2013), pp. 243–244.
5. *Ibid.*
6. Nicholas Longworth was Theodore Roosevelt's son-in-law, having married the colonel's daughter, Alice. It is a classic example

of politics making strange bedfellows because while Taft and Roosevelt had grown to be political enemies, Taft maintained a good working relationship with Longworth and, as a practical political matter, wanted him to retain his Republican seat in Congress.

7. The only other Democrat president during that time period was Grover Cleveland who was elected to non-consecutive terms in 1884 and 1892.

8. Berg. *Wilson*, pp. 246–247.

9. *Ibid.*, p. 259.

Chapter 20

1. Lewis Gould. "Why TR Lost the Republican Nomination in 1912: What New Research Shows." www.historynewsnetwork, April 30, 2008.

2. *Ibid.*

3. *Ibid.*

4. White. *The Autobiography of William Allen White*, 496.

5. "The Transformation of American Democracy: Teddy Roosevelt, the 1912 Election and the Progressive Party." *American Heritage*, June 11, 2012.

6. Goodwin. *The Bully Pulpit*, p. 737.

7. *Saturday Evening Post*, November 3, 2012.

8. Thayer. *Theodore Roosevelt: An Intimate Biography*, p. 324.

9. Novak's reflections are in connection with his book on the 1964 Republican convention that nominated Barry Goldwater.

10. Novak. *The Agony of the GOP, 1964*, p. 16.

11. *Ibid.*

12. *Ibid.*

13. Helferich. *Theodore Roosevelt and the Assassin*, p. 232.

14. Cowan. *Let the People Rule*, p. 279.

15. *Ibid.*

16. Helferin. Interview with onmilwaukee.com, February 3, 2014.

Chapter 21

1. "Blackstone Hotel." Chicago Department of Planning and Development, Landmarks Division, 2003.

2. The Cubs acquired Alexander in hopes of winning the National League championship in 1918. Then Alexander went off to war, seemingly eliminating their chances. But the Cubs went on to win the championship without him.

3. "Roosevelt Grips the Hand of Taft." *New York Times*, May 26, 1918.

4. *Ibid.*

5. *Ibid.*

6. Hess. "Big Bill Taft." *A Sense of History*, p. 581.

Epilogue

1. Thayer. *Theodore Roosevelt: An Intimate Biography*, p. 392.

2. *Ibid.*, p. 394.

3. Lewis L. Gould, *Chief Executive to Chief Justice: Taft Twixt the White House and Supreme Court* (Lawrence: University Press of Kansas, 2014), p. 14.

4. Hess. "Big Bill Taft." *A Sense of History*, p. 580.

5. Cowan. *Let the People Rule*, p. 289.

6. *Ibid.*

7. Marty Hamilton. "Bull Moose Plays an Encore: Hiram Johnson and the Presidential Campaign of 1932." *California Historical Society Quarterly*, September 1962, pp. 211–221.

BIBLIOGRAPHY

Books

American Heritage Pictorial History of Presidents of the United States. New York: American Heritage, 1968.
Andersen, Kristi. *The Creation of a Democratic Majority*. Chicago: University of Chicago Press, 1979.
Berg, A. Scott. *Wilson*. New York: G.P. Putnam's Sons, 2013.
Broderick, Francis L. *Progressivism at Risk: Electing a President in 1912*. New York: Greenwood Press, 1989.
Bryan, William Jennings. *A Tale of Two Conventions*. New York: Funk & Wagnells, 1912.
Buhle, Mari, Paul Buhl, and Harvey Kaye. *The American Radical*. New York: Routledge, 1994.
Butler, Nicholas Murray. *Across the Busy Years: Recollections and Reflections*. New York: Scribner's, 1939.
Butt, Archie. *Taft and Roosevelt: The Intimate Letters of Archie Butt, Military Aide, Volume 2*. Garden City, NY: Doubleday, Doran & Company, 1930.
Chace, James. *1912: Wilson, Roosevelt, Taft & Debs—The Election That Changed the Country*. New York: Simon & Schuster, 2004.
Collier, Peter, and David Horowitz. *The Roosevelts: An American Saga*. New York: Simon & Schuster, 1994.
Cooper, John Milton, Jr. *Woodrow Wilson: A Biography*. New York: Knopf, 2009.
Cowan, Geoffrey. *Let the People Rule: Theodore Roosevelt and the Birth of the Presidential Primary*. New York: W.W. Norton, 2016.
Fiehinger, Brett. *The 1912 Election and the Power of Progressivism*. Boston: Bedford/St. Martin's, 2003.
Freeling, William. *The Road to Disunion: Secessionists at Bay, 1776–1854, Volume I*. London: Oxford University Press, 1990.
Gable, John A. *The Bull Moose Years: Theodore Roosevelt and the Progressive Party*. Port Washington, NY: Kennikat Press, 1978.
Garland, Joseph. *Boston's Gold Coast*. New York: Little, Brown, 1981.
Goodwin, Doris Kearns. *The Bully Pulpit: Theodore Roosevelt, William Howard Taft and the Golden Age of Journalism*. New York: Simon & Schuster, 2013.
Gould, Lewis. *Chief Executive to Chief Justice: Taft Twixt the White House and Supreme Court*. Lawrence: University Press of Kansas, 2014.
Gould, Lewis. *Four Hats in the Ring: The 1912 Election and the Birth of Modern American Politics*. Lawrence: University Press of Kansas, 2008.
Gould, Lewis. *My Dearest Nellie: The Letters of William Howard Taft to Helen Herron Taft, 1909–1912*. Lawrence: University Press of Kansas, 2011.

Helferich, Gerard. *Theodore Roosevelt and the Assassin: Madness, Vengeance and the Campaign of 1912*. Guilford, CT: Lyons Press, 2013.
LaFollette, Robert, and Allan Nevins. *LaFollette's Autobiography: A Personal Narrative of Personal Experiences*. Madison: University of Wisconsin Press, 1960.
Link, Arthur S. *Wilson: The New Freedom*. Princeton: Princeton University Press, 1956.
Longley, Lawrence D., and Neal R. Peirce. *The Electoral College Primer*. New Haven: Yale University Press, 1996.
Mason, Alpheus. *Bureaucracy Convicts Itself*. New York: Viking Press, 1941.
McPherson, James. *Battle Cry of Freedom*. Oxford: Oxford University Press, 2003.
Meacham, Jon. *Destiny and Power: The American Odyssey of George Herbert Walker Bush*. New York: Random House, 2015,
Middendorf, J. William. *Glorious Disaster: Barry Goldwater and the Origins of the Conservative Movement*. New York: Basic Books, 2006.
Milkis, Sidney M. *Theodore Roosevelt, the Progressive Party and the Transformation of American Democracy*. Lawrence: University Press of Kansas, 2009.
Milkis, Sidney M., and Michael Nelson. *The American Presidency: Origins and Development, 1776-2011*. Washington, D.C.: CQ Press, 2011.
Morris, Edmund. *The Rise of Theodore Roosevelt*. New York: Ballantine Books, 1979.
Morrison, Elting E. *The Letters of Theodore Roosevelt, Volume III*. Cambridge: Harvard University Press, 1951.
Mowry, George. *Theodore Roosevelt and the Progressive Movement*. New York: Hill & Wang, 1946.
1912 Republican National Convention booklet (reprint). Ann Arbor: University of Michigan Library, 2016.
Novak, Robert. *The Agony of the GOP 1964*. New York: Macmillan, 1965.
Perlstein, Rick. *Beyond the Storm: Barry Goldwater and the Unmaking of the American Consensus*. New York: Nation Books, 2009.
Roosevelt, Theodore. *The Autobiography of Theodore Roosevelt*. New York: Macmillan, 1913
Ross, Tara. *Enlightened Democracy: The Case for the Electoral College*. Dallas: Colonial Press, 2004.
Ruddy, Daniel. *Theodore the Great: Conservative Crusader*. New York: Regnery History, 2016.
A Sense of History: The Best Writing from the Pages of American Heritage. New York: American Heritage Press, 1985.
Skowronek, Stephen. *Building a New American State: The Expansion of National Administrative Capacities, 1877-1920*. Cambridge: Cambridge University Press, 1982.
Smith, Ira. Morris, Alex. *Dear Mr. President: The Story of 50 Years in the White House Mail Room*, New York: Julian Messner, 1949.
Thayer, William Roscoe. *Theodore Roosevelt: An Intimate Biography*. Boston: Houghton-Mifflin, 1919.
Traxel, David. *Crusader Nation: The United States in Peace and the Great War*. New York: Vintage Books, 2006.
White, William Allen. *The Autobiography of William Allen White*. New York: Macmillan, 1946.
Wolraich, Michael. *Unreasonable Men: Theodore Roosevelt and the Republican Rebels Who Created Progressive Politics*. New York: St. Martin's Press, 2014.

Other Sources

Blumgart, Jake. "America's Bizarre, Brawl-Filled History of Contested Conventions." *Rolling Stone*, April 7, 2016.

Bibliography

Bryan Tim. "Trump Is the Reincarnation of Teddy Roosevelt." *Lexington Libertarian*, January 5, 2017.
Cowan, Geoffrey. "Teddy Roosevelt Defends the Presidential Primary." *New Republic*, February 1, 2016.
Cowan, Geoffrey. "Riots, Guns, Bribes: TR's Contested Convention." *The Atlantic*, April 2016.
Fazio, Evan. "Is Trump the new Teddy Roosevelt?" *Chicago Tribune*, February 7, 2017.
"Fight in the Open." *Grand Forks Evening Times*, July 12, 1912.
Glass, Andrew. "Roosevelt Shot in Milwaukee Oct. 14, 1912." *Politico*, October 14, 2007.
Gould, Lewis. "Why TR Lost the Republican Nomination in 1912: What New Research Shows." *History News Network*, April 30, 2008.
Grimes, William. "Theodore Roosevelt's Sagamore Hill Home Cries Bully!" *New York Times*, July 9, 2015.
Hamilton, Marty. "Bull Moose Plays an Encore: Hiram Johnson and the Presidential Campaign of 1932," *California Historical Society Quarterly*, September 1962.
Huebner, Robin. "A Place in History: North Dakota Holds First Presidential Primary." *Dickinson Press*, February 1, 2016.
Klein, Christopher. "History in the Headlines: Shot in Chest 100 Years Ago, Teddy Roosevelt Kept On Talking." www.history.com/news/sht-in-chest-100-years-ago-teddy-rosevelt-kept-on-talking.htm.
Lemann, Nicholas. "Progress's Pilgrims." *The New Yorker*, November 18, 2013.
"Lessons from 1912: Why Trumpmanias Probably Won't Last." *Politico*, March 3, 2016.
Lord, Jeffrey. "The GOP and the Ghost of the 1912 Convention." *Conservative Review*, December 14, 2015.
Jensen, Colt, "The 2016 Election and its Echoes of 1912," *Huffington Post*, April 28, 2017.
"Maniac in Milwaukee Shoots Col. Roosevelt; He Ignores Wound, Speaks an Hour, Goes to Hospital." *New York Times*, October 15, 1912.
"My Hat Is Still in the Ring, Only It's a Bigger Ring, Says Roosevelt." *The Washington Times*, June 22, 1912.
Needham, Henry Beach. "Why Roosevelt Opposes Taft." *Saturday Evening Post*, May 4, 1912.
Orndal, Lloyd. "No Presidential Primary This Year." *Grand Forks Herald*, March 21, 2016.
O'Toole, Patricia. "The Speech That Saved Teddy Roosevelt's Life." *Smithsonian*, November 1912.
Polk, James. "Nine U.S. Presidents Attacked Since Civil War," *CNN*, March 28, 2011.
Pringle, Henry. "Publicist or Politician: A Portrait of Dr. Nicholas Murray Butler." *The Outlook*, October 17, 1928.
"The Revolution of the Primary Under Leadership of LaFollette." *Milwaukee Sentinel*, October 10, 1909.
"Roosevelt Has Inexhaustible Energy." *Outlook*, October 12, 1912.
Schambra, William. "The Saviors of the Constitution." *National Affairs*, Winter 2012.
Stewart, David O. "The Family Plot to Kill Lincoln," *Smithsonian*, August 28, 2013.
Sullivan, Mark. "President Had Place in the Sun," *Boston Globe*, July 29, 2004.
"Summer White House." Beverly Historical Society, Beverly MA, 2016.
"Taft Fears No Harm from Pinchot Row." *New York Times*, January 9, 1910.
"Taft Men Say They'll Win Today and That Col. Roosevelt Will Bolt." *New York Times*, June 18, 1912.
"Taft Victory in the First Clash; Root Chosen Chairman." *New York Times*, June 19, 1912.
"Teddy Roosevelt Survives Assassin When Bullet Hits Folded Speech in His Pocket." *New York Daily News*, March 12, 2013.
Throntveit, Trygve. "A 100-Year Legacy: The 1912 Election's Lasting Impact." Dartmouth College, June 6, 2012.

"The Transformation of American Democracy: Teddy Roosevelt, the 1912 Election and the Progressive Party." *American Heritage*, June 11, 2012.

"U.S. President William H. Taft's Turn-of-the-Century Weight Loss Diet Revealed." *New York Daily News*, October 15, 2013.

"Who Shot TR?" www.nps.gov/thrb/learn/historyculture/whoshottr.htm.

Index

Adams, John 3
Addams, Jane 139, 142, 155
Aldrich, Chester 77, 82
Aldrich, Nelson 49, 60, 71
Alexander, Grover Cleveland 173
"Alexander's Ragtime Band" 26
Allen, Henry, 120, 121, 187
American Legion 183
American Railway Union 144
The Apprentice 9
The Art of the Deal 11
Arthur, Chester 34, 40, 46
Astor, John Jacob 26
Atzerodt, George 32

Baker, Ray Stannard 24, 72
Baldwin, Simeon 127
Ballinger, Richard 62, 63, 64, 65, 182
Barnes, William 179
Barnum, P.T. 130
Bascam, John 72
Bass, Robert 77, 82
Bates, Edwin 29, 30
"Battle Hymn of the Republic" 105, 137
"Be My Little Baby Bumblebee" 26
Bell, Alexander Graham 21
Belmont, August 126
S.S. *Berlin* 57
Berlin, Irving 26
Biden, Joe 4
Blackstone, Timothy 171
Blackstone Hotel 171, 173, 175
Blackstone Theater 171
Blaine, James 34, 35
Blair House 212
Bloodgood, Joseph 150
Blythe, Samuel 118
Boehner, John 9
Booth, John Wilkes 32, 211
Boston Globe 118
Boston Red Sox 25
Bourne, Jonathan 82, 94, 182-183
Bradley, Joseph 34

Brady, James 212
Bremer, Arthur 212
Broadway 1
Brown, Margaret "Molly" 26
Brown, Walter 107
Browning, Robert 161
Brunt, Stellanova 185
Bryan, Tim 9
Bryan, William Jennings 12, 123, 124, 125,
    126, 127, 128, 168
Buchanan, James 31
Buchanan, Pat 4
Bull Moose party 12, 13, 134, 148, 151, 169, 211
Bulloch, Anna 37
"bully pulpit" 28, 59
Burnett, Ernie 26
Bush, George H.W. 2, 4, 12
Bush, George W. 4, 12
Bush, Jeb 12
Butler, Nicholas 152, 153, 187
Butt, Archie 5, 26, 52-57, 65, 67, 79, 92, 93,
    152
Butt, Clara 53-54
Butt, Kitty 56
Butt, Louis 53

Calhoun, John 180
California primary 96
Cameron, Simon 29, 30
Cannon, Joseph 58, 59, 123, 182
Carey, Robert 77, 82
Carnegie, Andrew 22
Carnegie Endowment for International Peace
Carnegie Hall 23, 74, 89
Carnegie-Mellon University 24
Carpenter, Fred 110
Caswell, I.A. 108
Cermak, Anton 211
Chancellor, John 1
Chase, Salmon 29, 30, 33
Chicago, Burlington and Quincy Railroad 47
Chicago Coliseum 7, 10, 109, 110, 165
Chicago Cubs 41, 173

Index

Chicago Herald 118
Chicago Tribune 91, 98, 100, 118
Cincinnati Times-Star 41
Clark, James "Champ" 123, 124, 126, 127, 128, 129, 186
Clay, Henry 180
Cleveland, Grover 32, 123, 125, 144, 167
Clinton, Bill 4
Clinton, Hillary 4, 15
Cohan, Geoffrey 104, 111
Cohan, George M. 88
Cohems, Henry 148
Coiniere, Ray 16, 19
Colby, Bainbridge 177
College of Cardinals 58
Collier's 64
Columbia University 152, 187
"Confession of Faith" speech 137–139, 154, 155, 156
Congress Hotel 104, 135
Connally, John 212
Coolidge, Calvin 10, 180, 181, 184
Council on Foreign Relations 181
Credentials Committee 104, 116, 117, 118, 119, 120, 135
Cruz, Ted 12
Cummins, Albert 99, 106, 121, 187
Cunningham, Clarence 64
Curtis, Charles 185
Czolgosz, Leon 211

Daugherty, Harry 183
Davis, David 34
Davis, Gray 184
Debs, Eugene 144, 145, 146, 147, 162, 164, 180
Declaration of Independence 15
Democratic Convention 123–131
Democratic Party platform 190–195
Depew Chauncey 68
Dixiecrats 10
Dixon, Joseph 132, 134, 135, 143, 183
Doan, Cozy 88
Dole, Robert 4
Dred Scott decision 31

Edison, Thomas 21
Eisenhower, Dwight 2, 3, 10, 168, 169, 176
Elkins Act 47
Emporia Gazette 23, 119
Evans, Maria 141

Fayle, R.G. 150
Fenway Park 25
Ferris, Woodbridge 185
For Whom the Bell Tolls 187
Forbes, Steve 4
Ford, Gerald 2, 4, 11, 170, 212
Ford, Henry 21
Ford's Theater 32, 211
"Forty-five Minutes from Broadway" 88
Foss, Eugene 127
Foster, Jodie 212

Frawley, William 26
Fremont, John 31
French Revolution 79
Fromme, Lynette "Squeaky" 212
Fuller, Melville 55

Garfield, James A. 34, 46, 123, 211
Garfield, James R. 72, 132, 182
Gaynor, William 127
General Electric 62
Gilded Age 21, 22
Gilpatrick, M.P. 147
Girrard, A.O. 148, 149
Glasscock, William 77, 82
Glavis, Louis R. 64
Goldwater, Barry 1, 11, 15, 16, 169
Gorbachev, Michel 16
Gore, Albert 4, 10
Gould, George 55
Gould, Louis 165
Graham, Lindsey 12
Grant, H. Roger 23
Grant, Robert 80
Grant, Ulysses 32, 33, 34, 40, 123
Great Depression 10, 16
Great Northern Railroad 47
Greeley, Horace 31, 32
Gruin, Edward 150
Guggenheim, Benjamin 26
Guiteau, Charles 211

Hadley, Herbert 8, 77, 82, 101, 102, 107, 110, 111, 115, 116, 118, 132, 184
"Half-Breeds" 34, 168
Hamilton, Alexander 133
Hanna, Mark 45
Harding, Warren 10, 121, 122, 175, 180, 181, 184, 187
Harland and Wolff Corp. 26
Harmon, Judson 125, 127
Harriman, Edward 47
Harris, Henry 26
Harris, Julian 134, 135
Harrison, Benjamin 34, 39, 42, 43, 123
Hayes, Rutherford 33, 34, 43, 123
Haymarket Riot 7
Hemingway, Ernest 187
Henry, Patrick 124
Hepburn Act 147
Hill, James 47
Hilles, Charles 109, 110, 130, 166, 184–185
Hinman, Harvey 179
History of Standard Oil 24
Hoover, Herbert 10, 168, 175, 181, 183, 185, 187,
Hotel Astor 151
Hotel Gilpatrick 147
Houdini, Harry 26
House Rules Committee 58
House Ways and Means Committee 60, 125
Houser, Walter 112

Howard, Perry 132, 134, 135, 183
Howell, R.B. 108
Hughes, Charles Evans 66, 88, 107, 121, 177, 180, 187, 188, 181, 186

"I Love Lucy" 26
Illinois primary 91–92
Insurgents 70, 71, 82
International Workers of the World (IWW) 144
Interstate Commerce Commission 66
Ismay, J. Bruce 26
"It's a Long Way to Tipperary" 26

Jackson, Andrew 133
Jackson Daily News 135
James, Ollie 127
Jamison, Frank 158
Jefferson, Thomas 3, 15, 133
Johnson, Andrew 32, 33, 46
Johnson, Hiram 75, 78, 82, 96, 97, 107, 111, 115, 133, 139, 162, 181, 184
Johnson, Lyndon 15, 169
The Jungle 25, 49

Kansas-Nebraska Act 31
Kasich, John 12
Kefauver, Estes 2
Keirsey, David 16, 19
Kennedy, John F. 2, 16, 212
Kern, John 127, 128
Kipling, Rudyard 119, 133
Knox, Frank 85, 133, 185, 186

LaFollette, Robert 13, 69–73, 74, 75, 76, 82, 83, 86, 88, 89, 91, 92, 94, 96, 98, 105, 106, 110, 112, 113, 121, 130, 132, 146, 166, 180, 187
Landon, Alf 186
League of Nations 10, 177, 180, 181
Lewis, J. Hamilton 127
Library of Congress 5
Lincoln, Abraham 15, 29, 32, 33, 34, 46, 77, 91, 133
Lincoln Memorial Commission 180
Lisner, Meyer 107
Lodge, Henry Cabot 78, 79, 82, 100
Longworth, Alice Roosevelt 7, 38
Longworth, Nicholas 160
Lorimer, George 175
Lorimer, William 91, 92, 95
Louisiana Purchase 31
Lugar, Richard 4

MacArthur, Arthur 44
MacArthur, Douglas 44
Macy's 26
Madison, James 3
Madison Square Garden 150, 158
"Make America Great *Again*" 11
Manson, Charles 212
Mantle, Mickey 2

Marquard, Rube 88
Marshall, Thomas 127, 128, 174, 187–188
Martin, Albert H. 148, 149
Maryland primary 96
Massachusetts primary 94–95, 96
Mathewson, Christy 88
Mays, Willie 2
McCain, John 4, 12
McClure, S.S. 24, 25
McClure's 24
McCutcheon, John 98
McGovern, Francis 112, 113, 114, 166
McGovern, George 1, 212
McGrath, John 149
McGraw, John 88, 173
McKinley, William 3, 4, 17, 35, 36, 40, 44, 49, 119, 123, 148, 150, 151, 168, 180, 211
Meat Inspection Act 48
"Melancholy Baby" 26
Michigan state convention 96
Miller Center 5
Millet, Francis David 56
Milwaukee Auditorium 147
Minnesota Progressive League 130
Missouri Compromise 30, 31
Missouri Pacific Railroad 55
Mollison, Willis 132
Monroe, James 4, 50
Monroe Doctrine 50
Moore, Sara Jane 212
Morgan, J.P. 22, 47
"muckrakers" 24, 25, 48
"Mugwumps" 35
Munsey, Frank 117, 118, 119, 133

Nader, Ralph 10
National Association for the Advancement of Colored People 183
National Conservation Commission 182
National Irrigation Conference 63
National Progressive League 72, 82, 86, 183
National Wholesale Liquor Dealers Association 66
"Nearer My God to Thee" 26
Nebraska primary 93–94
New Deal 168
"New Freedom" papers 154, 155
New Jersey primary 98
"New Nationalism" speech 67, 137, 154, 155
New York Central Railroad 23
New York Evening Post 60
New York Giants 88, 173
New York Highlanders 88
New York primary 88–89
New York Sun 79
New York Times 87, 96, 106, 109, 122, 145, 150, 174
New York Tribune 31
New York World 74, 79, 158, 167
New York Yankees 25
Newett, George 179

228 Index

Newlands, Francis 48
Newlands Reclamation Act 48
Niedeerhaus, Thomas 108
Nixon, Richard 16, 212
Norris, Edwin 101
North Dakota primary 87
North Iowa Area Community College 5
Northern Pacific Railroad 47
Northern Securities 47
Norton, C.D. 42, 54, 109
Norton, George 26
Novak, Robert 9, 28, 167

Oak Leaves 3
Obama, Barack 4
"Oh, Isn't He a Darling" 30
Ohio Constitutional Convention 77
Ohio primary 96–98
O'Laughlin, John 118
Omaha Bee 100, 118
Omaha World-Herald 118
Oregon primary 93–94
Orme, Gordon 134
Osborn, Chase 74, 77, 82, 130, 132, 185
Osborn, Lillian 185
Oswald, Lee Harvey 212
Outlook 72

Paine, Lewis 32
Pan-American Exposition 211
Panama Canal 49–50
Parker, Alton 126
Parker, Fess 2
Parker, John 134, 186
Patronage 34
Patterson, Thomas 10
Payne, Sereno 60
Payne-Aldrich Tariff Act 58–62, 66
Pearson, Richmond 108
Peck, Mary Hulbert 143
Pennsylvania primary 92
Penrose, Boise 92, 110
Periodical Publishers Association 75,
Perkins, George 117, 132, 186
Perot, Ross 10, 170
Philadelphia Athletics 115
Philadelphia Phillies 173
Philpott, A.G. 118
Pinchot, Amos 116, 132
Pinchot, Gifford 48, 60, 62, 63, 64, 65, 66, 72, 132, 181–182
Plaza Hotel 74
Primary elections 82–87
Princeton University 1, 75, 147, 159
Progressive Party (Bull Moose) 130, 134–145, 147, 154, 156, 167, 181, 182, 186
Progressive Party Platform 201–207
Progressives 12, 13, 21, 22, 28, 36, 58, 59, 61, 66, 73, 74, 75, 76, 77, 78, 81, 82, 83, 94, 96, 105, 106, 111, 112, 132–139, 154, 156, 164, 168, 177
Pulitzer Prize 187

Pullman Palace Car Company 144
Pure Food and Drug Act 48, 66.

Ransom, Matt 54
Reagan, Ronald 2, 11, 16, 17, 170, 212
Redmund, Sidney 132, 134, 135, 136, 183
Reeves, George 2
Republican National Committee 99–108, 117, 119, 166, 185
Republican Party Platform 196–200
Richmond Times-Dispatch 118
"The Right to Work" 24
"robber barons" 21
Rockefeller, John D. 22, 47
Rockefeller, Nelson 1, 169
Rogers, Will 176
Romney, George 11
Romney, Mitt 12
Romudka Trunk Company 147
Roosevelt, Alice Hathaway Lee 38
Roosevelt, Anna 37
Roosevelt, Corrine 37
Roosevelt, Edith Carow 39, 104, 151, 160, 177
Roosevelt, Eleanor 103
Roosevelt, Elliott 37
Roosevelt, Franklin 10, 16, 103, 132, 168, 169, 185, 186, 211
Roosevelt, Martha 37, 38
Roosevelt, Philip 148
Roosevelt, Theodore, Jr. 134, 183–184
Roosevelt, Theodore, Sr. 37
Root, Elihu 18, 78, 100, 111, 112, 114, 115, 117, 118, 119, 120, 122, 132, 140, 153, 166, 179, 180, 181, 188
Rosenwald, Julius 171
Rosewater, Victor 110, 118
Rough Riders 27, 35, 44, 46, 48, 58, 74, 85, 111, 133, 164, 185
Ruby, Jack 212
Ruth, George Herman "Babe" 25
Ryan, Thomas 126

St. Louis Republic 79
San Juan Hill 40, 44, 46, 50, 52
Saturday Evening Post 167, 175
Sawyer, Philetus 69
Schrank, John 148, 150, 151, 211
Schwarzenegger, Arnold 184
Scranton, William 11
Sears & Roebuck 171
Seibold, Louis 158, 167
Seward, William 29, 32
Sherman, James 67, 88, 121, 132, 152
Sherman, John 34
Sherman Anti-Trust Act 35, 47
Shurz, Carl 29
Sinclair, Upton 25, 49
Skipper, Jim 3
Smith, Bennett 5
Smith, James Clinch 26
Socialist Party 144, 145, 156, 162; platform 208–210

Index

Sorbonne 20
South Dakota primary 98
Spanish-American War 7, 19, 27, 35, 40, 44, 49, 50, 52, 54, 85, 184, 185
Square Deal 23, 77, 169
"Stalwarts" 34, 70, 168
Standard Oil Co. 22, 67
Stead, William T. 26
Steffens, Lincoln 24
Stevens, Thaddeus 29, 30
Stevenson, Adlai 2
Stimson, Henry 78, 100
Stratton. F.A. 150
Strauss, Ida 26
Strauss, Isador 26
Stubbs, Walter 77, 82, 132
Sulzer, William 127
Surratt, John 33
Surratt, Mary 33
Swalm, Frank 132

Taft, Alphonso 40, 41
Taft, Charles 41, 159, 160
Taft, Charles P., II 176
Taft, Charlie 121, 122, 163
Taft, Henry 41
Taft, Horace 41, 65
Taft, Louisa 40, 41, 65
Taft, Nellie 5, 42, 43, 55, 62, 65, 114, 115, 121, 122, 125, 130, 141, 142, 159
Taft, Peter 41
Taft, Robert 168, 169, 176
Taft, Robert, Jr. 176
Taft, Robert, III 176
Taft, William Howard 1, 2, 4, 5, 7, 9–13, 17–19, 26–28, 35, 36, 39–45, 49–56, 58–62, 64–68, 71, 78–80, 82–89, 91, 93–96, 98–121, 132, 136–138, 140–143, 146, 153–155, 158–165, 167–168, 171–176, 179–181, 187–188
Tammany Hall 126
Tarbell, Ida 24
Tennessee Coal and Iron Company 67
Terrell, Scurry 149, 150
Thayer, William Roscoe 76, 167
Theodore Roosevelt Center 5
Thomson, T. Kennard 88
Thorson, Thomas 108
Thurmond, Strom 10
Tilden, Samuel 34
Time magazine 182
Tippett, J.D. 212
Titanic 21, 26, 27, 28, 57, 92–93
Truman, Harry 16, 44, 212
Trump, Donald 4, 7, 8, 9, 10, 11, 12, 13, 29, 79, 169
Tuskegee Institute 171
"Tweed Days in St. Louis" 24

Underwood, Oscar 125, 127–128
United States Civil Service Commission 39, 40
United States Forest Service 181
United States Steel Corporation 67
University of Cincinnati 42
University of Colorado 184
University of Wisconsin 69

Vanderbilt, Cornelius 21, 22, 23
Vaughn, Hippo 88, 173

Wagner, Stubby 88
Waldorf-Astoria Hotel 26
Wallace, George 10, 212
Wallace, Henry 10
Washington, Booker T. 171
Washington, George 17, 27, 95, 132
Washington Nationals 115
Washington Post 87
Washington University 184
Wasson, Henry, 108
Watergate 16
Watson, James 110, 116
Webster, Daniel 180
Westinghouse 62
"What's the Matter With Kansas" 118
Wheeler, Burton K. 183
"When Irish Eyes Are Smiling" 26
White, William Allen 23, 72, 76, 79, 82, 104, 107, 119, 129, 143
White Star Line 26
Whiting, Borden 108
Wichita Daily Beacon 187
Wickersham, George 64
Willard, Dwight 81
Wilson, Ellen 161
Wilson, Nell 161
Wilson, James 64
Wilson, Woodrow 1, 4, 9, 10, 12, 13, 75, 124, 125, 126, 127, 128, 129, 130, 141, 143, 146, 147, 152, 154, 156, 164, 171, 177, 179, 180, 181
"Wisconsin Idea" 70
Wisconsin primary 89–90
Wood, Leonard 44, 184
Wright, Orville 21
Wright, Wilbur 21

Yale University 173, 179
York-Davies, E. Nathan 43
Young Men's Christian Association (YMCA) 186

Zangara, Giuseppe 211

www.ingramcontent.com/pod-product-compliance
Lightning Source LLC
Chambersburg PA
CBHW032050300426
44116CB00007B/673